FILM IN CANADA

FILM IN CANADA

☐ JIM LEACH ☐

OXFORD
UNIVERSITY PRESS

OXFORD
UNIVERSITY PRESS

70 Wynford Drive, Don Mills, Ontario M3C 1J9
www.oup.com/ca

Oxford University Press is a department of the University of Oxford.
It furthers the University's objective of excellence in research, scholarship,
and education by publishing worldwide in

Oxford New York

Auckland Cape Town Dar es Salaam Hong Kong Karachi

Kuala Lumpur Madrid Melbourne Mexico City

Nairobi New Delhi Shanghai Taipei Toronto

With offices in

Argentina Austria Brazil Chile Czech Republic France Greece

Guatemala Hungary Italy Japan Poland Portugal Singapore

South Korea Switzwerland Thailand Turkey Ukaraine Vietnam

Oxford is a trade mark of Oxford University Press
in the UK and in certain other countries

Published in Canada by Oxford University Press

National Library of Canada Cataloguing in Publication Data

Leach, Jim
Film in Canada/Jim Leach.

Includes bibliographical references and index.
ISBN-13: 978-0-19-541951-1
ISBN-10: 0-19-541951-0

1. Motion Pictures—Canada—History.
2. Motion picture producers and directors—Canada. I. Title

PN1993.5.C3L42 2006   791.43'0971   C2005-906430-7

Cover design: Brett Miller
Text design/composition: Valentino Sanna, Ignition Design and Communications

1 2 3 4 - 06 05 04 03
This book is printed on permanent (acid-free) paper ∞ .
Printed in Canada.

Contents

Acknowledgements

I would like to thank Cliff Newman for initiating this project, Lise Creurer for her encouragement and advice as it developed and for her tenacity and patience in pursuing copyright permissions for the stills, and Richard Tallman for his careful and thoughtful copy-editing.

Not Just Another National Cinema

When one delves into the very notion of the thing called Canadian cinema, one is sinking one's rubbers in something much more sensitive, complex, and problematic than just another national cinema.

—Geoff Pevere (2002a: 103)

What is a national cinema if it doesn't have a national audience?

—Andrew Higson (1989: 46)

National cinemas always turn out to be more complex and problematic than they first seem to be, but Canada's is certainly more difficult to pin down than most. It is far from the only national cinema to have difficulty finding a national audience, but Canada's status as part of Hollywood's domestic (North American) market has created a situation in which the achievements of Canadian filmmakers have been virtually invisible to most Canadian filmgoers. This situation is further complicated by the production of films in both of the nation's official languages, leading to divisions in an already limited market and provoking claims that there are two national cinemas rather than one. In recent years, thinking about the national cinema has also had to deal with Canada's increasing ethnic diversity and the emergence of a global media marketplace.

I will address all these issues in this book, but my main focus will be on the films themselves. Ideally, as Andrew Higson (1989) suggests, the study of a national cinema should take into account not only the films produced by the domestic film industry, but also the distribution and exhibition systems through which those films are shown (or not shown). In Canada, of course, these systems have been largely owned or controlled by the Hollywood studios, and, while it would be useful to situate Canadian films in relation to the Hollywood films in circulation at the time of their release, this will not be my main concern here. I will place the films in the context of the critical discourses and government policies that helped to shape them and their reception, and I have organized each chapter around a specific topic that raises important issues for understanding the national cinema.

In this introductory chapter, I will look first at how the situation I have just identified came about before moving on to deal with questions of national identity and the complex ways in which films engage with the political, cultural, and mythic dimensions of national life.

Blame Hollywood

When film was invented at the end of the nineteenth century, Canada was a vast and sparsely populated country and in no position to exploit the new technology on an industrial basis. In 1925, D.W. Griffith, who was probably the most famous film director in the world at that time, visited Toronto and told his Canadian audience that 'you should have your own films and exchange them with those of other countries' (Morris, 1978: 175). However, the Canadian government proved reluctant to follow the lead of other nations by enacting measures to protect the domestic film industry, which was, in any case, virtually non-existent.

The British government did enact a quota system in 1927 to protect Britain's more developed, but crisis-ridden, national film industry. British cinemas were required to screen a specified (and gradually increasing) percentage of British films, leading to a growth in the number—and eventually the quality—of films produced. As a result of a provision that allowed films made in the Empire to count as British for the purposes of the quota, Canada experienced its first production 'boom' when Hollywood producers came north to make 'quota quickies' in British Columbia. It came to an abrupt end when the loophole in the British legislation was closed in 1938, and the low-budget productions that resulted were hardly calculated to convince skeptical critics and policy-makers of the value of a commercial film industry in Canada. Instead, the federal government chose in 1939 to establish the National Film Board of Canada (NFB) as a public institution geared to the production of documentaries in the national interest (see Chapter 1).

A few independent filmmakers did make feature films, but these were always produced in very difficult circumstances and never achieved the commercial success needed to sustain an industry.[1] The federal government came under some pressure to enact a quota system, but when it seemed that legislation might be introduced after World War II the Hollywood studios intervened and negotiated an agreement with the government. Under the Canadian Co-operation Project, which came into effect in 1948, the government dropped the idea of a quota, and, in return, the studios agreed to include references to Canada as often as possible in their films (to promote the tourist industry) and to make a few films in Canada—the most distinguished of which turned out to be *I Confess*, Alfred Hitchcock's thriller made in Quebec City in 1952.

Film audiences declined in Canada as elsewhere with the introduction of television in the 1950s, but the new medium provided an outlet for NFB documentaries and encouraged innovative approaches that finally paved the way for feature film production. In the early 1960s, several young filmmakers produced low-budget feature films using techniques and equipment developed originally for documentaries, and their modest critical and commercial success convinced the government that a film industry in Canada was now a viable proposition (see Chapter 2). Accordingly, it created the Canadian Film Development Corporation (CFDC) in 1967 to subsidize filmmakers and thereby encourage the growth of a private sector that would hopefully become self-sustaining. However, subsidies, unlike quotas, target production, rather than distribution and exhibition, and many films that received support from the CFDC were never shown in Canadian cinemas, and very few made money.

Hollywood has always claimed to give the people what they want, and the failure of the Canadian films was often attributed not to distribution problems but to their lack of appeal to audiences. The CFDC was faced with a contradiction between its economic and cultural mandates and came under attack for failing on both counts. On the one hand, the Corporation was responsible for investing public money and expected to generate a profit. On the other, as a public institution, it was under pressure to ensure that the films that it supported were culturally respectable and/or distinctively Canadian. It was open to attack when it invested in films with strong commercial potential but no apparent cultural pretensions, like David Cronenberg's *Shivers*, which sparked a lively debate in 1975; but it was also criticized for poor business practices when the films it supported did not make money.

As we shall see, the tension between commercial and artistic or cultural goals in Canadian film policy remains a highly contentious topic. Commercial motives came to the fore as a result of the Capital Cost Allowance Act, which allowed a 100 per cent tax deduction on investments in Canadian films and provoked a short-lived boom in production between 1978 and 1980. This approach did produce some commercial successes—most notably teen comedies such as *Meatballs* (Ivan Reitman, 1979) and *Porky's* (Bob Clark, 1981), and horror films such as *Prom Night* (Paul Lynch, 1980) and more Cronenberg films—but most films were either never released or quickly forgotten (see Chapter 3).

The failure of most of the films produced under the Capital Cost Allowance Act, and the general disrespect for those that succeeded, led to a change of policy at the CFDC, accompanied by a change of name in 1984. Telefilm Canada, as the name suggests, envisaged television (and soon video) as a solution to the distribution problem, and the new body began to invest in smaller-budget films with explicitly Canadian settings and distinctive cultural identities. In addition to the money from Telefilm, the budgets for these films were often patched together from a number of different sources, including provincial initiatives to support local film production, regional arts councils, and television networks. Two early successes that demonstrated the potential of this approach were *Le Déclin de l'empire américain* (Denys Arcand, 1986) and *I've Heard the Mermaids Singing* (Patricia Rozema, 1987).

The recent emergence of the Alliance Atlantis media empire—modest by Hollywood standards but a major player in the Canadian context—has provided a more secure basis for production and distribution. But the most publicized development in recent years has been the phenomenon of 'Hollywood North', a term that emphasizes economic factors but has taken on several different connotations over the years.

Originally it was used by those lobbying for the formation of what became the CFDC, simply to designate the goal of establishing a Canadian film industry. Thus Michael Spencer, the Corporation's first executive director, insisted that Hollywood North is 'not a location, but a concept: that the success, glamour, and all-American dream of the motion picture industry can be recreated in Canada' (2003: 1). In this vision, the concept was a highly positive one that envisaged no conflict between the American dream and Canadian reality. During the capital cost allowance years, however, it became attached to Canadian films that imported American actors and concealed their Canadian locations. According to Martin Knelman, the film industry at this time became 'an accidental comedy' (1987: 30), a judgement endorsed by Peter O'Brian's satiric comedy *Hollywood North* (2003), set during this period but released well after the term had acquired a third meaning.[2]

It now refers not to Canadian films at all but to the 'runaway' Hollywood productions that have brought a new prosperity to the film industries in many Canadian cities. The Hollywood studios were not slow to 'blame Canada' for perceived economic problems in an industry that had historically dominated film screens throughout the world, thereby inverting the long-established tradition of complaints by Canadian filmmakers (and critics) that Hollywood dominance worked against the development of a domestic film industry in Canada. In fact, the economic impact of Hollywood North on California has been greatly exaggerated, since employment rates in Hollywood remain high as a result of the demands of the burgeoning media industries. Ironically, one of the main effects has been that Canadian filmmakers now have to compete for crews, equipment, and studio space with Hollywood productions with much larger budgets (Saunders, 2001: 97–8). In other words, the long-standing problem of competing with Hollywood has been internalized at the level of production as well as distribution and exhibition.

Screening the Nation

In the circumstances, blaming Hollywood is understandable and, to a large extent, justified. However, the frustration generated by Hollywood's business practices often leads to an indiscriminate denigration of its films and the people who consume them. During the first half of the twentieth century, commentators condemned commercial movies as products of a new 'mass culture' that undermined traditional cultural standards as well as distinctive national cultures, and there was widespread concern that popular movies virtually hypnotized their audiences, causing them to lose contact with reality. Canadian cultural policy was accordingly designed to protect the national culture, still largely identified with British and French traditions, from the supposedly shoddy and meretricious products of American popular culture. The popular appeal of Hollywood movies could only be explained by treating the audience as 'cultural dopes' who passively consumed the illusions concocted in the 'dream factory' and lacked the discrimination to appreciate true art.

When a film industry did eventually appear in the 1960s, this tradition encouraged filmmakers and critics to attribute the disinterest of Canadian audiences to the effects of Hollywood's cultural imperialism, an attitude hardly likely to convince Canadians to support a Canadian cinema that would rescue them from their own poor taste. The link thus forged between national identity and cultural standards is also apparent in the emergence in the 1970s of a critical canon that identified certain kinds of film as typically or ideally Canadian because they were more 'realistic' than Hollywood films with their emphasis on illusion and spectacle (see Chapter 2).

This prescriptive approach, based on judgements about what the national cinema should be, tends to obscure the full range of Canadian film production—English-Canadian and Québécois, documentary and fiction, commercial and avant-garde. However, any account of a national cinema is bound to be selective, especially if it does not want to become a mere listing of titles, and the main concern in my account will be with feature films, the fiction films that would be regarded as 'mainstream' if Canadian audiences had more chance to see them. Important areas of filmmaking will not appear (animation, for example) or will receive only brief treatment (documentary and the avant-garde), not because they are somehow less Canadian than feature films (indeed, many would argue the opposite) but because national cinemas are usually defined by the kinds of stories they tell and by the myths of national identity on which they are based.

Films provide spectators with cues that establish the terms on which they want to be judged, and I will attend to these cues through close readings of selected films (so there will be inevitable omissions even here). These films have rarely received close critical attention and are often dismissed as failing to live up to the standards set by

Hollywood popular cinema or European art cinema. While value judgements are important, Jim McGuigan has argued that 'a cultural performance may be deemed "good" or "bad" of its kind, that is, within its own discursive field' (1996: 45). I will thus also look at the 'discursive field' that frames Canadian cinema, notably the critical reception of the films, to suggest why they have so rarely been treated on their own terms. Of course, spectators do often read films in quite different ways from what their makers intend, and there is no guarantee that the cues given by a film will be coherent or in accord with the conscious intentions of the filmmakers. My strategy will be to suspend value judgements, as far as possible, in my initial response to the films.

One judgement that will be readily apparent is my conviction that Canadian cinema has produced many films that have been unjustly neglected, but I certainly do not believe that all Canadian films are equally valuable. I will discuss these films in relation to the cultural, industrial, and political contexts in which they were made.[3] The main focus will be on how they represent Canada visually and on the stories they tell about the nation, but this is not to suggest that the national context exhausts the interest of these films. I will not use the contexts to explain the films, or to argue that some kind of 'Canadian psyche' can be read off from the films in any straightforward way. I will also, for the most part, resist 'allegorical' readings that regard the characters in films as personifications of national traditions but that often close down meanings too quickly.[4] Rather, I will explore the complex and unstable relationships between the films and the already complex and unstable idea of the nation.

Identifying the Nation

In order to explore these relations, we first need to have a sense of what a 'nation' is. It has become customary to cite Benedict Anderson's definition, according to which a nation is an 'imagined political community' whose members have a sense of shared interests with other people with most of whom they do not come into personal contact (1991: 6). In this sense, the nation exists because people believe that they belong to it, and it thus becomes a component of their sense of personal identity. It is also a political institution, a symbolic apparatus usually referred to as 'the state', with a constitution and laws that establish its boundaries as well as the rights and duties of its citizens.

Both the imagined and the symbolic nations are essentially fictions, but they have a very real impact on people's lives. From a nationalist perspective, the ideal situation occurs when national feeling coincides with the political institutions of the state, creating a strong sense of the 'nation-state'. However, this is rarely the case, as people's personal interests often place them in a critical relation to certain aspects of national life and its political and legal systems, even if they still feel a strong attachment to the nation in principle. As Slavoj Zizek puts it, there is a 'gap that separates every particular nation from its ideal notion' (2001: 24), and this means that most people's sense of national identity involves elements of identification and criticism.

In Canada, the tensions between the ideas of nation and state are most apparent in the ongoing uncertainty about the status of Quebec. For many among the French-speaking majority in Quebec, the present political structure threatens the survival of their language and cultural traditions, and they regard Quebec as already a nation but not yet a state. The situation for the rest of Canada seems to be the opposite: there is a widespread idea that English Canadians lack a distinct cultural identity that distinguishes them from the larger and more powerful nation to the south. Indeed, Seth Feldman describes them as citizens of 'a nationless state', although he adds that 'in their daily lives, most individual English Canadians are sufficiently secure in their regionalism and ethnicity' to accept this situation (2002a: xii).

The troubled relations between nation and state in Canada also create problems of definition for any study of the national cinema. It is therefore necessary to justify my decision to treat English- and French-language films together in this book. The bilingual structure of the film industry divides the already small market for Canadian films and, for many critics, this division undermines any sense that we are dealing with a single national cinema. In one of the first books on Canadian cinema, published in 1968, Gilles Marsolais argued that we should speak instead of '*two* cinemas: the "Canadian" and the "Québécois", whose interests are divergent' (1968: 104). More recently, in a book called *Canadian National Cinema*, Christopher Gittings nevertheless adopts a similar position, arguing that there are 'two very different national cinemas: Québécois and Anglophone Canadian cinemas', although he does later admit that there are 'dynamic moments of intersection and imbrication' (2002: 77, 105). On the other hand, in her more imaginatively titled book, *Weird Sex and Snowshoes*, Katherine Monk affirms that, despite the 'obvious and distinct differences between the two cultures', their films 'offer more similarities than difference' (2001: 158).

The 'two cinemas' view receives support from two other recent books. In his Preface to his *Quebec National Cinema*, Bill Marshall discusses the implications of his title and reports that a publisher refused to consider the book for a series on national cinemas on the grounds that Quebec 'is not a nation' (2001: x). Marshall is well aware of the complexities, political and cultural, attendant on his project, and in his first chapter, entitled 'Producing and Envisioning the Nation', makes clear that he will be dealing with 'Quebec cinema not as coherence but as patterns of incoherence' (13). A rather stronger claim is made in the Introduction to *North of Everything*, an anthology of essays on recent English-Canadian films, in which William Beard and Jerry White justify their editorial decision to exclude Quebec cinema on the grounds that 'the idea that there is a coherent Canadian national self, composed of both English and French elements, seems to us somewhat naive' (2002: xviii).[5]

My decision to deal with films in both languages, and to discuss them together rather than in separate chapters, should not be taken to imply that I believe in 'a coherent national self'. Indeed, I would be skeptical of such a claim even if it applied only to English-language films, as Beard and White seem to assume (although the range of films discussed in their book proves otherwise). Nor should my approach be seen as a denial of the distinctive qualities of Quebec culture, which include a much clearer sense of a 'national self' than in the rest of Canada. Whatever the differences, however, the situation is much more complex than suggested in one attempt to 'theorize the global range of national cinemas', in which English-Canadian cinema is consigned to the category of 'Imitating Hollywood', while Quebec cinema belongs in 'Regional/Ethnic Cinemas' (Crofts, 1993: 49, 56–7). Like most national cinemas, Canadian cinema is 'a messy affair' (O'Regan, 1996: 2), and there is a great range and variety of productions to account for in both languages.

Recent work in cultural studies and postmodern theory calls into question the existence of a coherent self even in individuals, and the idea of a 'national character' is best seen as a fiction or a myth, albeit a very powerful one, that seeks to unify a host of shifting, and often conflicting, identifications. Discussions of national cinemas often contribute to this unifying effort by distinguishing recurrent themes and motifs that are then interpreted as symptoms of the national character. In his pioneering study of German cinema, first published in 1947, Siegfried Kracauer studied the national cinema to discover why the German people succumbed to the National Socialist ideology. According to Kracauer, his method did not imply 'the concept of a fixed national character', but it did rest on the claim that 'the technique, the story content, and the evolution of the films of a nation are fully understandable only in relation to the actual psychological pattern of this nation' (1947: 8, 5).

Kracauer's approach has been widely criticized on the grounds that it uses films to explain social processes of which they themselves are a product. Few critics now explicitly acknowledge his influence, but the discussion of Canadian cinema is almost inevitably based on the underlying assumption that the films reveal something about the social and cultural context in which they appear. This assumption begs two major questions, which are relevant to most national cinemas but especially urgent in the Canadian context: How can films be said to reflect the psychology of a nation if most of the nation's citizens never see the films and often reject them when they do? In any case, is there really a single 'psychological pattern' that can account for the responses of citizens regardless of gender, class, racial, and linguistic differences?

The idea of a coherent national identity has also been disturbed by political, economic, and technological developments that place great pressure on the traditional forms of both nation and state. Several states—the former Yugoslavia, for example— have disintegrated because of an upsurge of national feeling among groups for whom the state no longer represented their 'imagined political community'. Similar feelings motivate separatist movements in many other states, including Canada, but these pressures from within have been accompanied by the establishment of multinational institutions, including political and economic unions such as the European Union and trading blocs such as the North American Free Trade Agreement, as well as business conglomerates that operate on a global scale. At the same time, the emergence of new communications technology—the proliferation of television channels, video cameras and recorders, and the Internet—allow for the sharing of images and information among groups with common interests throughout the world, unconstrained by regional and national boundaries.

Traditional concepts of national identity have also been challenged in many countries by the growth of diasporic communities founded by people who left their homelands to start new lives in safer or more prosperous nations. In Canada, the government sought to manage this challenge in 1971 by officially proclaiming Canada a multicultural, as well as bilingual, nation; and the members of these communities have become increasingly active and visible within Canadian culture. At the same time, Canada's Native peoples have claimed 'First Nations' status, calling into question the claims of English- and French-speaking Canadians to be the nation's 'founding' cultures (see Chapter 10).

All these complicating factors will be discussed in later chapters, but they do call into question the point of studying national cinemas at all in the contemporary context. Andrew Higson has argued, in the context of British cinema, that 'new types of film-making have embraced multiculturalism, transnationalism and devolution' and that 'such films should be seen less as products of a national cinema, more as post-national films' (2000: 35). This is an attractive suggestion in many ways, not only because it attends to the new developments but also because it acknowledges the contradictions and tensions already present within the idea of the 'nation'. However, rather than abandon the concept of national cinema and leave the field open to Hollywood—or perhaps we should now say the global media marketplace—it seems better to seek to incorporate what Higson calls 'the instability of the national' into our understanding of national cinemas and the myths of national identity they contain and with which they engage.

In the chapters that follow, I begin by destabilizing the notion that Canadian cinema has its roots in the realist tradition. Chapter 1 questions some basic assumptions about realism and traces how Canadian films, from the NFB's direct cinema documentaries to contemporary mockumentaries, have themselves questioned these assumptions. In Chapter 2, I examine the formation of the Canadian film canon around two direct cinema feature films, *Nobody Waved Good-bye* (Don Owen) and *Le Chat dans le sac* (Gilles Groulx), produced at the NFB in 1964 and argue that other films from the same year point in different directions. Since one of the tenets of the canon is that Canadian cinema is best seen as a regional cinema with a strong sense of place, Chapter 3 looks at the treatment of place in regional films in the direct cinema tradition and in films that conceal their locations either for economic reasons or to suggest the displacement of their characters.

While far from rejecting the importance of the realist tradition, I then go on to explore aspects of Canadian cinema that point in quite different directions. Chapter 4 explores the rich tradition of Canadian genre films, and Chapter 5 is devoted to the films of Gilles Carle and David Cronenberg as examples of the tension between the 'popular' and the 'national' in the discourses of Canadian cinema. In Chapter 6, I bring together a variety of films that are more concerned with imaginary worlds than external reality, from the fantastic cinema of Paul Almond to films that draw on Gothic and surrealist traditions.

The remaining chapters discuss groups of films related to specific topics that raise (sometimes awkward) questions about the national cinema. Chapter 7 discusses the challenge to mainstream cinema (itself a problematic term in the Canadian context) from filmmakers working on the margins, including the avant-garde and the work of Jack Darcus, William MacGillivray, and Jean Pierre Lefebvre. Questions of national identity are also bound up with representations of gender and sexuality, and Chapter 8 engages with these issues in Canadian cinema, looking at the commercial exploitation of sexuality, the work of women directors such as Léa Pool and Patricia Rozema, and that of gay filmmaker Thom Fitzgerald. Chapter 9 turns to 'art cinema' and the auteur theory and relates them to two Canadian directors whose work is most often discussed in these terms, Denys Arcand and Atom Egoyan.

The topics treated in the last three chapters involve new challenges to national traditions. Chapter 10 deals with films from the diasporic communities that have changed the previous French/English basis for national identity, as well as the work of First Nations filmmakers who also challenge the old ways of seeing. In Chapter 11, I look at two related responses to the changing conditions in the film industry: 'stupid' films, such as *Les Boys* (Louis Saia, 1997) and *Men With Brooms* (Paul Gross, 2002), that defy the conventions of good taste and 'smart' films, such as *Kissed* (Lynne Stopkewich, 1996) and *Maelström* (Denis Villeneuve, 2000), that function as a kind of postmodern art cinema. Finally, Chapter 12 raises questions about the relations of the global and the local, through a discussion of the films of Bruce Sweeney and Robert Lepage, and examines the relations of body and image in contemporary culture as they appear in *Lulu* (Srinivas Krishna, 1995) and *Emporte-moi* (Léa Pool, 1998). This concluding chapter will also bring us back to the question of value judgements and their entanglement with perceptions of the nation.

Realism and Its Discontents

The Canadian psyche seems better suited to information programming than to drama, partly because of the documentary traditions established in this country by John Grierson.

—Martin Knelman (1987: 103–4)

Realism is at the root of the Canadian psyche.

—Katherine Monk (2001: 10)

Alongside the absent audience, the other most salient characteristic of Canadian cinema is, according to most accounts, its roots in documentary realism. For many commentators, such as Knelman and Monk, this predilection derives from a specifically Canadian mindset that produces a distinct national identity. By such accounts, the realist bent did not originate with the NFB but rather provided a fertile ground in which John Grierson's project could flourish.

As we shall see in later chapters, the dominance of realism in Canadian cinema has been much exaggerated, but the persistence of this notion has played an important part in shaping how films have been interpreted and how questions about the national cinema have been posed. It is intricately entangled with the problem of the absent audience, since we might well ask why, if Canadians are such realists, they do not respond more enthusiastically to Canadian realist cinema. There is even the possibility that the perceived propensity towards realism accounts for this resistance: too many people regard Canadian films as 'depressing downbeat little pictures that nobody wants to see in our country or anywhere else' (Tadros, 1976: 37).[1]

I do not want to underestimate the importance of the realist tradition. In this chapter, I will argue that realist filmmaking in Canada is not the product of a naive belief that film can provide an objective view of reality. Rather, we shall see that this tradition, especially as it develops from the 1950s onward, becomes increasingly aware of the difficulty of adequately representing the real. The films are not straightforwardly realistic but investigations into the possibilities and limits of realism. Inevitably, the concerns at the core of this tradition have become even more urgent—to the point of throwing it into crisis—in the age of computer simulations and so-called reality television.

The National-Realist Project

The federal government established the National Film Board in 1939, acting on the advice of Grierson, who became its first commissioner. It was Grierson who first applied the term 'documentary' to cinema in 1927 and who famously defined it as 'the creative treatment of actuality' (Hardy, 1966: 13). He had already used state sponsorship in Britain to create a documentary film unit, working first for the Empire Marketing Board and then for the General Post Office. His goal was to intervene in well-established discourses of national identity and modify them in more progressive directions, balancing public relations with social change; in Canada the ties to the state were even more direct, but the myths of national identity were much less secure.

The NFB's mandate, as it was later defined in the Film Act of 1950, was 'to interpret Canada to Canadians and to other nations' (Morris, 1984: 283), and it had thus to foster a sense of an 'imagined community' essential to the survival of the nation. Grierson thought that documentary could provide evidence of shared interests among Canadians in different regions who had no direct contact with each other. I will thus refer to his vision as 'national-realist', on an analogy with the idea of the 'national-popular' developed at roughly the same time by the Italian political theorist Antonio

Gramsci (see Chapter 5). In many ways, their ideas and political goals were divergent (Gramsci was a Marxist; Grierson's generally socialist views were less clearly defined) and they could not have been aware of each other's work. Yet both advocated new forms of popular culture that would address the needs of the 'people' as citizens, rather than as consumers, by making them aware of the actual conditions that shaped their lives.

The NFB did not bring documentary filmmaking to Canada, nor was it the beginning of state-sponsored production. It replaced the Canadian Government Motion Picture Bureau, established in 1918 as the world's first government film unit. What Grierson brought with him was a new sense of social purpose, which was reinforced by the outbreak of World War II shortly after his arrival. Drawing on his work in Britain, Grierson produced films in which images, often taken from stock footage, provided the evidence to support the information and arguments in the commentary, scripted in advance and delivered by an authoritative 'voice-of-God' commentator.[2]

In the years after Grierson's departure in 1945, many filmmakers began to feel that this approach was not suited to the less urgent and, in some ways, more complex problems of a peacetime nation. As the Board sought to adjust to changing social and cultural conditions, new documentary forms emerged, but the national-realist project persisted. However, this project was always an unstable one, and the tensions and contradictions manifested themselves more visibly as a result of formal and technical developments as well as increasing pressures on the concept of national identity. The effects of these changes can be illustrated, fortuitously, by two NFB documentaries about the same family made 20 years apart.

Alexis Tremblay Habitant: The Story of a Farmer in Quebec (Jane Marsh, 1943) is a 37-minute documentary that distinguishes itself from the NFB's wartime style by its leisurely depiction of a year in the life of a farming family on the north shore of the St Lawrence River. Filmed in colour (also unusual for documentaries at this time), the images provide a record of rural life in Quebec in which the seasonal cycle is interwoven with the Church calendar. The voice-of-God commentary stresses the importance of tradition but also insinuates a few brief references to the benefits of modern agricultural methods—which, however, remain unseen.

Thus, a tension develops between the visual evidence of a life grounded in tradition and the verbal allusions to the NFB's 'progressive' outlook that often came into conflict with the dominant conservative ideology in Quebec politics at this time (see Leach, 1990–1). This imbalance points to the pressures generated by the film's effort to show that progress does not pose a threat to traditional values. In the context of the NFB's mandate, it also seeks to demonstrate what the family shares with rural families elsewhere in Canada, despite cultural and linguistic differences. The commentary tries to hold these elements together but, since the voice-of-God is male and speaks English, it essentially drowns out the voices of the film's French-speaking subjects—and that of its female director.

However, the voice of Alexis Tremblay was finally heard to great effect in *Pour la suite du monde* (Pierre Perrault and Michel Brault, 1963). The family had in the meantime moved to the Ile-aux-Coudres in the St Lawrence, where Perrault met them while making a series of radio documentaries on the island.[3] For the film, he persuaded a group of the inhabitants, led by Alexis's son Léopold, to revive the traditional practice of trapping beluga whales, which had once been the mainstay of the local economy. The film documents the placement of poles in the offshore waters, following the traces of the earlier traps, and the eventual capture of one whale, which Léopold and Alexis take to an aquarium in New York.

Apart from some captions at the beginning that acknowledge the filmmakers' intervention, there is no commentary, and the soundtrack consists of 'a network of interweaving voices defining life values through the energy of their speech' (Harcourt, 1984: 131). Alexis Tremblay's is not the only voice heard, but his creative use of a distinctively Québécois French (that had to be subtitled in France) made him into a key, but controversial, icon for the separatist movement.[4] While the film was widely interpreted as a celebration of the deep roots of Quebec culture, the rural setting and Alexis's insistence on respect for the 'ancestors' raised questions about the relevance of its vision for a modern urban society.[5]

The title of *Pour le suite du monde* emphasizes the idea of succession or continuity, an idea completely lost in the abbreviated English-language version, with an added commentary, called *Moontrap*. For Perrault, the film embodied a national identity rooted in 'our *acharnation*—our "stubbornation," that staggering word invented by Alexis Tremblay' (Lévesque, 1968: 126). The speech of the islanders, coupled with Brault's close-ups of their weather-beaten faces and striking long shots of the poles reflected in the water, created the complex sense of a national feeling grounded in lived experience.

The differences between *Alexis Tremblay Habitant* and *Pour la suite du monde* can be attributed to the gap between Canadian and Québécois cultural perspectives, but they are also the product of developments in the idea of documentary realism in the intervening years. In its refusal to guide the spectator's response through an authoritative, pre-scripted commentary, *Pour la suite du monde* belongs to a movement that began at the NFB in the 1950s and was usually referred to in Quebec as *le direct*. The corresponding English term was 'direct cinema', but this became very much entangled with the term 'cinéma-vérité'. Both designate films that make use of new lightweight equipment to create a more intimate and immediate relationship with the subjects and that investigate a situation rather than follow a preconceived script.

The two terms were often used to make a crucial distinction between films that simply claim to represent an unmanipulated reality and those that (like *Pour la suite du monde*) acknowledge the intervention of the filmmakers in that reality. Unfortunately, they were not defined consistently by filmmakers in different national traditions (see Feldman, 2003: 31–2). For the sake of convenience, I will refer to these films as direct cinema, because this term was widely used in Canada and was also applied to the fiction films that emerged from this tradition in the 1960s.

The possibilities of direct cinema were first explored in Canada by NFB filmmakers within Unit B, set up during a major reorganization in 1948, and *l'équipe française*, an emerging group of francophone filmmakers. A key early film from Unit B was *Corral* (Colin Low, 1954), in which the filmmakers, under the leadership of producer Tom Daly, dispensed with the intended commentary so that its lyrical shots of a rancher rounding up wild horses were accompanied only by a solo guitar.[6] For the

Board's francophone filmmakers, the equivalent breakthrough film was *Les Raquetteurs* (Gilles Groulx and Michel Brault, 1958), a short and often humorous film documenting a snowshoers' convention in Sherbrooke.

The direct cinema documentaries not only rejected the authoritarian structures of the Griersonian tradition but also responded to emerging concerns about the ideological implications of realism. In an influential article, David Clandfield argued that *l'équipe française* reinvigorated documentary filmmaking through 'the "impassioned" involvement of the filmmaker in his pro-filmic material, the social "milieu"', while the Unit B filmmakers adopted a less innovative strategy of 'dispassionate empiricism' (1984: 113). As might be expected, the Quebec filmmakers were more politically explicit in their project, but the Unit B films, while certainly less involved with their subjects, also often implicated the spectator by drawing attention to the processes by which their images of reality were constructed.

Unit B consolidated its approach in a series of films made for the CBC television series *Candid Eye* (1958–9). The first film shot for this series was *The Days Before Christmas* (Terence Macartney-Filgate, 1958), in which several filmmakers spread out through Montreal in the pre-Christmas season. It presents a series of observations of everyday life with a sparse and unassuming commentary delivered by one of the filmmakers (Stanley Jackson). As Seth Feldman has pointed out, the style is 'candid', not just in its claim to reveal reality but also in its acknowledgement of the technology that makes this revelation possible. Feldman argues that the film's final revelation is that there is no 'ultimate direction here, no single metaphor' and that the meaning of Christmas is 'nothing other than all the things we can see and hear at that time of year and all the ways we can see and hear them.' The process of editing a film from the varied material shot in the course of a few days demonstrates only that 'the more we edit them, the more disparate they become' (2003: 44).

A few years later, an even larger army of filmmakers set out to document the life of a working-class section of Montreal in *À Saint-Henri, le 5 septembre* (Hubert Aquin, 1962). The aim was to inject a more political engagement with Quebec culture into the work of the *l'équipe française*. The film's producer, Fernand Dansereau, later disowned its methods on the grounds that they still 'involved an *outsider's* observations, despite the makers' good intentions' (Morris, 1984: 2). However, this judgement is already incorporated into the film itself through its self-reflexive commentary, written by Jacques Godbout, which raises the issue of the relationship of the filmmakers to the people they are filming and finally admits that 'Saint-Henri has still not yielded its secret.'

The 'failure' of these two films to uncover an underlying and unifying reality points to the ways in which direct cinema raises questions about the national-realist project, to which it was still ostensibly committed. For the Unit B filmmakers, the changes in documentary form reflected a more tentative sense of the nation, as a mosaic of different groups whose identities are shaped by many, often contradictory, factors. The Quebec experience involved a stronger sense of the nation, but it is clearly an exaggeration to suggest, as Feldman once did, that '*Les Raquetteurs* and the films like it . . . brought forth in their straightforward iconography perceptions emblematic of the new national identity' (Clandfield, 1984: 112). While the iconography in these films may support the nationalist cause, the loss of the voice of authority opens the films to more diverse interpretations. It becomes increasingly clear that national myths are constructions and that documentary, Grierson's tool for nation-building, can also be used to expose the complexity that the myths conceal as well as the fictions that we often take for reality.

Too Real? A Married Couple and Les Ordres

Realism came under heavy attack in the 1960s. Drawing on the ideas of German dramatist Bertolt Brecht and French political philosopher Louis Althusser, a new generation of critics argued that most forms of realism function as a vehicle for the dominant ideology and thus as an obstacle to social change. This argument was taken up in Britain by a group of film theorists associated with the journal *Screen*, who developed the notion of 'the classic realist text', a broad category that encompassed Hollywood features and most documentaries. According to this argument, a realist film 'denies its own status as articulation' and offers the spectator 'a point of view from which everything becomes obvious' (MacCabe, 1974: 9, 16). Needed instead are films that expose the contradictions in the social order by drawing 'the viewer's attention to his or her relation to the screen in order to make him or her "realise" the social relations that are being portrayed' (MacCabe, 1976: 25).

This argument against realism turned Grierson's position against itself: if the realist image was a means of showing the way things are, it thereby served the interests of those opposed to social change. In any case, according to this argument, the conventional NFB documentaries did not simply represent reality but showed a selective version, thereby transforming public service into public relations. The NFB itself responded to this kind of thinking in 1967 by introducing a new program called Challenge for Change.

Ironically, this program grew out of a film called *The Things I Cannot Change* (Tanya Ballantyne, 1966), a documentary intended to expose the conditions of poverty in which many Canadians lived. Using direct cinema techniques with no commentary, the film depicts the everyday life of a Montreal family; but the publicity it generated when shown on CBC television had less to do with the topic of poverty than with its exploitation of the family.[7] The Challenge for Change program sought to avoid this problem by putting 'the means of communications into the hands of people' and thus, as the official mandate stated, 'to prepare Canadians for social change' (Morris, 1984: 60–1). Its greatest success came with a series of films made in 1968 by Colin Low with the inhabitants of Fogo Island, Newfoundland.[8]

Although the program began in 1967, it only received official government support in 1969, at which time it was expanded to include a French-language counterpart under the title 'Société nouvelle'. However, the idea of social change in Quebec was almost synonymous with the independence movement, a situation that posed major problems for a federally funded institution like the NFB. The program did make possible the feminist films of the *En tant que femmes* series (1973–4), produced by Anne

Claire Poirier; but the limits of its definition of 'change' became apparent in the treatment of Denys Arcand's *On est au coton* (1970), a feature-length documentary on the textile industry in Quebec.

This film was not part of the series and was conceived, at least in part, to expose how the NFB sought to manage rather than promote change. The NFB banned it for several years after the Canadian Textile Institute objected to its depiction of unhealthy working conditions, union-busting tactics used by owners in the past, and the impact of unemployment caused by the closure of mills the companies deemed unprofitable. Since the workers were francophone and most of the owners were anglophone, separatists pursuing social change on their own terms adopted the film, and illicit video copies found larger audiences than the film would have attracted without the ban.[9] The title is a colloquial French expression meaning 'we're fed up', and the film captured the widespread discontent of many young people at this time, although it was later criticized for its focus on workers who were apparently resigned to their fate.

The Challenge for Change program continued until 1980, but it lost much of its impetus in its later years and was 'allowed to quietly wither away' (Morris, 1984: 61). However, the NFB continued to contribute to the questioning of the documentary myth of objectivity, especially in films in which the filmmaker becomes an on-screen participant. These include the diary films of Michael Rubbo, an Australian-born filmmaker who developed an ironic and probing screen persona in films such as *Waiting for Fidel* (1974), in which he travels to Cuba but fails to meet Castro, and *Daisy: The Story of a Facelift* (1983), in which he takes off from a colleague's plastic surgery to explore the social implications of physical appearance.[10] Similarly, Jean Chabot's *Voyage en Amérique avec un cheval emprunté* (1987) sends the filmmaker on a journey that becomes a meditation on Quebec's 'américanité', while Alanis Obomsawin also often appears in her own films about First Nations people (see Chapter 10).[11] All these filmmakers, and others pursuing similar strategies, had to deal with objections from those—like CBC television programmers—who claimed that their films were not sufficiently balanced and objective.

The ideological debate over realism came to the fore in the critical response to two controversial but apparently quite different films, Allan King's *A Married Couple* (1969) and Michel Brault's *Les Ordres* (1974). While King's film placed pressure on the public gaze of the documentary tradition by applying it to the intimate spaces of domestic life, Brault addressed the public events of the October Crisis of 1970 but used fictional strategies to bring out the personal experience of the many innocent people who were arrested. These two films were far from the only—or the first—to blur the boundaries between documentary and fiction, but the controversies they generated posed the questions in an acute form. Both films provoked new terms to describe their strategies, 'actuality drama' in King's case and 'documented fiction' in Brault's (Kael, 1974: 135; Marsolais, 1975: 12).

King had already run into trouble with *Warrendale* (1966), a documentary on the unconventional methods used in a home for disturbed children, which was intended for television but refused by the CBC, ostensibly because of the language used by the children.[12] The use of hand-held cameras and wide-angle lenses to get close to the children in highly emotional situations proved as controversial as—and strangely analogous to—the home's therapy of hugging troubled inmates until they became calm. For his next film, King advertised for a couple whose marriage was in crisis and who would be willing to be filmed in their home over a period of several weeks. He eventually settled on Antoinette and Billy Edwards, a middle-class couple living in a Toronto suburb, and shot 70 hours of footage before editing it into a feature film for theatrical release.

The debate over the film often turned on the question of how the presence of the filmmakers affected the couple's behaviour. Critics tended to assume that King's aim was to film the couple going about their everyday lives as they would if the camera were not there. Cameraman Richard Leiterman indeed described the 'invisible barrier' created by the 'ground rule that we would have no communication with them, nor would they communicate anything to us' (Rosenthal, 1970: 23). On the other hand, the presence of the camera obviously precipitated many of the situations: the couple quarrel about how they will spend the money they are going to receive for making the film, and, at one point, Antoinette defends herself for not using the car as planned by saying that 'Allan was here until 10:45.' King himself insists that 'people, at least in the films I've done in cinéma-vérité style, are always aware of the camera because that's the reason they get involved in the first place' (Stone, 2003: 34).

A 'Brechtian' filmmaker (like Jean-Luc Godard) might have drawn explicit attention to the actual 'reality' of the situation, perhaps by showing the couple signing the contract that preceded the filming.[13] Yet the presence of the camera is implicitly acknowledged, and part of the experience of the film is an awareness of the role it has played in influencing the behaviour we witness. King's use of this consciousness represents a highly sophisticated exploration of the fictional element in documentary and the theatrical element in everyday life. His approach belongs to the kind of cinéma-vérité practised by the French anthropologist and filmmaker Jean Rouch, who argued that the truth (*vérité*) that emerges is specifically cinematic, 'a new truth . . . which has nothing to do with normal reality' but is the product of the camera's presence as 'an incredible stimulant for the observed as well as the observer' (Yakir, 1978: 7–8).

The film opens with Billy and Antoinette showing out (unseen) friends whose visit has obviously been something of a strain. We are thus immediately conscious of penetrating behind their public images. As Billy begins to undress and the camera follows them to the bedroom, they argue about things that they do not have and that (presumably) they plan to buy with the money they will get for allowing King to film them. The film thus draws attention to the suppression of its apparatus and to our situation as voyeurs viewing behaviour that is ambiguously coded as 'real' or 'performed'.

The evident ways in which the couple perform for the camera led some critics to contest the film's realist credentials. Pauline Kael objected to the 'elaborate games of role-playing' and complained that 'we don't know enough about the Edwardses' forms of faking or about King's methods of selection.' She pointed out that the couple had 'previous connections with acting' and felt their attempts to improvise became 'a parody of Method acting' (1974: 136–7). On the other hand, Philip Strick thought that

'Billy and Antoinette play their part beautifully' and that 'their exchanges flow with the ease and logic of any scripted marital drama' (1970: 219).

As Strick suggests, the film often evokes fictional models, such as the squabbling couples in television sitcoms or the marital struggles in the plays of August Strindberg and, to take a more contemporary example, Edward Albee's *Who's Afraid of Virginia Woolf?* (1962). King admitted that the material was not edited in chronological order and explained that 'all I do is take episodes and put them into a dramatic structure that works for me' (Rosenthal, 1970: 14). In his review, Ron Blumer agreed that 'the film, as a whole, is as tight as any pre-scripted work' and argued that it gains its power because 'cinema's little-explored ability to transmit whole chunks of reality is thrown in as an extra bonus' (1971: 472).

What Strick calls the productive 'ambiguity of Allan King's method' (1970: 220) is apparent not only in the film's temporal structure but also in its *mise en scène*. When Billy enters the bathroom, we see a framed reproduction of a Rembrandt painting, usually known as 'The Jewish Bride' but also as 'The Married Couple', and when Antoinette discusses her problems with a friend in a café, a storefront full of mannequins is visible in the background. Such moments function much as they would in a fiction film, as symbolic commentary on the couple's life, but we remain uncertain about the extent to which these juxtapositions are coincidental or arranged by the filmmakers.

The film thus hovers between claims to documentary authenticity and fictional artifice. King insisted that 'what is going on isn't really acting', but he recognized that 'they were making things up—and therefore it's not real' (Stone, 2003: 33). While he acknowledged that the Billy and Antoinette seen in the film are not the same as in 'actual real life', he also pointed out that 'we all, at all times, and to varying degrees perform, or perform as if we were different people' (Rosenthal, 1970: 15, 13). As Robert Fulford put it, the film is 'not a voyeur's delight, but a new way of exploring reality' (1974: 34), and this new way depends on accepting that elements of fiction, theatricality, and artifice are part of reality.

Although—or perhaps because—it acknowledges that Billy and Antoinette are performers, the film led one reviewer to write that, 'time and time again, one finds oneself wincing and looking away from the screen because what is coming from it is obviously too real' (Blumer, 1971: 471). The same reviewer also felt that *Les Ordres* was 'haunting like no other political film partly because it's so close to home and partly because it's so understatedly real' (Blumer, 1975: 77). In both cases, the effect of the 'real' was created by a process of distillation: whereas this process occurred during post-production in *A Married Couple*, Brault shifted it to pre-production, during which he interviewed many people who were imprisoned under the War Measures Act, imposed after members of the Front de Libération du Québec (FLQ) kidnapped a British diplomat and a Quebec cabinet minister.

He then condensed their stories into a few exemplary cases, and the characters thus created are played by actors who introduce themselves and their characters when they first appear. This acknowledgement of the production process is a 'distancing' device in the Brechtian tradition, and Gilles Marsolais called the film 'a perfect application of the theories of Brecht to the cinema' (1975: 13). Other critics—sympathetic and otherwise—stressed the emotional power of the film. Thus Robin Wood objected that, after the actors introduce themselves, 'Brechtian distance is abandoned in favor of the encouragement of straightforward identification with nice people and "correct" liberal-humanist emotions' (1975: 28). Robert Fulford, on the other hand, admired the film because 'Brault's direction is so involving, and his use of the actors so skilful, that our identification is complete' (1984: 3).

For some critics, the extreme situations depicted in the film had more in common with the nightmare visions of Franz Kafka than with Brecht's political theatre or any form of realism. André Leroux thought that Brault creates 'an unreal universe where everything is simultaneously logical and illogical, tangible and intangible, precise and imprecise' (1975: 120). The film begins with an argument in which a mother annoys her daughter by demanding that she come straight home from school, and the subsequent events thus become a monstrous fulfillment of this fear of the outside world.

This emphasis on the personal experience of the victims led to accusations that Brault ignored the political issues and reduced the October Crisis to a human problem, a criticism often directed at classic narrative cinema. Fulford felt that this approach gave the film 'a kind of universal dimension by forcibly readjusting the audience's views not only of the Montreal political prisoners it depicts but of *all* prisoners in *all* jails' (1984: 3). René Lévesque, then leader of the Parti Québécois, also praised the film as 'a very beautiful and poignant illustration of the how', but he noted that 'what is missing . . . is the why. And also, of course, the who' (1975: 124). For Pierre Vallières, who had been a leading member of the FLQ, this was a crucial omission, and he argued that the film even misrepresented the 'how' by not showing that 'the immense majority of the people arrested on 16 October were Québécois who were politicized and committed' (1974: 19–20).

The charge that the film lacked political analysis could also be laid from a very different ideological perspective, as it was by Nat Shuster, who also asked why the film ignores 'the causes for these arrests' but thought 'there is something quite ludicrous in attempting to turn this comic-opera police-state escapade into a cause calling for a revolutionary response' (1975: 24). This uncompassionate reading implies that the film covertly supports the FLQ position, but a more balanced assessment came from Robert Fulford, who argued that the omissions work 'to make us want to know a great deal more about this crucial event in our history' (Fulford, 1984: 4).

The film is, in any case, not completely silent about who was responsible. It begins with a caption quoting an earlier affirmation of civil rights by Pierre Trudeau, the Prime Minister who invoked the War Measures Act, and a later caption identifies Jean Drapeau, the Mayor of Montreal, as the authority who determined that there was a need to 'protect society against the seditious plot and apprehended insurrection'. As the film goes on to demonstrate, the 'orders' from the political establishment become a screen behind which the police and army can hide. Just before one of the prisoners is released, a policeman tells him that 'terrorists' should not think that they can 'go pushing decent people around', but what the film shows is that, as Michel

Brûlé put it, 'ordinary people were accused of fomenting a plot against society, but . . . on the contrary there was a plot against these people' (1974: 15).[14]

One of the most important, but much questioned, aspects of the film's style was the insertion of colour sequences into what is predominantly a black-and-white film. Some reviewers found this effect 'rather arbitrary' or 'a nuisance and a puzzlement' (Fulford, 1984: 4; Shuster, 1975: 24). According to Bill Marshall, it was adopted because 'money was not available for a complete colour feature' (2001: 40), but, if this was the case, it is another example, among many in Canadian cinema, of an economic exigency being adapted to aesthetic purpose. It works as a distancing device (since it calls attention to the medium) but, simultaneously, it functions as an intensifier of the emotional impact.

When one of the arrested men describes his first experience of prison, he comments on the colours that got on his nerves. At this point, the film turns from black-and-white into colour. Several others also comment on the colours in the prison and, when one of the women is released, the colour drains from the image as she walks away. Even during the central sequences in the prison, all shots of the world outside are in black-and-white, except when one prisoner is taken in custody to attend his father's funeral. The use of colour thus implies that the crisis created a sense of heightened reality—and, as the prison sequences show, communal awareness—among the victims. After their release, the whiteness of the snow suggests that mundane reality has been reinstated and that nothing has been achieved, with the Québécois people being left bewildered and resentful.

The critical debates that erupted around *Les Ordres* and *A Married Couple* reveal an uncertainty about the aesthetic and ideological implications of realism. Brault challenged his audience with what Marsolais called a 'layered structure' that establishes 'subtle dialectical relations between the real and its representation, the present and the past, commentary and witness' (1975: 12–13). Both films sought to deepen and renew the realist tradition by scrambling the distinctions on which the arguments for and against realism depended.

Faking It: The Canadian Mockumentary

The debate over realism during the 1970s, and especially the ethical concerns regarding films like *A Married Couple*, may seem rather quaint in the age of so-called reality television. Cameras have become such a presence in contemporary culture that Denys Arcand could plausibly follow the rise and fall of a supermodel in his *Stardom* (2000) using only images (supposedly) taken from newsreels, television shows, and home movies. This was a fiction film satirizing celebrity culture, but popular television series have now turned the lives of ordinary people into a form of entertainment that makes King's documentaries seem quite discreet. As parodied in Michel Poulette's *Louis 19, le roi des ondes* (see Chapter 11), the public gaze of documentary regularly crosses into areas once regarded as private.

Digital technology also makes possible the creation of reality effects that have no existence in actuality. Whereas the documentary tradition always defined itself in opposition to a cinema of illusion, we now live in a culture in which, according to Jean Baudrillard, 'illusion is no longer possible, because the real is no longer possible.' What Baudrillard is claiming is that the technological ability to reproduce reality has become so powerful that, instead of experiencing the real as something that resists our efforts to represent it, the real has become 'not only what can be reproduced, but *that which is always already reproduced*' (1983: 38, 146). In this 'postmodern' world, the loss of a secure sense of reality erodes many cultural distinctions, including that between documentary and fiction, but it also inspires desperate efforts to reinstate the real, including religious and other kinds of fundamentalism.

In contemporary films and television programs, the characteristics of direct cinema, such as hand-held cameras, jump cuts, and grainy images, have become familiar devices in fictional as well as documentary contexts, contributing to what Timothy Luke calls 'the proliferation of second-hand authenticity' in media texts (1991: 6–7). Such works simulate the truth claims of traditional documentary and, in doing so, threaten to undermine the impact of those documentaries that still seek to provide evidence about actuality. One manifestation of this state of affairs is the emergence of a genre often known as the mockumentary or mock-documentary.

There have been many such films, in Canada and elsewhere, and this is not the place to go into a detailed history of the genre.[15] In some cases, they still make documentary truth claims, as in the films of Michael Moore, which develop the idea of the filmmaker as on-screen provocateur that Rubbo had pioneered at the NFB.[16] More commonly, the mockumentary is a disguised fiction film, but they all play with the uncertain status of realism in contemporary culture, while the extent to which they collude with or critique this culture varies considerably. Two recent Canadian examples suggest that digital video is the contemporary equivalent of the new equipment that enabled the earlier direct cinema films. They also follow to a logical conclusion the blurring of the distinction between fiction and reality in those films.

Both *La Moitié gauche du frigo* (Philippe Falardeau, 2000) and *FUBAR* (Michael Dowse, 2002) begin with credits that attribute the films to the fictional directors who appear in them, although the latter is preceded by a disclaimer from Odeon Films explaining that it is a fiction and apologizing to people who appeared in it thinking it was a documentary. It is characteristic of the genre that it is impossible to tell whether this caption expresses the genuine concern of the distributors about possible legal action or is just part of the mockery. In both films, a filmmaker sets out to document the everyday lives of his subjects: in *La Moitié gauche du frigo*, Stéphane (Stéphane Demers) makes a film about Christophe (Paul Ahmarani), his unemployed roommate, as he searches for a job in Montreal; in *FUBAR*, Farrel (Gordon Skilling) enlists the collaboration of Dean (Paul J. Spence) and Terry (Dave Lawrence) to explore 'headbanger' culture in Calgary.

Although both (fictional) filmmakers have serious ambitions, their efforts correspond to a trend that has developed out of the use of hand-held cameras to 'reject professionalism for a more general amateurism which is seen as being more truthful or "authentic'" (Roscoe and Hight, 2001: 39). In these films, however, this claim to authenticity is itself called into question.

Stéphane's film seems to be more truthful before he attracts funding from Radio-Canada (which did, in fact, back Falardeau's film) and hires a crew. Yet his status as an observer is ambiguous from the beginning. He provokes confrontations to bring out Christophe's plight as a qualified engineer who cannot find a job in Quebec, where companies are laying off employees despite making huge profits. At one point, an anglophone executive tells him that he is 'a poor Michael Moore', and his efforts do not help Christophe, who tires of being followed around. He complains that he feels like the character in *Louis 19 le roi des ondes*, who becomes the star of a reality television show, and he eventually moves to Vancouver, where, according to the final captions, he is currently working as a music teacher in a high school—and it is now Stéphane who is unemployed.

The allusion to *Louis 19* is a reminder of the closeness of the film to the broad comedies that proved very popular in Quebec in the 1990s. *FUBAR*, whose title is an acronym for 'Fucked Up Beyond All Recognition', is even more tied to the popular comic tradition, since it grew out of characters developed by the lead actors in impro-vised stage routines. The distinction between the comic and the documentary is, in any case, very blurred since one of the funniest sequences involves actual 'headbangers' who (apparently) thought the documentary was genuine. While the opening of the film seems to be completely complicit with the aimless and hedonistic lives of its subjects, it gains momentum and becomes more complicated when Terry is diagnosed with testicular cancer and the director dies in a swimming accident. The 'real' intervenes in a potentially traumatic way, even if these developments are fictional and quickly drawn into the general mock-serious tone.

Both films include sequences in which the filmmakers follow their subjects away from the city. When Christophe drives 1,000 kilometres to apply for a job only to be told he is not qualified, he pokes fun at the clichés associated with Canada's 'wide open spaces'. Dean and Terry decide to spend the last weekend before Terry's operation in the country, where they drink a lot of beer and persuade their director to take his ill-fated plunge. Even the natural environment, a major factor in Canada's cultural traditions (see Chapter 3), no longer seems to function as a meaningful cultural symbol—or even as the last refuge of the real for the urban citizens of the new global economy.

This erosion of a sense of the real, often seen as a symptom of postmodern culture, poses a major challenge in these films not only to the national-realist project but also to the documentary mode itself. However, this challenge is less a negation of the Canadian realist tradition than a development from within it, and one that suggests the possibility of new and unpredictable collaborations between documentary and fiction.

1964 Revisited: The Sense of a Beginning

To tabulate what these two films have in
common is to underline their differences—
not only differences between the two films
but between the two cultures.

—Peter Harcourt (1980: 64–5)

Canonical lists raise questions not only
about what is *included* but also about
what is *excluded*.

—Peter Morris (1994: 31)

In a highly influential article, Peter Harcourt identified 1964 as 'the Beginning of a Beginning' for Canadian cinema. He discussed two films produced in that year, Gilles Groulx's *Le Chat dans le sac* and Don Owen's *Nobody Waved Good-bye*, and stressed their roots in 'the tradition of observational documentary established at the Film Board throughout the fifties'. Both films were NFB productions, made by young directors who used the budgets originally intended for short documentary projects, but Harcourt also stressed their cinematic and cultural differences, arguing that while Owen's film 'stands on the shoulders' of the documentary tradition, Groulx 'contests it' (1980: 64).

Despite this distinction, Harcourt's article reinforced a critical position that was already emerging whereby these two films became the founding features in a distinctively Canadian tradition of documentary-influenced 'realist' films. For many years, it was assumed—by supporters and detractors alike—that most Canadian films, or at least the best or most typical of them, belonged to this tradition. Like most critical canons, this one plausibly identified some aspects of the new Canadian cinema, most notably its condition as a 'poor cinema', but it also tended to obscure the diversity of film production in Canada and to downplay the differences between even those films that did apparently fit into the tradition.

The canon first came under serious scrutiny in the debate set off in 1985 by avant-garde filmmaker Bruce Elder in an article entitled 'The Cinema We Need'. In this debate, Canadian cinema was both attacked (by Elder) and defended as a realist cinema with its roots in documentary traditions (see Chapter 7), and not until the 1990s did critics begin to question this basic premise. By examining the critical discourses about Canadian cinema, Peter Morris identified the two major—and interlinked—canonical criteria as a 'realist tendency' and a 'nationalist orientation' (1994: 35, 33). In effect, then, the canon was an extension of Grierson's 'national-realist' project.

The idea that 1964 was the 'beginning' of a feature film industry in Canada has since been further questioned by critics and historians who point to significant films made a few years earlier. These include several small-budget films produced in the late 1950s and early 1960s in an effort to develop a commercial film industry in Canada, notably: *The Mask* (Julian Roffman, 1961), a horror film that became the first Canadian feature distributed by a major Hollywood studio (Corupe, 2003–4: 21); *À tout prendre* (Claude Jutra, 1963), regarded by Morris as 'the most surprising omission' (1994: 31) and presumably disregarded because of the elements of fantasy and subjective vision that complicate its evident debt to the 'direct cinema' tradition; and Donald Haldane's *Drylanders*, made at the NFB a year before *Nobody Waved Good-bye* but released later, whose blend of drama and documentary in a historical narrative about early settlers in Saskatchewan seemed less adventurous at the time, but which is the subject of a recent article urging a reconsideration of 'the complexity of this major Canadian film' (Moen, 2001: 29).

Yet another version of the 'beginning of the beginning' emerges from the recollections of Michael Spencer, a self-proclaimed 'cultural bureaucrat' who worked at the NFB in the 1960s and became the first Executive Director of the Canadian Film Development Corporation in 1967. Spencer does not even mention *Nobody Waved Good-bye* or *Le Chat dans le sac*. Instead he credits Gilles Carle's *La Vie heureuse de*

Léopold Z (1965) as the film whose commercial success gave momentum to the campaign that led to the creation of the CFDC (2003: 22). Carle's film was also made at the NFB and originally planned as a documentary (on snow removal), but its comic and romantic plot discouraged critics from taking it as seriously as the two films produced in much the same way in the previous year (see Chapter 5).

Spencer also refers in passing to other pockets of production that encouraged the supporters of a Canadian film industry. Three of these endeavours generated films in 1964 that initially seemed even more promising than their NFB counterparts. *The Luck of Ginger Coffey* was produced by veteran Canadian filmmaker Budge Crawley, who wanted to expand from the production of documentaries and short films into the mainstream feature market. *Trouble-fête* was the first film produced by Coopératio, a company founded by Pierre Patry (the director), Jean-Claude Lord (the screenwriter), and Robert Blais, who each invested $2,000 (Spencer, 2003: 16). *Sweet Substitute* was the second small-budget feature directed in British Columbia by Larry Kent, a recent immigrant from South Africa. The year 1964 may not have been the real beginning, but these films—along with the two canonical films—illustrate the problems and the possibilities involved in the creation of a new Canadian cinema.[1]

Beginning Afresh

Nat Taylor, the Canadian film distributor who produced *The Mask*, argued that Canada's proximity to the US should be seen as an advantage that would allow the production of films 'practically indistinguishable' from the Hollywood product (Magder, 1993: 106). Budge Crawley took the opposite position, insisting that a Canadian film industry could succeed only if it created 'something distinct that has sales appeal because it's a production unique to Canada' (Magder, 1993: 94). Whereas *The Mask* carefully concealed its Canadian origins, *The Luck of Ginger Coffey* foregrounds its Montreal locations. On the other hand, Crawley's nationalist orientation did not prevent him from hiring British actors for the major roles and a largely British crew, led by American director Irvin Kershner (who went on to direct many large-budget Hollywood films but had previously worked mainly in documentary and television). As a result, the film 'wasn't considered "Canadian" by critics when it was first released', although it did win the award for Best Feature at the Canadian Film Awards in 1965 (Wise, 2001: 134).

The British connection is most apparent in the film's narrative and style. A series of working-class realist films, beginning with *Room at the Top* (Jack Clayton, 1958), had established a 'British New Wave', drawing on the British documentary movement but also on theatrical and literary traditions. Like all the British films, *The Luck of Ginger Coffey* was adapted from a literary source, in this case a novel by Brian Moore, an Irish writer who drew on his own experiences as an immigrant to Canada. Its two British stars were experienced stage and film actors, although not usually associated with the Irish accents required in this film: Robert Shaw (Ginger) most often played villains in British genre films but had recently appeared in the film version of Harold Pinter's

The Caretaker (Clive Donner, 1963), while Mary Ure, who plays his long-suffering wife, had a similar role in the adaptation of John Osborne's *Look Back in Anger* (Tony Richardson, 1959).

This British tradition of 'quality' cinema rooted in realism accords well with Canadian critical discourses of the time (see Morris, 1989). *The Luck of Ginger Coffey* is basically a character study about a 'new Canadian' who finds that Montreal does not provide the opportunities he had expected. His wife leaves him when she finds that he has spent the money they had saved to return to Ireland, and, when their teenage daughter chooses to stay with her father, he is unable to cope with this responsibility. Although Ginger is middle-aged and Irish, Shaw invests him with what one critic called 'a childish gawkiness' (Burgess, 1964: 57), and he has much in common with the adolescent males in the low-budget 'direct cinema' films that came to form the canon. In particular, the gulf between his qualifications and the jobs he expects anticipates Pete's experiences in Toronto in Don Shebib's *Goin' Down the Road* (see Chapter 3).

The film establishes its setting, as well as the pressures of time and money against which Ginger struggles, in its opening shot of a clock bearing the name of the Bank of Montreal. During the credits sequence, long shots of the city's snow-covered streets recall the urban landscapes of the British films, and one enthusiastic British reviewer praised the film's depiction of 'a real place fixed in a definite time in history' (Johnson, 1965: 31). Yet, while critics often accused the British filmmakers of making their bleak settings look picturesque, the depiction of Montreal was seen as authentically oppressive. One reviewer commented that 'the winter light is mean and sparing like so much else in this inimical place' and another suggested that cinematographer Manny Wynn 'has photographed Montreal very acutely . . . , but the film won't make you want to live there' (Sussex, 1965: 149; Burgess, 1964: 57).

Apart from its unsuitability as an incentive to tourism, the film sets up a tension between Ginger's optimism and resilience and the frequent humiliations he suffers because of his refusal to accept the reality of his situation. In a darkly comic ending, he gets drunk after losing two jobs in one day and is arrested for indecent exposure when he urinates on a public building. Although his trial brings the family together again, there is little sense that the reunion will be permanent or that Ginger will be able to settle down. This uncomfortable vision must have made it hard to sell the film, despite its stars and good reviews; and its commercial failure discouraged Crawley from pursuing his interest in feature films.[2]

As Ted Magder asks: 'If a well-capitalized and able producer such as Crawley could not sustain feature film production, how much greater would be the obstacles encountered by a less established producer?' (1993: 93–4). The filmmakers who formed the Coopératio collective overcame these obstacles, at least temporarily, by beginning on a much smaller scale. *Trouble-fête* was shot in 25 days on a shoestring budget and was 'an immense commercial success' (Marsolais, 1968: 87). However, Patry dissociated himself from the direct cinema tradition, and instead positioned his film as a first step towards a Quebec popular cinema. Whereas *The Luck of Ginger Coffey* only briefly acknowledges the francophone population in Montreal, there are no signs of the English in *Trouble-fête*.

The film's plot hinges on a student rebellion against the restrictions of an educational system controlled by the Catholic Church. Although the school depicted would already be rather anachronistic by 1964, the demands for a more modern curriculum and increased personal freedom reflect the ideas of the Quiet Revolution, which had brought major changes to Quebec culture and whose triumph was symbolized by the election of Jean Lesage's Liberal government in 1960. By 1964 the break with the past was expressing itself more urgently in a bombing campaign by the FLQ, which is not directly represented in the film but to which some critics attributed the violent atmosphere that envelops its style and plot (Marsolais, 1968: 88). On the other hand, the violence, along with the car chases and lively jazz score, might be attributed to what Bill Marshall calls the 'very American' ambience of a film that seeks to adapt the pleasures of Hollywood cinema to the Quebec context (2001: 64).

Near the beginning of the film, a priest lectures his class on the need for 'a modern hero' to arrest the decline of moral values in society. Lucien (Lucien Hamelin), who walks out during this sermon, is the film's modern Quebec hero, but he rejects the terms on which the priest defines heroism. He tries to channel the rowdiness of his fellow students into coherent action, but the authorities refuse to listen to his requests for reform. The Principal rejects the idea of a 'mixed film club', but the meetings of a theatre society and a jazz club (where Lucien and his friends are arrested in a police raid) evoke the cultural ferment of the time. As the tensions escalate, Lucien defends the students by arguing that they may act like 'babies', but this is the only way to get the authorities to listen to them. The Principal replies that it is easier to destroy than construct, and Lucien's efforts come to nothing when he is shouted down at a meeting by his fellow students chanting that he is a 'troublemaker'.

Gilles Marsolais thought the film 'does justice to the photogenic diversity of Montreal', a quality enhanced by shooting the film in summer (1968: 90). However, much of the action takes place at night, and the opening shots establish the setting with cars speeding through city streets, headlights blazing and tires screeching. Lucien defuses the first threat of violence when the gang he is with terrorizes a couple of lovers exposed by the headlights, but he gradually becomes engulfed in a nightmare world, captured through extremes of light and dark reminiscent of film noir.

The film asserts its 'realism' through the contrast between Lucien's everyday family and school life and the heightened language of the play in which he rehearses. It is this poetic dialogue, however, that releases the film to increasingly involve the viewer in his subjective vision. Devices normally associated with direct cinema, such as hand-held camera shots and jump cuts, come to signify the pressures on the '*trouble-fête*' as he tries to shake up a reality he finds stifling. These pressures increase when his mother dies (for which his father holds him responsible), and the final crisis occurs when he accidentally pushes a man making sexual advances into the path of an oncoming car. He screams and holds up his arms in a Christ-like posture, as a crowd gathered for a parade turns on him, and the camera pans away from him to waving figures on the floats as the parade goes on.

The attractions of modernity in *Trouble-fête* expose the inadequacy of traditional values, but the ending testifies to an underlying anxiety about what is replacing them.

A similar uncertainty is evident in *Sweet Substitute*, and the two films do have much in common. Both use small-band jazz scores—inflected with rock rhythms in the case of *Sweet Substitute*—to evoke the energy of the new youth culture, and both develop a style in which, as Dave Douglas says of Kent's early films, 'objectivity is constantly subverted by ... excess' (1996: 88). The equivalent to the priest's sermon is a high school English class on *Macbeth*, a distinction that reveals the more secular context for the conflict between tradition and modernity in the Vancouver-based film. Tom (Robert Howay)—this film's modern hero—knows that Macbeth's 'tragic flaw' is ambition, but he is more interested in gazing at the legs of his female classmates (another difference from the all-male school in *Trouble-fête*).

Despite the different contexts in which they worked, Larry Kent shared common ground with Budge Crawley regarding the future of film in Canada. He argued that 'we have to find what is uniquely Canadian because without that uniquely Canadian attitude, you are just making very cheap American movies' (McLarty, 1974: 19). Some critics felt that this was precisely what Kent was doing, and they were probably confirmed in their opinion when *Sweet Substitute* proved to be 'a considerable commercial success' largely based on its performance in US cinemas (Morris, 1984: 286). Yet it did receive a Canadian Film Award and was invited to several film festivals, and Piers Handling later compared its 'restless' style to the films of the French New Wave (1986: 11).

Handling also commented on Kent's 'uneasy relationship to the dominant realist tradition' (1986: 16). The sequences in which the youths aimlessly wander through the streets of Vancouver are shot in the observational style of the Candid Eye films. In the opening shots, for example, the camera tracks behind a car and then picks up the youths playing a pinball machine, walking along the street, looking in a store window advertising topless bathing suits, and ogling passing young women. Although the shooting was carefully planned in the interest of economy (Douglas, 1996: 93), the dialogue is largely improvised, and Tom's dilemma rarely takes on the nightmare quality found in *Trouble-fête*.

The 'excess' in this film stems rather from its depiction of adolescent sexuality and, in particular, from the way it involves the spectator in Tom's sexual desires and fears. After he picks up a woman on the street and goes to her room, he is overcome by panic when she undresses, and he runs away, as a swaying hand-held camera follows him down the dark stairwell. In another sequence, a more experienced friend takes Tom and two other young men to the home of a woman who agrees to have sex with all of them. Tom, who is clearly uneasy, arranges to go last and is relieved when her father returns home unexpectedly.

It is thus not surprising that the film defines Tom's dilemma through his relations with two young women. He often studies with Kathy (Carol Pastinsky), who wants to travel and would like to find a place that is 'unspoiled, untouched by Coca-Cola'. She plans to have a career and refuses to wear makeup. On the other hand, Elaine (Angela Gann) is first seen working on her makeup in a mirror and looks forward to leaving school. Tom finds her attractive and takes her to a television pop music show and to the latest Beatles and James Bond movies. Ironically, it is Kathy who gets pregnant, while the seductive Elaine, following her mother's advice to put security before short-term 'fun', refuses to have sex before marriage. As an added irony, after Tom's friends persuade him not to marry Kathy, the film ends with Tom and Elaine kissing, as she displays her new engagement ring. Her insistence on 'sex for a price' equates marriage and prostitution, but it is little different from the promise made by Tom's father that he will buy him a car if he gets a scholarship.

Re-viewing the Canon

Although each of these films could be regarded as 'realist' in some sense of the term, none were admitted to the canon when it began to emerge in the following decade and to shape critical discussions of Canadian cinema as well as academic course outlines. In turn, the emphasis on realism in the critical reception of the canonical films tended to obscure the extent to which they, and others in the direct cinema mode, unsettle basic realist conventions. After all, the attraction to fiction on the part of the NFB film-makers grew out of a dissatisfaction with documentary, which was already apparent in the questioning of the principles of objectivity and dispassionate observation in the work of Unit B and *l'équipe française* (see Chapter 1). The question then becomes how the perceived realism of *Le Chat dans le sac* and *Nobody Waved Good-bye* differentiates them from the other films of 1964.

Groulx and Owen made direct cinema documentaries at the NFB and continued to work in documentary after their feature film debuts. Their films both emerged from documentary projects concerned with the 'youth problem' and apply direct cinema techniques to fictional plots. They both depict young men searching for a sense of identity in a society that cannot meet their needs, and they treat this search in the context of the breakdown of a sexual relationship. In *Le Chat dans le sac*, Claude (Claude Godbout) tries to establish himself as a journalist in Montreal but finally moves to the country, while Barbara (Barbara Ulrich), his Jewish anglophone girlfriend, stays in the city to pursue her career as an actress. In *Nobody Waved Good-bye*, Peter (Peter Kastner) leaves his family home in the Toronto suburbs but finally drives off in a stolen car, leaving his pregnant girlfriend Julie (Julie Biggs) beside the highway.

The main actors in both films share the same first names as their characters, and there is a strong sense that they are familiar with the situations in which the characters find themselves. By eliminating the distance between actors and characters as much as possible, both directors were able to rely heavily on improvisation to make their films 'as spontaneous as possible, starting from a fixed scenario' (Groulx, quoted in Marsolais, 1968: 85). Groulx explained that he spoke to the actors separately so that 'each one did not know what the other was going to say' (Bonneville, 1979: 395), and Owen, too, often 'gave the players incomplete or conflicting instructions so as to create genuine surprise and tension' (1971: 104). Nevertheless, detailed scenarios ensured that the films could be shot quickly, and the result was what Natalie Edwards called, referring to *Nobody Waved Good-bye*, an 'extraordinary marriage of spontaneity and control' (1977: 165).

What Harcourt and other critics immediately noticed, however, was that, despite their common features, which could all be attributed to the direct cinema tradition, they were very different films. The significance of these differences, and the extent to which they corresponded to cultural differences, remained open to some debate. Shortly after their release, Harcourt argued that *Nobody Waved Good-bye* seemed like 'a logical extension' of the open-minded spirit of inquiry that he found in the Unit B films, whereas *Le Chat dans le sac* developed out of *l'équipe française*, whose work lacked 'any reference outwards to the larger world beyond Quebec' (1977a: 76). By 1980, his account of the difference had shifted in favour of the Quebec film: 'unlike *Nobody Waved Good-bye* which sets out to charm us, *Le Chat dans le sac* sets out to confront us' (1980: 66).

It is certainly true that *Le Chat dans le sac* is the more analytic and the more politically aware of the two films. According to Groulx, the film depicts 'a society that is living through pre-revolutionary times' and seeks to individualize 'a collective problem' (Fieschi and Ollier, 1965: 57). The FLQ bombing campaign began while it was in production, and newspaper headlines were incorporated into the film. It was fairly easy, then, to read the film as 'a reflection of the societal awakenings and unease that many artists and intellectuals were manifesting' (Evans, 1991: 94) and to see its depiction of the relationship between 'an anglophone and a francophone who cannot understand each other' as 'symbolic of the situation in Canada' (Prédal, 1967: 47–8).

Groulx set out to achieve a form of realism that would 'abolish the boundaries between documentary and fiction' (Bonneville, 1979: 394), thereby retaining the 'truth' of his work in documentary while bringing a 'critical perspective' to bear (Fieschi and Ollier, 1965: 56). However, he acknowledged that the film's political and symbolic meanings are complicated by an awareness that it bears witness to 'a reality that is very obscure and very difficult to make out' (Fieschi and Ollier, 1965: 57).

This sense of uncertainty emerges from the opening sequence in which Claude describes his situation: 'I am French-Canadian, therefore I am searching for myself.' The title derives from a phrase used by Claude to describe his feeling of being trapped by the lack of options in his life, a situation he attributes to the colonial status of Quebec. Barbara claims that it applies equally to her situation as a woman and a Jew, but Claude gradually becomes convinced that she cannot understand his problems and aspirations. An opening caption informs us that this is a relationship without a future, so the focus is on *why* it ends and on the problem of combining the personal and the political.

Claude applies for jobs with several Quebec publications, but one editor tells him that 'in this society, you'll never succeed by being yourself.' As an actress, Barbara is prepared to play different roles, but she is aware that her accent will limit the parts she can get in Montreal. The basic tension in the film is thus between acting and being, the qualities necessary for practical success and those required to satisfy the individual conscience. Although Claude's political interests seem more 'realistic' than her theatrical pursuits, he cannot find a basis for action, and she accuses him of being a 'dreamer'. The problems of bringing their interests together are accentuated by their separate monologues that convey both their inability to communicate and the impotence generated by a society that does not allow the individual to express him or herself.

There are several references to Bertolt Brecht, a cultural figure who combined Barbara's passion for theatre and Claude's interest in politics, and the film draws on Brecht's idea of the 'separation of elements'.[3] Its narrative is frequently interrupted by still images, written texts, spoken statistics, and music that interact and comment on each other. As Harcourt puts it, 'the film establishes a series of "texts" . . .—texts which we have to "read" as we experience the film in order to make sense of what is going on' (1977a: 142). The discontinuous structure reminded critics of the French New Wave, especially the films of Jean-Luc Godard. Yet, while some felt that the film's style was 'highly derivative' (Morris, 1984: 63), a French critic argued that Groulx had achieved 'what Godard has never been able to produce—a subjectively political film' (Marcorelles, 1973: 72).

The film acknowledges its debt to Godard when Barbara poses next to a still of Anna Karina in *Vivre sa vie* (1962) on the cover of an issue of the Quebec film journal *Objectif 63*. This allusion has a complex effect since it suggests an affinity between Groulx's film and Godard's; but it is just one in a series of media images of women seen throughout the film that evoke the commodification of sexuality in the new consumer society, a topic that Godard addresses in his film about a young prostitute. The cover photo and Barbara's posing raise questions about how to avoid complicity in the system, and Claude's break with Barbara becomes a rejection of this culture 'for its falsity and distortion of . . . the "authentic" individual or nation' (Marshall, 2001: 56).

It seems rather perverse, however, to object, as Gary Evans does, to 'the film's uncomplimentary portrayal of the female [as] the archetypal seductress, a self-absorbed *bourgeoise*' (1991: 94). While the film doubtless is mainly interested in Claude's subjectivity, Barbara speaks for herself and emerges as someone equally caught up in the contradictions of her situation. It remains uncertain to what extent the film wants the viewer to identify with Claude, and this uncertainty is maintained in its ambiguous ending. In her final monologue, Barbara is reflected in a mirror, as so often in the film, putting on makeup and talking of why she must break with Claude's 'defeatism' and 'fear of life'. Claude receives a letter informing him that she cannot come to visit him in his cottage in the country, and he contemplates himself in the bathroom mirror. In the final image, he stands in the snow watching a young— presumably Québécois—woman skating on a frozen pond.

According to Groulx, Claude's retreat is only 'provisional'; he is just conserving his strength and 'will return to his milieu with a more realistic view, now that he knows what to expect' (Bonneville, 1979: 395). The final images, however, are quite enigmatic. A long pan across the snow-covered landscape is followed by an extreme long shot of Claude standing disconsolately, which then freezes for the final credits. The stillness is accentuated by the baroque classical music (Vivaldi, Couperin) that dominates the soundtrack after the move to the country. This music contrasts with the jazz (John Coltrane) heard during Claude's self-questioning and when he recites figures indicating the colonized situation of Quebec, implying a parallel between the

French-Canadian experience and that of the blacks in the US, soon to be more fully developed by Pierre Vallières in his book *Nègres blancs d'Amérique* (1968).[4]

At one point, Coltrane fades into the muzak of a shopping mall, which in turn gives way to a marching band, denounced by Claude as 'the new folklore of alienation'. He also refers to the hope of the blacks in the US that the Jews would understand their situation because 'they too have suffered', and he tells Barbara that, because of her 'nationality', she might have understood his problem. As Bill Marshall suggests, however, the ending implies that it is Claude who 'cannot deal with the Otherness of Barbara, either as femininity or as anglophone Jew' (2001: 57).

The effect of this ending depends on the contrast between its stillness and the disjunctive editing and visual style marked by 'the omnipresence of the camera' in the rest of the film (Daudelin, 1980: 101). In comparison, the fusion of documentary and fiction in *Nobody Waved Good-bye* seems much less complicated. According to Piers Handling, this film's aesthetic is based on an 'attempt to disguise the camera's eye or turn it into a neutral, documentary observer' (1986: 11). Yet, while 'the break was generational (Oedipal), not sociopolitical, as it was in Quebec' (Evans, 1991: 102), Owen's approach has more in common with Groulx's than most critics acknowledge. As Harcourt noted, the film seeks to retain 'the documentary authenticity that characterized the work of Unit B' (1977a: 142), but the result was aptly described by Joan Fox as an 'uncertain style' that is 'neither earnest documentary nor clear-cut drama' (1977: 158).

Peter is significantly younger than Claude and just finishing high school. His family life consists mainly of arguments about his future, but his parents can see this future only in social and economic terms. His father calls him 'a bad investment', and his mother tells him not to become too involved with Julie because his energies should be devoted to gaining the education required to become a lawyer. When Peter leaves home to escape from these pressures, he quickly finds that he cannot cope with the economic realities of life in the city. Although the city is quite visibly Toronto, the film presents it as what I have elsewhere called, borrowing from Northrop Frye (see Chapter 3), an 'obliterated environment', dominated by concrete highways, suburban streets, and parking lots (Leach, 1980: 278). The only signs of nature are the cemetery where Peter and Julie wander in the opening sequence, the urban parkette where Peter sleeps after he leaves home, and the lake on which the couple enjoy a brief, idyllic boat trip. As they drift across the lake, they discover a half-submerged sofa, an item from domestic space whose intrusion into their escape into nature suggests its illusory quality.

Despite his contempt for his father's job as a car salesman, Peter is fascinated by cars, and his two major acts of rebellion are car thefts. He rejects his parents' insistence on 'responsibility' and 'security' but is unable to articulate alternative values. His failure is most fully apparent in a sequence in which he discusses his views with a Québécois youth of his own age over a game of chess. He stresses the need for an individual identity and insists he does not want to become part of a collective vision such as that developing in Quebec. The emphasis is on Peter's inability to define what he believes in, and the sequence ends with his opponent saying, 'Your move, Peter.' Since Peter's views are not unlike the ideals of individual freedom and the suspicion of Quebec nationalism that formed the basis of Pierre Trudeau's political success at the time, this sequence works to expose a lack within the project of establishing a new basis for national identity in Canada.[5]

At the end of the film, Peter steals a car from the parking lot where he works as an attendant, and plans to drive away with Julie. When she announces that she is pregnant, he rejects her plea for a 'secure' relationship and drives off alone in the stolen car into the void of a neon-lit urban expressway. This kind of bleak ending was to become a characteristic of the direct cinema films that followed, one often seen as a hallmark of Canadian culture and as a reason for their commercial failure (see Chapter 1). However, Harcourt, at least in his first response to the film, declared that 'the quality of the film transcends the negativity of its theme' (1977a: 142).

If it does so, it is because its realist style, much less fragmented and more tied to a coherent narrative than *Le Chat dans le sac*, is far from the observational mode to which it seems to belong. Owen does use devices that give many sequences a documentary 'authenticity': the hidden camera shots of parking lot patrons discovering that Peter has short-changed them; the hesitations in improvised dialogue that bring out Peter's uncertainty and the ways in which the adults fall back on learned formulas. Yet the style also has a playful quality that has been much less often acknowledged. It was well described by a French critic as 'a sort of impressionism' in which 'the elements are juxtaposed in discontinuity' and in which 'Don Owen moves in a spiral around a whole world, around a reality, trying to disengage its meaning' (Martin, 1966: 77). This hardly sounds like Handling's 'neutral, documentary observer'.

The film's 'uncertain style' frequently unsettles the spectator by setting up tensions within and between images and between what we see and what we hear (in the spirit of Brecht, if less overtly than in *Le Chat dans le sac*). In the opening sequence, we see Peter and Julie playing among tombstones, accompanied by the plaintive lyrics of a folksy love song (sung by Peter, as we discover later in the film) and by his fumbling attempts to find words to describe his dissatisfaction with the death-in-life existence of his parents. He tells Julie that 'we've been living in this kind of set-up for so long we've lost all perspective.' The problem is that he must deal with adults—his parents, the probation officer, the owner of the parking lot—who are certain that they know what is best for him, an assumption the film challenges more through its style than through Peter's often highly inadequate attempts to put his feelings into words.

Peter never does gain the critical perspective for which he is looking, but Owen constantly disrupts the surface of the film to prevent us from being pulled into the position from which Peter can only experience the situation as hopeless. These disruptions were often attributed to the film's budgetary constraints, but Owen asserts the potential of a 'poor cinema' in a sequence in which Peter berates his sister's boyfriend for taking her to see *Cleopatra* (Joseph L. Mankiewicz, 1963), the epic that was at the time the epitome of Hollywood extravagance. His diatribe illustrates how Owen sets up tensions in the film: we can sympathize with Peter because we understand his disgust at the consumer society and its cinema, but his self-assured contempt for his sister's inoffensive boyfriend seems excessive. But, then, his apparent self-assurance seems like a mask to hide a basic insecurity. Caught between empathy and critical detachment, the spectator is discouraged from becoming a passive consumer of the film but must grapple with strategies that simultaneously parallel Peter's fragmented experience and prevent a complete immersion in his vision.

An Impossible Beginning?

What unites all these films from 1964, despite their many differences in other respects, is that their 'realism' serves to depict characters who refuse to 'be realistic', in the sense of accepting the situations in which they find themselves. In this sense, these characters were like the filmmakers themselves, who, as Claude Jutra put it, had 'to deny the impossibility' of their projects in order to produce their films; but, whereas Jutra felt that the result was 'an incredible freedom', the characters experience freedom only rarely and briefly (1966: 24).

The Luck of Ginger Coffey differs from the other films, both in the age of its title character and in the relatively comfortable production circumstances. It is, therefore, less heavily marked by a tension that works, in various ways, in the other films: on the one hand, there is a feeling of liberation—the camera freed from the tripod and roaming through actual locations, producing images to be reassembled in editing practices that disregard the rules of continuity; on the other, these stylistic choices underline the instability of characters who feel alienated from reality and trapped in their environments. Yet the 'free style' shares with these characters a reluctance to accept the established conventions and an uncertainty about what should take their place. There is an 'overwhelming sense of instability', says Handling of *Sweet Substitute* (1986: 11), but this could also be said of *Le Chat dans le sac* (despite its more apparent critical perspective), *Nobody Waved Good-bye* (despite Handling's claim to the contrary), and *Trouble-fête* (despite Patry's disdain for direct cinema).

The films, including *The Luck of Ginger Coffey*, also share a strong emphasis on the specificity of their geographical settings, or what critics often referred to as their 'milieu'. Owen pointed out that 'there was nothing more deadly in 1964 than the word "local"' (Edwards, 1977: 164), but these films depend on the idea that, to 'comprehend the choices' made by their characters, 'we must feel part of their milieu' (Douglas, 1996: 93). The relative critical and commercial success of the low-budget films, along with the failure of Crawley's endeavour, encouraged a sense that the future of Canadian cinema would develop from such films. However, few later films in the direct cinema tradition proved commercially successful, and the discovery that Canadians (especially outside Quebec) did not usually experience a strong sense of pleasure in recognizing their own localities on screen gave support to those who felt that Canadian films could succeed only if they concealed their national identity. We will examine this issue more closely in the next chapter.

Traces: Space, Place, and Identity

A locality is the trace of an event, a trace of what had shaped it. Such is the logic of all local myths and legends that attempt, through history, to make sense out of space.

—Mikhail Bakhtin (1981: 189)

Doesn't suburban Montréal resemble suburban Pittsburgh . . . in many significant ways?

—Peter Urquhart (2003: 68)

The ongoing debate over whether Canadian film policy should emphasize cultural or economic objectives is closely related to another question that divides critics and filmmakers: should Canadian films deal with specifically Canadian stories set in Canadian locations? In their concern to reach broader international audiences, some Canadian filmmakers (following Nat Taylor's lead) have preferred anonymous or non-Canadian settings, a strategy that has rarely reaped the desired commercial benefits. Others, as we shall see, cultivate a deliberate sense of placelessness for other than commercial motives. Both groups defy one of the basic assumptions of the realist tradition: that the more grounded in a distinct cultural landscape, the more likely a film is to interest audiences everywhere.

Budge Crawley's attempt to build a commercial film industry in Canada with distinctively Canadian films proved no more successful than Taylor's approach, but critics have tended to value films that visually, and by implication thematically, acknowledge their national origins. The privileging of the direct cinema films was largely based on their exploration of specific local environments, but the rethinking of the canon also called this criterion into question. Peter Urquhart, for example, castigates critics who ignore 'films in the popular idiom' and forcefully rejects 'the notion of a setting necessarily having to represent itself' (2003: 67–8). On the other hand, Bruce Sweeney, who makes his films in British Columbia in the shadow of Hollywood North (see Chapter 12), insists that 'a film has a lot more truthfulness and validity if it's actually set somewhere' (Spaner, 2003: 159).

As societies develop, they construct and organize the spaces they occupy, creating a distinctive cultural geography. Landmarks and landscapes become visual signifiers that help to shape the nation as an imagined community, a process in which the conjunction of time and space, history and geography, creates a distinctive sense of place. In a similar manner, the emergence of film as a mass medium depended on techniques that translate space into place. The development of the system of continuity editing, in Hollywood and elsewhere, made possible a powerful illusion of three-dimensional space within which spectators could become involved with the characters and events. Through the analytic breakdown and reconstruction of space, popular cinema created a sense of place that functioned as an imaginary alternative to their everyday reality—in other words, a utopia (literally, a no-place).

The continuity system facilitated a form of storytelling that became known as 'classical narrative cinema', often defined as 'realist' even though its critics, including André Bazin and John Grierson, pointed out that it depends on an illusion. Through the seamless blending of studio and location sequences, the films contruct plausible worlds, which may be highly artificial in some genres, and invite the audience's intense and subjective involvement in their stories. Because the spectator shares this experience with millions of others, the effect is to create a kind of 'imaginary community' that transcends national boundaries.

Since, as Erin Manning puts it, 'the narrative of the nation-state is a powerful modern enunciation that defines the ways in which we configure space and time', the cinematic construction of place is intricately bound up with myths of national identity (2003: xxx). From the national-realist perspective, the appeal of Hollywood 'escapism' is both superficial and a threat to the national culture, and Canadian film-makers must not only develop counter-narratives but also ground them in the specifics of actual and recognizable places.

'Vrais films de chez nous'

Between 1944 and 1953, a cycle of films appeared in Quebec, made in local studios and rooted in the traditions of French-Canadian society and culture. The producers had the support of the Catholic Church and the Union Nationale government of Maurice Duplessis.[1] While the immediate impetus for local production was the disruption in the supply of French films caused by World War II, the Church and government were, in any case, highly suspicious of the liberal and secular trends in modern French culture. They were even more anxious to combat the influence of Hollywood glamour and the modernizing propaganda associated with the NFB.

In their plots and iconography, these films propagate an ideology of *conservation* that, as described by Christiane Tremblay-Daviault, stressed the importance of the land as 'the only guarantee of the perpetuation of the Catholic faith and French culture, the city being a place of perdition and industry, an invention of the devil' (1981: 54). This ideology had already been celebrated on film by Maurice Proulx, a priest who documented the colonization of the Abitibi region in the 1930s; but—ironically— one of its clearest statements is found in the NFB's *Alexis Tremblay, Habitant* (see Chapter 1), with its idyllic vision of family life grounded in the rhythms of nature and the religious rituals. The Quebec films, however, placed much more emphasis on the struggle to clear the land in remote areas and in a harsh climate.

They were studio-based productions, whose theatricality disturbed the direct cinema filmmakers of a decade later, who, in any case, were much more concerned with modern city life than with rural traditions.[2] While there were enough location shots to situate the narratives within specific regions of Quebec, it was the characters and situations that most appealed to audiences as expressing the typical features of traditional French-Canadian culture. Thus a critic in *La Presse* welcomed *Un Homme et son péché* (Paul Gury, 1948) as 'un vrai film de chez nous' because it did not seek to 'overwhelm or shock in imitation of Hollywood or Paris' (Lever, 1988: 481).

As this comment suggests, the ideology stressed the need to maintain the distinctive-ness and purity of Quebec's cultural traditions. Richard Arès, one of its most influential advocates, insisted that anything that separated the people from the land 'prepares us for *métissage*, duplicity and betrayal' (Tremblay-Daviault, 1981: 54–5).[3] Ironically, in view of this concern to protect the culture from outside influences, the first film in the cycle, *Le Père Chopin* (1944)—which, in many ways, offered the fullest expression of the values of rural life—was directed by Fedor Ozep, an expatriate Russian filmmaker. It tells the story of two brothers, one a music teacher who lives in the country, the other a businessman in the city, but the film ends with their reconciliation and the prospect of reforming the city by incorporating the values associated with the rural family.

This utopian ending does not strictly adhere to the ideology of *conservation*, according to which the city is beyond redemption, and even deeper tensions emerge in the later films. Although the clearly defined moral oppositions are rooted in the literary and artistic traditions of Quebec, they also have much in common with the popular domestic melodramas produced by Hollywood at this time, and the affinity with the Hollywood studio system often seems to contradict the films' ostensible ideological projects. The rural settings may look idyllic, but the stories acted out within them point to a 'collective malaise' in post-war Quebec that parallels the disturbances found in the urban environments of post-war Hollywood film noir (Tremblay-Daviault, 1981: 41). This kinship would later provide the impetus for Robert Lepage's *Le Confessionnal* (see Chapter 12), in which he treated Alfred Hitchcock's *I Confess* (1952), made on location in Quebec City, as an expression of the 'great darkness' of the Duplessis years (Caron, 1995: 28).

Five years before *I Confess*, Quebec produced its own film noir set in Quebec City. *La Forteresse* (1947, also directed by Ozep) was made simultaneously (with different actors) in French and English versions (the latter released as *Whispering City*). Its visual style depends on the contrast between the picturesque sites of the old city (glimpsed only briefly) and the mean streets and shadowy interiors of the generic film noir city. The nightmare city corresponds to the distrust of modern urban society in the ideology of *conservation*, but the sunlit countryside of most of the other films hardly offers a straightforward alternative. They are steeped in the iconography and culture of the *habitant*, but the twin pillars of that culture, the Church and the family, invariably fail to protect the innocent. Michel Brûlé even suggests that they demonstrate 'the impossibility of life in the country' (Lever, 1988: 482).

The two most popular films in the cycle, *Un Homme et son péché* and *La Petite Aurore l'enfant martyre* (Jean Yves Bigras, 1951), feature, respectively, an old miser who torments his young wife and a sadistic woman who tortures her stepdaughter to death. Both films have their roots in the past: *Un Homme et son péché* was adapted from a best-selling novel by Claude-Henri Grignon, first published in 1933, that had already provided the basis for a popular radio serial; *Aurore* was based on a very popular play first performed in 1920. *Un Homme* is set in the past—the opening narration gives the date as 1889—and *Aurore* seems to be, until a modern car parked behind the village green appears in one sequence towards the end of the film. The 'old-fashioned' effect is enhanced by the use of a solo organ for its background score, evoking silent cinema as well as the religious connotations of martyrdom. Despite this backward-looking impression, both films regularly appeared on television in the following decades, and *Un Homme* spawned a sequel, *Séraphin* (Gury, 1950), a long-running television serial, and, recently, an enormously successful remake (Charles Binamé, 2002).

The opening narration in *Un Homme*, accompanied by shots of forests and hills, explains that the settlement of the lands to the north of Montreal—*les pays d'en haut* (the Laurentians)—was inspired by the 'violent enthusiasm' of a priest.[4] As in the opening of *Alexis Tremblay Habitant*, the narrator then enumerates the regions of France from which the settlers came, calling them 'authentic descendants' with a mission to 'prolong the civilization of *la belle France*.' He describes the place as a 'land of mountains, of dreams, and of misery' and then suggests that the harshness of the land has provoked the equal harshness of the miser's heart.

Séraphin Poudrier (Hector Charland), in fact, has two 'sins': his greedy obsession with the sacks of money stored in his attic (over which he gloats during the opening credits) and his cruelty to his young wife, Donalda (Nicole Germain), whom he has married against her wishes (to pay off her father's debt). She was engaged to Alexis (Guy Provost), a young man who returns from a logging camp where he has gone to earn the money for their marriage. He finds it hard to settle down, and he promptly loses the money in a card game. His prodigal ways place him at the opposite extreme from the miser, and the film can be (and was) read as a conservationist text contesting 'the increasing materialism in Quebec society', showing that money is 'dirty' and should be left to 'people who lead "bad lives"' (Lever, 1988: 102–3). Yet it is clear that Séraphin is a product of the traditional culture, and Alexis is hardly a strong symbol of conservative self-discipline.

The tensions within the rural community are even more apparent in *La Petite Aurore*. It opens with a close-up of a fire from which a blacksmith removes a red-hot horseshoe, and the camera pans with his movement as he carries it to a barrel of water. This shot evokes the idea of torture that governs the melodramatic plot, but it is here associated with the routines of everyday life. The cinematic fluidity of this shot is contradicted by the following shots introducing Théo (Paul Desmarteaux), talking to the blacksmith about his wife's illness and then getting angry with another customer who makes insinuations about his relations with Marie-Louise (Lucie Mitchell), a widow who is nursing his wife. Avoiding the shot/reverse-shot structure on which the continuity system depends, the director stages both conversations in a series of two-shots in which the only editing consists of jump cuts to closer positions.

The construction of this opening sequence avoids the need for an establishing shot, and the countryside is seen only from the inside looking out. It also refuses point-of-view shots, thus intensifying the stress on the gaze of Aurore (Yvonne Laflamme) when she observes Marie-Louise poisoning her mother and destroying the medicine that might save her. The film thus engages the spectator's look with Aurore's perspective and her suffering, an effect that reaches its height in a subjective shot of Marie-Louise, who is now her stepmother, as she pushes a hot iron into her victim's face. Since most of the film is shot in a 'frontal' style reminiscent of early cinema, the long martyrdom of Aurore occurs as if in a different space, from which the other characters are detached and in which they cannot intervene. The spectator becomes caught in the perverse dynamic of the relationship between torturer and victim, Aurore stubbornly refusing to address Marie-Louise as 'mother' and her persecutor smiling with pleasure every time she inflicts a new punishment.

This shooting style was undoubtedly adopted partly for economic reasons, a factor that becomes even more apparent in the final sequence in which, after Aurore has finally succumbed to her injuries, the trial of Marie-Louise takes place in an abstract space with no set to represent the courtroom.[5] The high-angle shots of the defendant when the judge imposes the death sentence intensify her anguish and suggest that she is being punished by more than strictly human justice, while also allowing the audience to disavow any complicity in the cruelty that has been depicted at such length. However, as Brûlé suggests, the film depicts 'a completely degenerate world where everybody is in the final account complicit with the martyrdom of a child' (Lever, 1988: 482).

Although *La Petite Aurore* soon became known as an exemplary text of the 'great darkness' from which the Quiet Revolution rescued Quebec, Yves Lever insists that its plot is 'in absolute contradiction with the official ideology' (1988: 105). Heinz Weinmann also argues that it exposes the regressive ideology and anticipates future developments (1990: 27–50). A lot depends on the spectator's response to the traditional figure of the village priest and the scientific authority of the doctor. While one critic refers to 'the eminently positive figure of the "good curé"' (Weinmann, 1990: 21), another opposes his impotence to 'the prosaic dynamism' of the doctor who finally exposes Marie-Louise, but neither traditional religion nor modern science can save the poor child (Tremblay-Daviault, 1981: 223).

Obliterated Environments

These Quebec films represent a specific place through a conventional iconography that depends on stereotypes (which the films may reinforce or call into question). The English-Canadian equivalent to the ideology of *conservation* may be found in the tradition of landscape painting associated with the Group of Seven. However, while these paintings of the northern wilderness often serve as emblems of the national culture, the effect is very different from the ties between land and nation in Quebec. Whereas the emphasis in Quebec was on the human effort to occupy an inhospitable environment, the English-Canadian tradition stressed the emptiness of the land (thereby excluding the Native peoples who lived there) and the sublime grandeur of untamed nature. According to Northrop Frye, this image of 'Canada, with its empty spaces, its largely unknown lakes and rivers and islands' constitutes an 'obliterated environment' because its vastness cannot be comprehended by the human imagination (1971: iii).

This tradition did not accord with the vision of a modern national culture developed under Grierson at the NFB, and the direct cinema filmmakers were more concerned with the other kind of obliterated environment identified by Frye, the modern city as the product of an emerging 'global civilization' (1971: iii). It was *Nobody Waved Good-bye* rather than *Drylanders*, in which the family's struggle with the land helps to build the nation, that pointed the way forward for English-Canadian filmmakers. The only film to engage directly with the Group of Seven landscape tradition directly was *The Far Shore* (Joyce Wieland, 1976) (see Chapter 6). The direct cinema films tend to suggest the irrelevance of this tradition to modern urban life.

These filmmakers were more in tune with Frye's insistence that 'identity is local and regional' and that the tension between the 'political sense of unity and the imaginative sense of locality is the essence of whatever the word "Canadian" means' (1971: ii–iii). Their films offer sharply observed regional settings, but they also develop the tensions within the idea of 'realism' found in the 1964 films (see Chapter 2).

While their visual appeal stems from their attention to recognizable and distinctive locations, the narratives deal with characters who want to escape from these locations. The failure to integrate regional identity into a unifying idea of the nation is linked to the economic deprivation of the local communities and the frustration of the male protagonists who live there.

In *The Rowdyman* (Peter Carter, 1971), Will Cole (Gordon Pinsent) dreams of leaving his job in a Newfoundland lumber mill for a better life on the mainland, while Jim King (Donnelly Rhodes) in *The Hard Part Begins* (Paul Lynch, 1973) tours northern Ontario with his country band and refuses to admit that he will never obtain a contract with a major record label. Such films as these came closest to fulfilling the criteria for a national cinema set out in the emerging critical canon, but they rarely found a national audience. Whether this was due to the structural problem of distribution or to their low production values and downbeat narratives was open to debate. However, one film in this cycle, *Goin' Down the Road* (Don Shebib, 1970), did achieve critical recognition and a modest commercial success that raised the hope that the CFDC could reconcile its cultural and economic imperatives.

The film's opening sequences clearly define the geographical co-ordinates of the narrative. An aerial shot reveals an island, which is immediately identified as Cape Breton in the lyrics of the accompanying song by Bruce Cockburn, who composed the film's score. As the song continues, the following shots emphasize first the natural beauty of the landscape but then the ruined buildings that testify to the economic decline described in the lyrics. These shots provide the motivation for the departure of Joey (Paul Bradley) and Pete (Doug McGrath) and lead into a montage sequence of their journey. When they drive into the city, it is immediately named by Joey, who shouts exuberantly, 'Look out Toronto, here we come.' Shebib then cuts to another aerial shot in which their car is hardly visible among the high-rise buildings, foreshadowing the imminent collapse of their illusions.

As Robert Fothergill suggests, 'the audience discovers Toronto along with them, and from their perspective' (1977b: 362). Yet the film rarely involves us with their point of view, as in classical narrative cinema; rather, it adopts the observational style of direct cinema, stressing the 'documentary' authenticity of its locations. The shots of the city exceed their function as establishing shots and create a strong sense of the texture of the environment (Yonge Street at night, the Salvation Army hostel at which Pete and Joey spend their first night, an encounter with a street person drinking cheap booze). Near the end of the film, the two men, now destitute and disillusioned, find themselves downtown amid Christmas festivities, and the camera pans away to the new City Hall, proclaiming a prosperous society from which they are excluded.

The setting thus functions (like Cockburn's songs) as an often ironic commentary on the narrative, and our response to the two men is likely to involve a mixture of identification and exasperation. Initially, it is Pete who is most convinced that 'it's going to be *so* different' when they reach Toronto, but his lack of 'realism' soon becomes apparent. He applies for a job in an advertising firm and vainly pursues beautiful women who have no interest in him. Joey is both more adaptable to reality and less aware of his alienation, and he is quite willing to settle for marriage when his girlfriend gets pregnant. Yet, after they are laid off from the one menial job they are able to find, it is Joey who stops looking for work and Pete who takes demeaning part-time jobs so they can afford the cramped apartment where he now lives with Joey and his family.

It is also Joey who violently attacks a supermarket employee when they try to leave without paying and Pete who phones for medical help for the injured man. The final irony is that Joey's desire to stay with his wife becomes 'unrealistic' and Pete's urge to move on corresponds to the reality of their situation. We are invited to identify with Pete's longing for something better (even if this is highly unrealistic) and with Joey's urge to settle down (even if this shows a lack of imagination), a dichotomy captured in the inscription 'My Nova Scotia Home' on the car in which they leave and continue to drive throughout the film. When they go to a nightclub, a singer celebrates 'Canada from Nova Scotia to Vancouver', but the film underlines the emptiness of this vision of national unity. It ends with them on the road once again, heading west.

To get from Nova Scotia to Toronto, Pete and Joey would, of course, have passed through Quebec, but this part of their journey is not depicted in the film.[6] Quebec's linguistic and cultural difference makes it the most distinct region of Canada and, of course, many in Quebec believe that it should be regarded as a nation rather than a region. In the Canadian context, Quebec perhaps represents an extreme form of the impossibility of aligning regional identity and national unity, but it also contains its own regional differences. Like their English-language counterparts, many Quebec films of this period use direct cinema techniques to depict regional locations in which young males undergo crises of identity, but they also have to contend with the charged meanings of rural landscapes in Quebec's cultural tradition.

Entre la mer et l'eau douce (Michel Brault, 1967) and *Le temps d'une chasse* (Francis Mankiewicz, 1972) both adapt the country/city opposition of 1940s Quebec to the new situation. In Brault's film, Claude Tremblay, a successful singer (played by the popular *chansonnier* Claude Gauthier), looks back on his life since he left his home on the north shore of the St Lawrence. He leaves his Indian girlfriend behind but meets Geneviève (Geneviève Bujold), a shy young waitress, in Montreal, where he takes on a succession of menial jobs. After his eventual success, he loses contact with her and realizes that his reality will never match the romantic dreams expressed in his songs. The film's title, taken from the words of the explorer Jacques Cartier quoted in *Pour la suite du monde*, refers to the transition from salt to fresh water in the river and is a metaphor for Claude's sense of being caught between two worlds. In the context of the 1960s, his uncertainty suggests Quebec's search for a new identity after the Quiet Revolution, but the distrust of the city and material success recalls the ideology of *conservation*.

Le temps d'une chasse reverses the trajectory as three middle-aged men from Montreal return to nature for a weekend's hunting. Richard (Marcel Sabourin) brings along his young son Michel (Olivier L'Ecuyer) and, while the trip is supposed to be a traditional initiation into manhood for him, he becomes witness to their childish behaviour. The natural beauty of the woods contrasts with the shabby motel where the men get drunk and harass the waitresses, and the film ends with a freeze-frame from behind Michel as he discovers that one of the drunken hunters has accidentally shot his father. As Mankiewicz noted, the characters are 'city-dwellers, out of place in the country, who have lost all authentic contact with nature' (Marsolais, 1978: 13). Although the film is something of a fable about cultural and masculine identity, critics stressed its 'undeniable climate of authenticity' rooted in the contemporary Quebec experience (Marsolais, 1978: 13).

The critical viewpoint of an adolescent boy on adult behaviour was also a key element a year earlier in *Mon oncle Antoine* (Claude Jutra, 1971), a film that was quickly identified as a Canadian classic. Like *Le temps d'une chasse*, it was photographed by Brault, an important figure in the development of direct cinema at the NFB; but this film represents a partial break with direct cinema techniques. The intense engagement of the film with the subjective experience of Benoît (Jacques Gagnon), an orphan living with his uncle (Jean Duceppe) in a small town beside an asbestos mine, pushes the film away from the public gaze of documentary. His gaze functions much like Aurore's, but the success of Jutra's film stems largely from the way its darker themes gradually emerge from its apparently nostalgic or 'folkloric' view of the past.

As in *Goin' Down the Road*, the film opens with panoramic shots of a landscape, accompanied by lyrical (this time wordless) music. The initial impression of natural beauty is quickly dispelled when the camera reveals dust spewing from a mine. A superimposed caption declares that the film is set '*au pays du Québec dans la région d'amiante y'a pas si longtemps*'. Although Erin Manning claims to have seen a version in which the caption reads '*Dans la nation de Quebec*', the term '*pays*'—translated as 'country' and 'land' in two different versions of the English subtitles—is a more ambiguous one that captures the uncertain status of Quebec implied by the narrative (2003: 121).

The temporal reference to 'not so long ago' is also deliberately vague, apparently referring to the beginning of the Quiet Revolution. In an interview, Jutra confirmed that the historical period was indeed the 1940s, and he underlined the political significance of locating the action in 'the asbestos country, one of the first hotbeds of the political agitation and labour unrest' (Even, 1973). Yet there is little sign of protest in the film, and the visual cues ambiguously suggest either an earlier or more recent period. The simultaneous specificity and vagueness with regard to space and time raise questions about the extent to which modern Quebec differs from the downtrodden society viewed by Benoît (see Leach, 1999a: 137–41).

The importance of location shooting to the sense of place in these films becomes apparent in the critical response to *Wedding in White* (1972). Directed by William Fruet, who wrote the screenplay for *Goin' Down the Road*, and based on his own stage play, the film is set in Canada during World War II, but shot in a studio. When a young woman (Carol Kane) becomes pregnant, her father (Donald Pleasance) forces her to marry an old friend to save the family honour. As one critic put it, the style pays 'scrupulous attention to the nuances of character' and places the story in a setting in which 'every detail is vintage 1943' (Hudecki, 1972: 29–30). Yet the period setting, in an old-fashioned home, is iconographically more British than Canadian, and critics have sometimes been confused about precisely where it is set.

The stage directions in the play define the location as 'somewhere in Western Canada' (Fruet, 1973: A5), and most viewers seem to have assumed, as the director presumably intended, that this also applies to the film. However, it was shot in Toronto, and John Harkness used it, in an article denouncing the concealment of Canadian locations in films produced with the tax breaks provided by the Capital Cost Allowance Act (CCA), to illustrate the importance of telling 'specifically Canadian stories'; it was, he said, 'the best portrayal of life in a small Ontario town ever made' (1982: 23, 25). More recently, George Melnyk asserts that the film is set in the Maritimes, and uses it to support the bizarre argument that, following *Goin' Down the Road* and *The Rowdyman*, 'the continued production of stories set on Canada's East Coast ... provided a lopsided view of Canadian society because it was so weighted toward one region and one class' (2004: 116). Perhaps this confusion attests to the universality of a narrative that transcends time and place, but it also suggests that the translation of space into place depends heavily on the mind of the viewer.

A Sense of Placelessness

Location shooting is not in itself a sufficient condition for the production of a sense of place, and Fruet himself went on to use locations extensively in many genre films set in unspecified places. Although *Goin' Down the Road* and *Mon oncle Antoine* encouraged those who thought the future of Canadian cinema lay with small-budget realist films with distinctive Canadian settings, the frequent failure of later films in this mode, many of which received little or no distribution, called this strategy into question. The direct cinema films rarely received strong support from Canadian critics, but there was wide-spread dismay at the trend towards films that disguised their locations in an attempt to attract audiences outside Canada.

One notable exception was Robert Fothergill. While endorsing the canonical view that 'Canadian filmmaking has been artistically most successful when it has sailed close to the winds of realism', Fothergill nevertheless acknowledged that 'concealment of the locale is not necessarily a crime; certain kinds of fiction positively require a vague location, free of specific associations' (1977b: 348). Many genre films indeed depend less on specific markers of place than on iconography that locates them in relation to other films in the same genre. The mean streets of film noir, for example, evoke Frye's obliterated urban environments, and it often matters little whether they belong in a specific city. As we saw in the discussion of *La Forteresse*, when such locations can be identified, the tension between genre space and local space becomes an important element in a film's meanings and effects.

Many of the films produced during the CCA boom were such genre films. *My Bloody Valentine* (George Mihalka, 1981), for example, belongs to the then very popular cycle of slasher movies. Its serial killer is apparently seeking revenge for a fatal explosion in a coal mine, caused by negligence. Predictably, the film was not well received by critics, but one did note that it at least depicted 'unmistakable Nova Scotian locations' (Dowler, 1981: 67). Yet, while coal mining is indeed a major industry in Nova Scotia, the major indicator of location is a product placement for a local beer, and when a waitress in a pub asks, 'Who ordered the Moosehead?' the question seems rather superfluous, since everyone in the crowded bar is drinking this brand.

For those spectators who knew the region, the setting would be readily apparent, and many CCA films operate on this principle of showing but not naming the location. Some films were explicitly set in Canada, including *Suzanne* (Robin Spry, 1980), an adaptation of a novel by Ronald Sutherland about a Montreal woman

(Jennifer Dale) torn between her mixed English and French ancestry during the Quiet Revolution, and *The Grey Fox* (Philip Borsos, 1982), a western in which an aging train robber (Richard Farnsworth) tries to revive his dying profession in Canada.[7] There were, however, many films that did not simply refrain from identifying their Canadian locations but identified them as somewhere else. In *The Changeling* (Peter Medak, 1979), captions identify an Ontario landscape as 'Northern New York State' and Vancouver as 'Seattle'; *Prom Night* (Paul Lynch, 1980), another slasher movie, was, according to the final credits, 'filmed in Ontario', but the high school is introduced by a shot of a flagpole flying the Stars and Stripes.

In many of these films, the masquerade was enhanced by the importation of American actors, such as George C. Scott in *The Changeling* and Jamie Lee Curtis in *Prom Night*. Their names were used to sell the projects to the many small investors needed to exploit the benefits of the CCA and in the (usually unrealized) hope that they would attract audiences. On the other hand, the names of Canadian directors carried very little weight, and Shebib and Jutra—just a few years after making films acclaimed as Canadian 'classics'—both found themselves working in circumstances in which they were far from comfortable.

Both did manage to make films based on projects in which they had been interested for some time, but the results were shaped by the production context of the CCA period. Shebib's *Heartaches* (1981) was based (although not acknowledged in the credits) on *The Bottle Factory Outing*, an English novel by Beryl Bainbridge, to which Shebib had acquired the rights some years earlier (Kelly, 1981: 61–2). In some ways, it is a female version of *Goin' Down the Road*, dealing with two women who arrive in a city in which they struggle to survive. As Robert Fulford pointed out in his review, the city is not named, even though 'Torontonians, and many other Canadians, will recognize the skyline as Toronto's.' He also noted some 'anomalies' (the use of the American term 'councilman' and an American $10 bill), which, he reported, 'Shebib explains as concessions to the producers' who believed that 'no one outside this country is interested in a Canadian story' (1982: 61).

The shots of the city include familiar landmarks, but they function like conventional establishing shots, and there is little sense of the texture of a specific location. As Piers Handling suggests, the stylistic difference from *Goin' Down the Road* also reveals a difference in attitude: 'the city liberates Bonnie and Rita', and, unlike Pete and Joey, 'the characters in *Heartaches* are all perceived as moving forward into the future, not regressing into old, restricting habits.' While this positive ending might be taken as a welcome break from the downbeat endings in earlier Canadian films, Handling sees it as evidence of a calculated 'sentimentality' based on Shebib's eagerness 'to please and court his audience' (1982: 48).

The film works fairly well as a light comedy, thanks largely to the performances of its leading actors, who included two Americans (Annie Potts, Robert Carradine) as well as a Canadian (Margot Kidder), well known to international audiences for her recent starring role as Lois Lane in *Superman* (Richard Donner, 1978).[8] Jutra was not so fortunate with the cast of *Surfacing* (1980), in which the presence of American actors encouraged the elimination of the negative depiction of 'Americans' (some of whom are Canadian) in the Margaret Atwood novel on which the film is based. Jutra only became involved in this production at a very late stage, as a favour to producer Beryl Fox, who agreed to help him mount his own current project. She accordingly produced *By Design* (1981), but on a reduced budget and abbreviated shooting schedule, because potential investors balked at a comedy about lesbian fashion designers (Hynam, 1981: 28). However, its one American 'star' (Patty Duke Astin, best known for her US television series) fitted into the production quite seamlessly.

Jutra's career after *Mon oncle Antoine* had suffered from the commercial failure of his next two films, *Kamouraska* (1973), a historical film that was at the time the most expensive film produced in Canada (see Chapter 6), and *Pour le meilleur et pour le pire* (1975), a more modest dark comedy about marriage. Unable to find work in Quebec, Jutra made English-language television films for the CBC before returning to the large screen through his collaboration with Fox. *By Design* was filmed and set in Vancouver, but the only city named is Los Angeles, where the designers must sell their clothes to be considered successful. The comedy centres on the desire of the lesbian couple to have a child, but the concern with the tensions between creativity and business must have been highly resonant for the filmmakers.

For many critics, the film lacked the passion and commitment of Jutra's work in Quebec, although Martin Knelman thought that it signalled 'the reemergence of Claude Jutra as Canada's finest writer-director' (1984: 21). According to Fox, even though 'most of the money people are looking for safe formulas', this film remains 'authentically Canadian and original' (Hynam, 1981: 27–9). Since the Canadian identity of the film is only implicit, as in *Heartaches* and many other CCA films, Fox implies that the cultural authenticity of *By Design* lies in its resistance to commercial pressures that lead to bland films following predictable formulas. Jutra's and Shebib's CCA films both make some concessions to these pressures, notably in their treatment of their locations, but it remains uncertain whether their lack of commercial success was due to these concessions or to the ways in which they resisted the expected formulas.

The few major box-office successes of this period were certainly formulaic: *Prom Night* was highly derivative of earlier slasher movies, while *Meatballs* (Ivan Reitman, 1979) and *Porky's* (Bob Clark, 1981) were raucous teen comedies, the latter set and filmed in Florida. Formulas are a basic feature of popular cinema and not necessarily as restrictive as the advocates of 'authentically Canadian' movies imply. However, popular cinema depends on a creative play with formulas that the CCA—with its emphasis on selling shares to small investors—did not encourage.

As Geoff Pevere puts it, 'one of the most elementary tenets of CCA-era feature filmmaking' was the desire to 'make more Canadian movies more like American movies'. He also points out that, after the CCA boom, many films made in Ontario exhibited 'a conspicuous sense of placelessness' so that 'Ontario often seems like it could either be anywhere in North America or, more unsettlingly, nowhere at all' (1995a: 12, 15). The implication is that the commercial logic behind the CCA films was symptomatic of a culture in which the loss of a sense of a 'home' environment is a common experience. Atom Egoyan thus captures the effect of his own films— and other films from this period—when he suggests that they deal with characters who 'never quite feel that they have the right to be where they are' (Harris, 1991: 17). While Egoyan claims that his films are 'very much the result of the city I made them in', he also points out that 'places in my films are concepts without a specific reference' (Romney, 2003: 12).

The placeless effect is not confined to Ontario films. The idea for *waydowntown* (Gary Burns, 2000) came from the 'Plus 15' system of walkways that link the buildings in downtown Calgary, and the film partially works as a critique of the kind of urban planning that this development represents. Although the system was designed to protect people from the cold winters, Burns felt that 'it's sort of against the Canadian character—you should just deal with the elements' (Peranson, 2000: 6). Katherine Monk also relates the film to the Canadian tradition of the struggle for survival in the Great White North and suggests that 'the characters are not oppressed by snow and death, but by mountains of paperwork and dead-end jobs' (2001: 79).

Burns's two previous films—*Suburbanators* (1995) and *Kitchen Party* (1997)— were low-budget realist films in which 'the Albertan landscape is a constant—a vast land of sky and cars, suburban bungalows and malls' (Corder and Blum, 2001: 12). However, it is easy to watch these films without being aware of the actual location, since they focus on young people whose identities are shaped less by their immediate environment than by a media-driven North American youth culture. In these films, Burns claims to have tried to convey 'a sense of where you are', as opposed to classical narrative cinema which, in opposition to most accounts of the system, he finds disorienting. In *waydowntown*, he reverted to a style 'more like a traditional Hollywood narrative', avoiding 'visual references that you could tie in settings together' in order to convey the maze-like effect of the spaces in the mall and office building (Peranson, 2000: 8).

According to Mark Peranson, 'a story that might well have been regionally specific takes on universal meaning for anyone who has worked in an office setting' (2000: 5). Although a few brief insert shots of maps of the mall indicate it is in Calgary, the glass-and-concrete buildings, fully equipped with surveillance cameras, are familiar features of life in most major cities. The story, about four young office workers who make a bet on who can go the longest without going outside, is told from the perspective of Tom (Fabrizio Filippo), one of the contestants, who uses dope to ease the edginess brought on by indoor living; and we see his drug-induced fantasies, in which the city is lifted into the sky by a super-villain, a superman figure rescues people who jump from the office building, and Tom himself flies through the mall.

The film was shot on digital video, except for the few shots of the streets outside, which were shot on 35mm film. Yet, as one character points out, people who leave the building do not find fresh air and open spaces but pollution-filled city streets dominated by high-rise buildings. Both nature and nation are virtually absent from this environment, and Tom's gradual recognition of his alienation points to the need for new configurations of place that will recognize the natural and cultural needs of the inhabitants.

In the age of globalization, the tension between specific local environments and generic locations, which has always been a part of Canadian cinema, is increasingly becoming a worldwide phenomenon. We will explore the contemporary implications of this development later (see Chapter 12), but in the next chapter we will look further at the question of genre in the context of the national cinema.

Are Genres American?

It is doubtful whether there have been
true genres in the cinema other than the
American genres.

—Christian Metz (1974: 252)

Their minds filled with prepackaged
memories provided by generic memory-masters,
genre film spectators have become the true
twentieth-century cyborgs.

—Rick Altman (1999: 191)

The concept of genre has proved very fruitful in the production, marketing, and critical understanding of Hollywood cinema. Through the familiarity of their iconography and narrative formulas, genres provide audiences with 'specific systems of expectation and hypothesis' (Neale, 2003: 161) and enable critics to analyze 'the relation between groups of films, the cultures in which they are made, and the cultures in which they are exhibited' (Tudor, 2003: 10). However, the international success of Hollywood genre films has led to concerns about the impact of American culture and values on other countries where these films are seen, with the result that popular genres often seem like a threat to national cinemas.

As categories that serve a variety of purposes, genres can be defined at different levels in relation to the totality of film production. Generic formulas work to frame and limit meanings by making some more 'probable' than others; but, because genre films are expected to operate within the laws of the genre rather than to provide a direct representation of social reality, they can tap into desires and anxieties normally unrecognized or repressed. Popular genres can thus be interpreted as symptoms of collective dreams and nightmares, whether these are seen as determined by the human condition or by specific cultural environments.

To the extent that genres reflect cultures, the international popularity of Hollywood genre films raises questions about the role of genre in other national cinemas. In a discussion of 'the problem of genre' in Australian cinema, Graeme Turner agrees with Metz that 'the genres are American' (or at least perceived to be so), a situation that provokes either a 'nationalist rejection of American genres' or, for those who seek to tap into their popular appeal, a struggle with 'the difficulty of adapting formal and structural devices from another culture without taking with them the meanings they most easily generate' (1993: 106, 110).

The Australian resistance to American genres, according to Turner, involved the promotion of national identity through 'quality' films and films dealing with the nation's history. In Canada, the dominance of the documentary tradition encouraged a concern with the present rather than the past, but Canadian critics also emphasized the need for 'quality', a term derived from British film critics of the 1940s. The direct cinema experience also reinforced the strong suspicion of pre-existing formulas found in critical traditions that dismissed all forms of 'mass culture'. However, although genres are, like much popular culture, formulaic, these critics tend to forget that all films filter reality through culturally developed ways of seeing.

It was precisely because of the close association between popular genres and American culture that Canadian filmmakers could use them to explore the impact on Canada of the powerful cultural influences from south of the border. The intersection of genre and national cinema is thus also a tension between popular pleasures and a more critical (and often elitist) response. As we have seen in Chapter 2, critics regarded genre films like *The Mask* as an obstacle to the development of a national cinema. However, genre films quickly became a major part of the Canadian film industry. With the emergence of video in the 1980s, many genre films were made with this new market in mind, and most received little or no critical notice. They were aimed mainly at the international market and often concealed their national origins, but some used their Canadian settings to reinvigorate the formulas. *My Bloody Valentine* is set amid the coal mines of Nova Scotia (see Chapter 3), while *Mob Story* (Gabriel and Jancarlo Markiw, 1989) amusingly confronts its Mafia gangsters with the intense cold of a Winnipeg winter.

While critics often preferred to ignore this Canadian cinematic underworld, they had to take notice of the enormously successful horror films of David Cronenberg (which will be discussed in Chapter 5), but other filmmakers also raised the possibility of distinctively Canadian genre films. As Cronenberg was making his mark in the 1970s, Denys Arcand turned to the crime film as a way of addressing the political tensions in Quebec after the October Crisis (see Chapter 9). Arcand theorized his own practice in terms close to Turner's account of the Australian situation, arguing that genre conventions bring with them ideological implications that must be contested at the level of 'the cinematic language itself' (1972: 11). During the 1970s, several other filmmakers, who (like Arcand) had been associated with documentary tradition, turned to genre in an effort to reach larger audiences, provoking ideological questions that are often addressed in the films themselves as well as in the critical discourses about them.

For English-Canadian filmmakers, this turn to genre involved the problem—to adapt Charlotte Brunsdon's discussion of the British crime film—of articulating the difference between 'the generic space of Hollywood' and 'the rather more literal space of the [Canadian] location' (1999: 148). The ease with which these two kinds of space could be conflated was, of course, an opportunity for those filmmakers who wanted to conceal the national origins of their films, but the difference was more readily apparent in Quebec. Yet genres could be used there in a similar way to explore what Bill Marshall calls 'the competing discourses of *Québécité* and *Américanité*' in Quebec society (2001: 12).

Inflecting American Genres

The final sequence of *Paperback Hero* (Peter Pearson, 1973) begins with a close-up of a traffic light shattering. There is a sudden cut to a high-angle long shot of a man in a cowboy outfit who twirls his gun as he replaces it in its holster. He proceeds slowly down the deserted street and calls out the sheriff. Spectators will recognize the cues that this is the inevitable showdown from the western genre, but, by this point in the film, there is no need for the anachronism of the traffic light to expose the illusions of Rick Dillon (Keir Dullea), a minor-league hockey player in a small Saskatchewan town who masquerades as the 'Marshal', exploiting the surname he shares with Matt Dillon, the marshal in a popular television series.[1] As the tension builds, it is suddenly broken by a farmer who drives his tractor down the street, oblivious to what is going on. The comic relief does not last long, and the film ends with the would-be western hero lying dead beneath a wheat silo bearing the word PIONEER, gazed at by uncomprehending townspeople.

This sequence forcefully brings out the collision between generic and national space on which Canadian genre films often depend, as well as their concern with characters who confuse the two kinds of space (much like the males in the direct cinema films who refuse to be 'realistic'). Another example is Chino (Chuck Shamata) in *Between Friends* (Don Shebib, 1973), who dreams of escaping from his drab reality in Toronto, where he works as a short-order cook, and of returning to California where he went to surf in his younger days. His obsession leads him to neglect his girlfriend Ellie (Bonnie Bedelia), and she begins an affair with Toby (Michael Parks), his American friend and old surfing buddy. All three become involved in a plan, devised by Ellie's father, Will (Henry Beckman), to rob the payroll of a nickel mine in northern Ontario. Chino's jealousy leads to tensions that distract the men during the robbery and result in a chaotic shootout in which Chino and Will are killed. The film ends with Toby and Ellie silently mourning their dead in the desolate landscape around the mine, before images of surfers remind us of the illusion that helped to create this reality.

Chino's jealousy provokes the catastrophe, but the plan seems doomed from the start. When Toby asks Will, who has just been released from prison, why he thinks the plan will work, he can only reply, not too reassuringly, 'I figure you can't lose 'em all.' It is hardly surprising that one of the key sequences is a funeral at which Will sings 'We Shall Gather at the River', a song that evokes the westerns of John Ford, over the grave of his friend who has died of a heart attack a few days before the robbery. As Peter Harcourt suggests, this is 'an allusion to an absence', with Ford's striking western landscape replaced by the slag heaps and chimneys of the polluted landscape (1977b: 216).

The emphasis is on the characters rather than the action, and the planning of the job is not simply complicated by their relationships, as in the typical crime film, but overwhelmed by them. In the genre narrative, Ellie functions as the femme fatale who causes Chino's death, but she gradually emerges as a figure of maturity and emotional depth who recognizes, but cannot change, the futility of the actions of the men around her. As Barry Keith Grant suggests, after the smoothly executed drug heist in California with which it opens, the film's style is 'in pointed contrast to the hyperkinetic, streamlined style toward which American crime films were already moving' (2002: 11). Its commercial failure could be attributed to this refusal to meet expectations, although, as so often, it was also a victim of poor distribution.

While the social alienation of the criminals is a constant motif in the American film noir, *Between Friends*, like *Paperback Hero*, stresses how Canadian reality blocks generic action. Quebec genre films are able to provide a more political (although usually still rather vague) explanation of this blockage, but one of the features that genre films in both languages share is the predominantly negative outcome of their plots. As Arcand's comments quoted earlier suggest, the effect is to provoke discomfort in audiences attuned to genre conventions, and it requires a shift in perspective to enjoy the hybrid pleasures offered by the tensions between genre and the national context.

These tensions were pushed to an extreme in *Pouvoir intime* (Yves Simoneau, 1986) and *Un Zoo la nuit* (Jean-Claude Lauzon, 1987), with highly controversial results. Just as Arcand's genre films of the 1970s reflected the mood in Quebec after the October Crisis, these films appeared at a time of widespread disillusionment after the 1980 referendum—when Arcand himself revived his career with *Le Déclin de l'empire américain* (1986), a film that linked the situation in Quebec to the international dominance of American culture. Just as Arcand came under attack for depicting a group of historians who had seemingly lost all interest in Quebec's past or future (see Chapter 9), Simoneau and Lauzon were often accused of betraying their cultural roots by turning to American genres.

The generic narrative in *Pouvoir intime* deals with the hijacking of a security van, which goes even more spectacularly wrong than the robbery in *Between Friends*. After the first setbacks, Théo (Jacques Godin), the gang leader, sounds rather like Will when he comments ruefully that 'it can't all go wrong'; but the situation goes downhill from there. In any case, the criminals are merely pawns in an elaborate scheme devised by two shady political figures to retrieve an incriminating document. Although these conspirators are francophones, the single word TRUST that appears in English on the security van (the film's English title was *Blind Trust*) becomes an ironic allusion to a larger political context marked by the absence of trust and by abuses of power.

Strikingly, both *Pouvoir intime* and *Un Zoo la nuit* begin with disembodied male voices heard over the telephone, voices of corrupt authority (political agents in the former, police officers in the latter) whose abuse of power sets off a disastrous chain of events. In both films, the forward momentum of the generic action is countered by a sense of claustrophobia that functions as a metaphor for Quebec's political situation, and their plots depend on the discrepancy between two narrative drives apparently pulling in different directions. Their disruption of genre conventions is also bound up with their highly contentious treatment of sexuality and gender codes.

Claustrophobia dominates the long central section in *Pouvoir intime*, in which a guard barricades himself in the security van and the robbers are trapped in their hideout while they try to get him out. The Quebec situation is present as a subtext throughout the film, but it only emerges as the dominant level in the final sequence, which takes place in the highly symbolic space of a ruined church in a rural landscape. Roxanne (Marie Tifo), the only surviving member of the gang, meets with Janvier (Jacques Lussier), the homosexual lover of the guard (who has also died). They have escaped with some of the money, and Roxanne now gives Janvier his share in return for a vehicle in which she drives off alone.

At least one critic saw this as a 'very American happy end' (Bonneville, 1986: 9), but, as Henry Garrity points out, this is hardly a conventional romantic couple. Roxanne joined the gang because they needed a woman to distract the guards but was almost rejected because her appearance was not sufficiently 'feminine'. Garrity thus argues that the film undercuts 'the audience's traditional image of homosexual men and androgynous women by making them the film's heroes and triumphant survivors' (1989–90: 32). Yet, since Janvier was not involved in the robbery until Roxanne thought of using him to win the guard's trust, their meeting comes as something of a surprise, and their muted exchanges are hardly triumphant. Simoneau claimed that he wanted the burned door, through which Janvier watches Roxanne leave, to represent an opening 'on the land, on nature, and on a still possible life' (Bonneville, 1986: 9); but it is an image that simultaneously refers back to Quebec's rural and religious past, seemingly irrelevant in the corrupt urban society that provides the setting for the film's generic action.[2]

The divergent responses to the film attest to the fine line between satisfying generic expectations and providing a critical perspective. Paul Warren criticized Simoneau, who would indeed go on to work in Hollywood, for his 'Americanism' (Garrity, 1989–90: 36); but, for Bill Marshall, the film 'refuses the pleasures and identifications of the Hollywood thriller' (2001: 130). The issues are so entangled that it is not clear whether Marshall's claim is refuted or confirmed by the complaint of a reviewer that the ending kills off 'the very characters the audience have come to *care* about' (Arsenault, 1986: 23).

Un Zoo la nuit initially seems to be more ready to satisfy generic expectations. The word 'zoo' in the title refers to the familiar 'urban jungle' metaphor, introduced early in the film by animal noises that accompany images of the city at night. On his final night in prison, Marcel (Gilles Maheu) is raped by a convict, with the connivance of a guard and as arranged by corrupt police officers, who want the money he made dealing drugs with which they supplied him. They persecute him after his release, but Marcel fights back and, with the aid of an 'American friend', he ambushes and kills the police officers in a seedy hotel. However, he has already confused his opponents by spending so much time with his dying father, Albert (Roger Lebel), a development they assume is a ploy to conceal his real goal of escaping with the drug money.

The generic action is presented in a style that might well be described as 'hyper-kinetic' and that contrasts with the more reflective Quebec narrative that emerges out of it. Marshall complains that the 'combination of *policier* violence and family drama' undermines the film's 'professed coherence' (2001: 115), echoing Michael Dorland, who called the film 'an uneasy assemblage of two genres' that failed to sort out 'the jumble of contradictory influences [in] contemporary Quebec modernity' (1987: 37). As Dorland's comment suggests, the film was often seen as a superficial 'postmodern' pastiche of the crime film, associated less with Hollywood than with the contemporary French 'cinema of the look' in the films of Jean-Jacques Beineix, Luc Besson, and Leos Carax.[3]

Lauzon's film may thus suggest that genres are becoming global rather than simply American, and, similarly, it represents the perceived threat to a distinctive Quebec culture as more diffuse. Albert lives next door to an Italian restaurant, and his living space is shrinking as the restaurant expands. The couple who run the restaurant are Albert's friends and treat Marcel as if he were their son, but the situation sets up a tension around the effect of the new 'ethnic' communities on Quebec's political future.

Ironically, the two 'plots' are linked by the use of guns. They appear prominently in the crime plot, of course, culminating in the shooting of the police officers, but they also figure in another key sequence that ties the film's title to the Quebec narrative. In an ironic allusion to 'the ancestral traditions of hunting', Marcel tries to satisfy Albert's wish to shoot a moose before he dies by taking him to a zoo where, in the absence of a moose, the old man shoots an elephant (Weinmann, 1990: 118). By this point, however, the pressures on the genre have become so extreme that the reality of what we see is called into question. Just as the visit of Albert's estranged wife to his bedroom in the middle of the night may be a real event (arranged by Marcel) or a product of the dying man's imagination, so Lauzon suggests that 'we can ask ourselves if Albert and Marcel really went to the zoo' (Bonneville, 1987: 18).

This bizarre sequence certainly anticipates the fantastic dimensions that Lauzon would take further in *Léolo* (see Chapter 6), but if it is an imaginary event we are left to decide exactly when the narrative lost touch with reality. The distinction between genre space and national space no longer seems relevant, and the vivid physicality of the final image, in which Marcel lies naked in bed with his dead father, becomes all the more moving if it is yet another allusion to an absence.

Deconstructing Genre

In a sequence midway through *I Love a Man in Uniform* (David Wellington, 1993), a police officer patrols a city street. He notices a car parked next to a fire hydrant. The owner appears and starts to make excuses and, when the officer reminds him of the seriousness of the offence, demands that he be given a ticket. The officer hesitates, and the man launches into a torrent of abuse, upon which the policeman hurries away. In context, the effect of this sequence depends on the spectator's awareness that the police officer is really Henry Adler (Tom McCamus), an actor wearing the uniform of his character in a television crime series. It is a situation rather like Dillon's masquerade as the Marshal in *Paperback Hero* and involves a similar confusion of genre space with everyday reality. However, this film systematically blurs the difference between genre and reality, and thus raises questions about the working of genre codes in contemporary culture.

According to Brenda Longfellow, the film points to 'the dissolution of a Canadian "real" into American simulacra', thus revealing that American popular culture is no longer 'something external or foreign, but . . . a deeply internalized facet of our national psyche'. She cites the director's observation that 'the camera expresses Henry's perception of every situation' but adds that, 'as spectators . . . we are not sutured into Henry's warped point of view' since his behaviour is 'observed at an ironic distance' (1996: 9–12). However, the film goes much further in implicating the spectator than the Canadian genre films discussed earlier, and, while it certainly makes us aware of Henry's obsessive behaviour, what we see does correspond disturbingly to his perceptions.

Henry gets a part in 'one of those slick, bloodthirsty cop shows shot in an anonymously-concealed downtown Toronto' and in which the police uniforms look more American than Canadian (Pevere, 1993b: 29). Yet the irate driver does not recognize the difference, nor do the 'real' police officers, with whom he becomes involved, whose uniforms are identical to the generic uniforms used in the cop show, with the same 'Metropolitan Police' insignia. Although the city is Toronto and the camera emphasizes the Ontario licence plate on the illegally parked car, it seems little different from the generic city it masquerades as in the television series.

While Henry's identification with his character may be, in the national context, a symptom of the loss of a distinctive Canadian culture, it also involves, in generic terms, a commitment to the 'law and order' position, familiar from many Hollywood films and from conservative politicians, that attributes the spread of crime to a liberal concern for the rights of criminals. His pathological behaviour can thus be read as a manifestation of the familiar Canadian identity crisis or, more generally, of the 'postmodern condition', or of the increasing difficulty of telling the difference.[4]

A rather more playful response to similar concerns emerges from three films associated with the Toronto-based actor, writer, and filmmaker Don McKellar. These films, like *I Love a Man in Uniform*, are not really genre films but films in which genre codes spill over into everyday life and interact with other cultural influences. The first two, *Roadkill* (1989) and *Highway 61* (1991), were directed by Bruce McDonald, with McKellar acting in both and contributing to their screenplays, and both are volatile mixtures of elements from several genres, including the road movie, rock 'n' roll movie, crime film, and screwball comedy. McKellar wrote, directed, and starred in *Last Night* (1998), a self-conscious Canadian version of the disaster movie.

Although both filmmakers belong to what Cameron Bailey calls 'Canada's first generation of feature filmmakers to make virtually no contact with the documentary tradition' (2000: 7), all three films draw on that tradition. *Roadkill* opens with a parody of a voice-of-god documentary; and, when Ramona (Valerie Buhagiar) is sent to northern Ontario to find a missing rock band, she meets a documentary filmmaker (played by McDonald himself) and his crew, who then follow her on the rest of her trip. There is no such figure in the other two films, but Chris Byford aptly refers to the 'rich documentary textures' in *Highway 61* (1998: 17), and André Loiselle comments that *Last Night*, 'unlike *Roadkill*, . . . does not explicitly reproduce the codes of documentary [but it] undoubtedly follows the axioms of realism' (2002b: 264).

These critics imply that realism is a residual marker of Canadian identity in these films, but they also recognize that this idea is not exempt from their general ironic stance. Among the strange characters that Ramona meets on the road in *Roadkill* is Russell (McKellar), who plans to become a serial killer and denounces the 'colonial attitude', which assumes that only Americans can succeed in this 'competitive field'. The film ends when Ramona finds the band, who are then massacred at a concert by gunmen working for her shady rock-promoter boss, after which the audience applauds enthusiastically, suggesting either that the bloodletting is imaginary or that it has been recuperated as spectacle.

In *Highway 61*, the American Jackie Bangs (Buhagiar) arrives in a northern Ontario town to retrieve a dead body in which drugs have been concealed, and persuades Pokey Jones (McKellar), a local barber and amateur trumpeter, to help her transport the coffin to New Orleans. He has dreamed of going to the US all his life and regards their journey down the legendary Highway 61 as a pilgrimage to the origins of popular music. Northern Ontario is thus the site of frustrated desire and death, while the US is the home of music, sexuality, and religious mania. As Byford suggests, the highway represents 'a mythological place' that is 'neither exclusively Canadian nor

American' (1998: 16), but the mythic land is populated by characters as absurd as the ones met by Ramona in the 'idiotic wilderness' in *Roadkill*. The oppositions that structure the myths of national identity—and underpin genre codes—fall apart.

According to Christopher Gittings, *Highway 61* 'takes Hollywood cinema, a device of cultural colonization, and transforms it into a representational system enacting an oppositional narrative of cultural decolonization' (2001: 158). This is a rather portentous way of describing the insidious way the film works to explode the terms of such an analysis. Documentary/Canada does not collide with genre/US in these films; rather, both become part of an array of cultural reference points whose interaction destroys any claims to dominance or purity.[5]

Last Night asserts the Canadian difference through the implied contrast between its representation of the end of the world and the spectacular special effects and heroic efforts to avert disaster in Hollywood blockbusters such as *Armageddon* (Michael Bay, 1998) and *Deep Impact* (Mimi Leder, 1998). However, the film relies on the spectator's memory to make this comparison and simply depicts the inhabitants of Toronto preparing for the ultimate catastrophe on the day the world is to end. There is some chaos and violence but, for the most part, the characters accept the inevitable end, the cause of which is never explained. While the film relishes the irony and absurdity of the juxtaposition of the mundane and the catastrophic, it ends with a moving sequence in which Patrick (McKellar) and Sandra (Sandra Oh), who have met by chance, agree to shoot each other at the very moment the world ends, represented only by a final fade to white.

Implanted Memories

Last Night aptly illustrates Rick Altman's claim that contemporary genre films 'implant in spectators the necessary memories, in the form of other genre films' (1999: 91). To some extent, this is how genres have always worked, and the change is not so much in the films themselves as in the cultural context, in which personal memories have become increasingly entangled with media images. At the same time, the distinction between genre films and 'art' films becomes difficult to maintain in a 'postmodern' culture in which the indiscriminate circulation of media images blurs the old boundaries between popular and 'high' culture. As Longfellow suggests, these developments also undermine the idea of the genres as American and question the possibility of distinct national identities.

Ginger Snaps (John Fawcett, 2000), which has already spawned two sequels, is a horror film set in a 'bland' or 'generic Canadian suburb' (actually Brampton, Ontario), but it intensifies the fusion of outer and inner space found in *Un Zoo la nuit* and *I Love a Man in Uniform*.[6] Its teenage sisters, Ginger (Katharine Isabelle) and Brigitte (Emily Perkins), resist the pressure to conform to the standards of 'normal' middle-class life by inventing gruesome 'death' games, while their community is disturbed by a mysterious dog-killer. When Ginger begins to menstruate, she is suddenly attacked by a werewolf and begins to turn into one herself and to infect those around her. The sisters are plunged into a nightmare world that embodies their sexual fears but also the resentment generated by the roles their culture expects them to play.

The film provides the blood and gore expected of its genre but grafts these onto the smart remarks and pranks of the high school movie. In this respect, it follows the example set by Hollywood films such as Wes Craven's *Scream* trilogy. But, while it similarly plays on the media awareness of the youth culture, it both feminizes the subgenre and grounds it in a sense of the return of what is repressed in our post-modern world, a quality that links it to the 'body horror' films of David Cronenberg. A similar situation in which games designed to counter the boredom of everyday life turn into a nightmare reality is found in *Foolproof* (William Phillips, 2003), a heist film in which a group of students find that their hypothetical scheme to rob a diamond merchant is taken over by real criminals, sparking a battle of wits between the professionals and amateurs.

The game-playing in these films, as in Cronenberg's *Crash* (1996) and *eXistenZ* (1999) (see Chapter 5), is in accord with Jean-François Lyotard's influential diagnosis of the 'postmodern condition' as one in which 'language games' replace the discredited 'grand narratives' of Western culture (1984: 10, 15). By incorporating games into their narratives, they remind us that genres are, in effect, games with rules and procedures that make sense in their own terms and create an alternative reality. However, while the collapse of the grand narratives may allow for more playful scrambling of generic rules, the effect can be disturbing in those films in which game-playing has real consequences or loses all contact with reality.

Since the idea of the nation is itself the product of a grand narrative, Canadian genre films play games with, among other things, cultural anxieties about nationhood. Lyotard's report on *The Postmodern Condition*, just cited, was commissioned by the Quebec government, with the aim of developing a more progressive education system, but his account of postmodernity raised awkward questions about the survival of Quebec's cultural traditions in a world of competing 'language games'. The implications of this situation for Quebec cinema have tended to focus on the role of popular genres in a film industry whose reputation has depended on the personal vision of its major directors.

This concern is forcefully expressed in articles by Julie Beaulieu (2003) and Pierre Barrette (2004a), both of whom accept that the genres are American and point to the increasing proportion of Quebec production devoted to genre films. Their discussion needs to be placed in the context of the recent policy and funding practices of Telefilm Canada, which serve the needs of producers rather than directors (see also Chapter 11). With regard to genre, Barrette summarizes the issue when he asks whether 'Quebec cinema should distance itself from genres to keep intact a separate cultural identity, closed in on itself', but he concludes by suggesting that the problem lies not in 'genre films in themselves but in the attitude that the filmmakers adopt towards them' (2004a: 11).

Two recent Quebec genre films, *Le Collectionneur* (Jean Beaudin, 2002) and *Sur le seuil* (Éric Tessier, 2003), owe much to developments in Hollywood, but their use of game-playing leads to extreme situations that speak to the anxieties within Quebec culture and the postmodern condition. The first is a serial-killer movie in which the killer dismembers his victims to construct a life-size statue of a family, apparently to exorcise his memories of an unhappy childhood. Tessier's film is a supernatural thriller in which a psychiatrist, investigating the reasons for a patient's attempted suicide, discovers a religious cult dedicated to evil. As these summaries make clear, the basic plots are hardly original, and both filmmakers were accused of stealing from earlier films. However, genre films are always derivative, and pastiche is a characteristic of postmodern culture. Whatever their merits, these films can be seen as symptomatic of tensions in contemporary Quebec culture.

Beaulieu describes *Le Collectionneur* as an example of 'a Quebec production copying the Hollywood model' (2003: 52–3). The dismissal of the film as a 'copy' misses the complexity of the cultural and cinematic influences at work within it. For one thing, Beaudin is a recognized Quebec auteur, noted for films dealing with characters, like the serial killer in *Le Collectionneur*, who carry 'the burden of a past from which they cannot escape' (Lavoie, 2002: 7). His best-known film is *J. A. Martin photographe* (1977), an understated study of a woman in nineteenth-century Quebec who defies convention by accompanying her photographer husband on his yearly travels through the country. Yet his first feature was a supernatural thriller, *Le Diable est parmi nous* (1971), released in English as *The Possession of Virginia*, and he has frequently returned to genre production.[7]

Le Collectionneur is 'loosely based' (as the credits put it) on a crime novel by Chrystine Brouillet, one of a series about Maud Graham, a police officer working in Quebec City. Critics compared the film to *The Silence of the Lambs* (Jonathan Demme, 1990), in which a female detective also hunts a monstrous serial killer, but the names of David Cronenberg and Stephen King were also invoked, as were the Frankenstein monster and Jack the Ripper. This critical response reveals a familiar concern with the purity of the national cinema, but it also points to an anxiety about new cultural forms that thrive on the combination of earlier texts and styles.

A similar anxiety is apparent in André Lavoie's observation about how the film represents Quebec City, sometimes making it look like a 'postcard' but also treating it as an 'anonymous city swarming with a fauna composed of formidable predators and easy prey' (2002: 8). The irony is that the shots of tourist sites function as a marker of the local context, raising the question of how to imagine a distinct cultural identity that would not depend on such visual clichés.[8]

While the film seems to follow genre conventions quite closely, it begins with a fragmented and dream-like pre-credit sequence set in a country home, outside of which a US flag is flying. A young boy, wearing a cowboy outfit and then a Zorro costume, watches his mother practising her poses as a bodybuilder and his father carefully gutting a fish, while an Elvis Presley song dominates the soundtrack. It seems that the film will be concerned, like its critics, with the impact of American popular culture in Quebec; but this sequence ends with a caption indicating that the main plot takes place 25 years later, and we quickly enter an urban environment in which any such influences have been thoroughly assimilated.

The presence of the US flag is explained when Maud (Maude Guérin) tracks the killer (Luc Picard) to his family cottage in Maine. He is from Quebec, and his grotesque artwork evokes the Holy Family and thus the Catholic traditions noticeably absent from a city where people gather in health clubs, disco bars, and video arcades rather than in churches. Following generic convention, the plot eventually imposes order, but the fragmentation of the opening sequence sets up a pattern of motifs related to the body and the family. It implies that the killer is driven by his traumatic memories, but the lack of clear psychological explanations accords with how images of the past, the genre's and Quebec's, circulate in postmodern culture, available for use in various combinations but without certain and fixed meanings.

Sur le seuil is Tessier's first feature, and critics have been divided over the question of its originality. It is generically very close to John Carpenter's *In the Mouth of Madness* (1995), and Élie Castiel notes its debts to a number of films, including *The Shining* (Stanley Kubrick, 1980) and *The Exorcist* (William Friedkin, 1973). But Castiel insists that 'Tessier does not copy, he is inspired. He does not imitate, he deconstructs' (2003: 42).

The film begins with a pre-credit sequence that presents itself as a 'live' television report on a massacre of schoolchildren in Montreal. This news special incorporates an amateur eyewitness video that consists of blurred and unstable images, familiar from many such videos included in actual news stories. The reporter identifies the gunman as a police officer, and she ends by asking what could have turned an apparently normal man into a savage killer. This opening grounds the film in the everyday terror of modern urban life, the potential for violence in familiar public spaces, and the way in which this terror is represented and intensified in the media. In effect, the film follows the efforts of Paul Lacasse (Michel Côté), who is seen apparently pondering the reporter's question in the final shot before the credits, to find the answer.

Barrette suggests that *Sur le seuil* presents 'a world overdetermined in large part by signs of its belonging to Quebec "normality"', but he objects that, in the context of this 'credible' setting, 'the supernatural machinations . . . appear strangely false and tacked on' (2004a: 10). This judgement, however, raises questions about the extent to which horror films invite our belief and, in effect, reproduces the skeptical attitude adopted by Paul in the film. His initial concern is to find out why Thomas Roy (Patrick Huard), a well-known writer, tried to commit suicide after cutting off his fingers, and he is disturbed to find that Roy had described the massacre and other atrocities *before* they occurred. As a scientist, he looks for a natural explanation, but he gradually unearths the story of a priest who has discovered the secret of evil (he explicitly states that it is not the Devil). The film ends with a bloody climax in which the priest attempts to pass on his powers to a child at the moment of its birth, with Paul resolving to observe the child as it grows up to see if he has become an evil spirit.

While it is unlikely that any spectators would believe this supernatural explanation, the film does speak to the crisis of faith in the new secular Quebec with its pluralism and multicultural population (not very evident in this film). It also implies that the repressed past can return to haunt the present, in distorted forms that attest to the fear that life has lost its meaning in the absence of grand narratives. If the resort to the supernatural is a desperate attempt to explain the apparently random acts of violence that fill our news broadcasts, the comfort it provides is highly ambivalent, since it posits evil as a force beyond human control. It may be that this ambivalence goes to the core of the appeal of genre films.

The tension between excess and containment that characterizes popular cinema is, for many critics, not something that Canadian filmmakers should seek to emulate, especially since it is usually heightened by the use of genre conventions identified with Hollywood. In the next chapter, we will explore these issues further in the work of two filmmakers who succeeded, not without controversy, in becoming popular within the framework of the Canadian film industry.

In Search of the National-Popular: Carle and Cronenberg

Our big-name producers do not see a great
deal of difference between themselves and the
Americans. Their films consistently prove two
things. First, that they believe they are American.
Second, that they are wrong.

—John Harkness (1982: 24)

I tend to view chaos as a private rather than
a social endeavour. That's undoubtedly because
I was born and raised in Canada.

—David Cronenberg (Rodley, 1992: 25)

In his 'Notes on a Tax-sheltered Cinema', John Harkness places the blame for the disappointments of the capital cost allowance era not on the commercial aspirations of those involved but on a failure of imagination in the way that producers conceived of commercial cinema. By eliminating recognizable Canadian settings and ignoring the directors of the direct cinema tradition, they produced bland imitative films that were rarely commercially successful (see also Chapter 3). On the other hand, while he accepted the canonical argument that 'we are a nation of realists' and argued that 'almost all our filmmakers tend toward the realist', Harkness saw this tendency as a 'problem' that contributed to the lack of popular interest in the national cinema' (1982: 25).

He identified only two exceptions to this realist bent, Gilles Carle and David Cronenberg. While they are not quite such isolated figures as Harkness suggests, their success suggested that a national-popular cinema in Canada might be possible, perhaps not quite in the sense intended by Antonio Gramsci, the Italian political and cultural theorist who spent the last years of his life (from 1926 to 1937) as a prisoner under Benito Mussolini's fascist regime. As Marcia Landy explains, Gramsci attributed the rise of fascism in Italy to the lack of a genuine 'national-popular' culture, which could create 'consensus among different regional groupings' (1994: 31). Although Carle and Cronenberg are not political filmmakers in any overt sense, they do have some of the qualities of Gramsci's 'organic intellectuals', not so much because they address 'stark disjunctions between theory and practice' (Landy, 1994: 30) but because they reconcile the opposing poles of commerce and culture in the discourses of Canadian cinema.

Yet, as Maurie Alioff points out in a retrospective review of Carle's *La Vraie nature de Bernadette* (1971), 'not unlike David Cronenberg's early films, Carle's work was an affront to institutional rectitude of the 1970s' (2002: 30). The controversy and critical resistance generated by their films provide an opportunity to explore the tensions between the idea of a national cinema and the practices necessary to reach a popular audience.

The Sins of Gilles Carle

Michael Spencer identified Gilles Carle's first feature, *La Vie heureuse de Léopold Z* (1965), rather than the more usual suspects, as the crucial film that persuaded the government to create the CFDC (see Chapter 2). This claim points to the way in which the film both exemplifies the direct cinema tradition and moves it towards a more popular idiom. Made at the NFB, where Carle had worked for several years, it was commissioned as a documentary on snow removal, and the finished film incorporates several sequences of snowplows clearing the city streets during a storm. Yet the central focus is on the frantic efforts of Léopold (Guy L'Ecuyer) to satisfy the various demands on his time. He must struggle against nature (the snowstorm that threatens to close the city down), a materialistic reality (the loan office where even the pen is chained to the table), and the myths that prevent him from rebelling against this reality (Christmas as a time for family and church). His dreams of escape are embodied in the nightclub singer Josita (Suzanne Valery), but he finally decides instead to hear his son sing at midnight Mass.

The tensions and incongruities in this film reappear in heightened form in Carle's later work, most successfully in the films he made in partnership with producer Pierre Lamy between 1970 and 1975. However, while *Léopold Z* is very much an urban film, critics often attacked the later films for their apparent retreat to the country, the privileged site of the traditional ideology of *conservation* (see Chapter 3), with its emphasis on church, family, and closeness to the land. It is true that a movement from city to country is a feature of many of the films (although some characters move in the reverse direction), and this movement is often associated with an exploration of the past. Yet Carle expressed his contempt for an ideology based on the idea of a 'unique, perfect country, resistant to all foreign influences' (Coulombe, 1995b: 50) and described his films as '*anti*-return to nature films' demonstrating that 'nature no longer exists' (Conseil québécois, 1976: 103).

Rubbing against Quebec's traditional iconography in Carle's films is the sexual revolution of the 1960s, which he saw, in common with anti-psychiatrists such as R.D. Laing and David Cooper, as entailing 'the death of the family' (Conseil québécois, 1976: 77). The loss of family ties is a source of unease for many of his characters, including Marie (Carole Laure) in *La Mort d'un bûcheron* (1972), who sets out to find her missing father, and the title character (also played by Laure) in *La Tête de Normande St-Onge* (1975), whose mother has been confined to an asylum. Although the various experiments with communal living, reflecting the hippie communes of the 1960s, usually collapse because they fail to come to terms with the irrational elements in human nature, the films stress the need for new forms of human relationship.

Carle refuses to provide solutions to the problems depicted in his films, and his refusal to adopt, or to allow the audience to settle into, a single, fixed viewpoint is based on the rejection of 'any orthodoxy, whether political, sociological or economic' (Tadros, 1973: 24). For Carle, dogma and orthodoxy represent the myths that society imposes on the individual from above to perpetuate the established order. This idea is most fully expressed in *Les Corps célestes* (1973), which he describes as 'a satire on ideologies' (Carle, 1973: 32). The 'heavenly bodies' are both the physical attributes of the prostitutes who distract the miners from the dark reality of their subterranean existences and the religious and political myths that come from the skies (via radio antennas). Since the film is set in 1938, the voice of Hitler dominates the airwaves, but the ending transcends time as we hear the voices of John Kennedy, Richard Nixon, and Pierre Trudeau.

The problems of Quebec are seen as an intensification of those of any consumer society; frustration and violence are a result of society's attempt to suppress contradiction. When Julie (Julie Lachapelle) discovers that she is pregnant in *Le Viol d'une jeune fille douce* (1968), her brothers turn the complexities of her life into a simple formula of honour violated. The gangster/businessmen of *Red* (1970) eliminate the contradiction represented by their Métis half-brother. The bosses in *La Mort d'un bûcheron* violently suppress the stirrings of independence among the workers. The lawyer in *Normande St-Onge* preserves his reputation by consigning his sister, an eccentric ex-stripper, to an asylum. In all cases, the attempt to eliminate contradiction defeats itself because of the violent means used to preserve social quiet.

Carle insisted that his films are 'a call to destroy big institutions and to do something as individuals', but he also stressed the need for collective action (Tierney, 1981: 44). *La Mort d'un bûcheron* probes the realities of a society structured around paper, a society of 'the lumberjack, the Scottish bosses of Canadian International Paper . . . , of the novel, of packing cases, and of electronic printing presses' (Carle, 1973a: 19). *Les Corps célestes* uses its basic metaphor of the brothel to equate prostitution and imperialism, and 'to show war as impotence, and not as a manifestation of power' (Carle, 1973b: 32). Yet, despite his desire 'to be some sort of collective filmmaker', Carle also acknowledged that 'I can't help having my fantasies, my ideas, my background' (Martineau, 1983: 17), and this tension between the personal and the political complicates the films' credentials as both national and popular cinema.

Although he insisted on the need 'to fight for a national cinema', Carle rejected the idea of 'a nationalist cinema' (Conseil québécois, 1976: 76), and his films seek to broaden rather than restrict the definition of national identity. Rather than lamenting the loss of a mythic past, they explore the possibilities of 'cultural *métissage*' (Bonneville, 1981b: 13). Characters like Reginald Mackenzie (Daniel Pilon) in *Red* and Marie in *La Mort d'un bûcheron* are literally Métis, divided by the forces within them that link them to the opposed worlds of whites and Indians. Even when his characters are not of mixed blood, however, they are full of contradictions and embody both the tensions and possibilities of diversity. According to one critic, Carle 'obstinately presents the bad conscience of a nation and makes it see its backside' (Gravel, 1996: 7).

The implications of living in a consumer society are central to *La Vraie nature de Bernadette*. The confined, bourgeois existence against which Bernadette (Micheline Lanctôt) initially rebels is imaged by the framed pictures of vegetables that decorate the walls of her suburban home. When she takes her son to live on a farm, she quickly finds that the reality of country life is far from her pastoral fantasy. Because she believes in 'free love', she is happy to satisfy the sexual needs of the locals, and when she apparently cures a sick child and water appears in a dry well she jokingly comments that she may be a new 'Saint Bernadette'. However, the media are quick to exploit this idea, and her house is besieged by a crowd who eventually ransack it in search of religious relics. At the end of the film, when farmers dump vegetables on a highway to protest against the low prices society is prepared to pay for them, the disillusioned Bernadette opens fire on the motorists who stop to load their cars with free vegetables. Her utopian aspirations are shattered by a mob whose idolatry relieves them of the responsibility for solving their own problems and masks a desire to get something for nothing.

This desire for guilt-free consumption is also apparent in the treatment of sexuality. Carle was accused of pandering to 'le milieu de "showbiz"' by following the 1960s view of social revolution as a 'struggle for sex' (Demers, 1973: 11, 13), and he caused minor scandals through his relations with his leading actresses, most notably Carole Laure and Chloé Sainte-Marie. Molly Haskell used the treatment of Laure in *La Mort d'un bûcheron* as an example of how 'a director, even with all good intentions, can hardly help turning a beautiful woman into a sex object', arguing that 'what starts as an exposé becomes exploitation' (1974: 345). But it is precisely the element of exploitation that prevents the film from becoming the kind of exposé that works up righteous indignation but leaves us essentially untouched (since the exploiters are always others).

The films dwell on the fine line between involvement and exploitation, between the erotic as a heightening of human experience and the erotic as a voyeuristic evasion of responsibility. Almost all include, literally or metaphorically, the rape of a sweet young girl, and this rape becomes a symbol of the processes of consumer society as well as film viewing. Our response to the attempted kidnapping and rape of Rita Sauvage (Andrée Pelletier) in *Les Mâles* (1971) is complicated by her evident enjoyment of the experience. While the two male dropouts offer a refreshing contrast to the hypocrisy of society, the sculptures carved by Sainte-Marie (René Blouin), which inevitably seem to take on the form of female breasts, express both the sexual frustration of the men in the wilderness and their treatment of women as objects. These absurd totem poles are part of the film's exploration of the relationships between the animal and the human, between nature and art, and between the subjective and objective in human relationships and in the experience of film.

Despite their alleged sins against morality, the films were more usually attacked for their offences against the rules of consistency, unity, and good taste. Thus Gerald Pratley objected that Carle 'doesn't give himself enough time to work out or properly motivate his screenplays, resulting in slap-dash ideas and incidents, superficiality, melodrama and ultimately confusion' (1972: 124). Nat Shuster similarly complained that in *La Mort d'un bûcheron*, Carle 'isn't just satisfied with merely telling a story' but 'rides off into umpteen directions, skipping and jumping' (1974: 49–50). And Léo Bonneville expressed concern that *Fantastica* (1980) creates 'the impression of watching two films at the same time' (1981a: 15).

Carle's response to such criticism was to insist that his approach reflected the contradictions he saw around him—contradictions rooted in the specific reality of Quebec but that have a much wider resonance. He traced this aesthetic back to his childhood experiences in northern Quebec: 'Our radio picked up Buffalo and Montreal, always together, never separate, so that the religious broadcasts always had a pleasant background of country music . . . . We seven children would thus recite our rosaries at a gallop, learning that in Quebec the most contradictory dreams are possible!' (1972: 17). Such unexpected juxtapositions form the basis of Carle's style and of his refusal to make 'films that seem profound because they deal with only one reality' (Tadros, 1972b: 20).

While most films tend to privilege either the dialogue or the image, Carle often creates tensions between the image and the soundtrack.[1] *Les Corps célestes*, for example, opens with a shot of a radio antenna and a Union Jack, while the voice of Hitler is heard on the soundtrack; and the film is built out of the contrasts between the menacing broadcasts and the sexual escapades depicted in the images. In *Léopold Z* and *Bernadette*, the cheerful music, Caribbean and country respectively, creates an uneasy lightheartedness in view of the frustration expressed in the images. Marie's letters to her illiterate mother and unknown father, read on the soundtrack of

La Mort d'un bûcheron, provide a contemplative counterpoint to the urgency and confusion shown in the images.

The excess and discontinuity in these films are designed to break down the conventional structures of film viewing in order to encourage a more open and less conditioned response to social structures. Their narratives are, therefore, 'necessarily complex and diffuse' (Tadros, 1972b: 20), and Carle claimed that he preferred to 'run the risk of a clumsy truth rather than a beautiful cinematic lie' (Conseil québécois, 1976: 19). The films expose social myths that conceal contradictions and constantly unsettle the audience by their shifting tones and genres. The arrival of the three brothers in *Le Viol* turns a romantic comedy into a modern version of the revenge western. Similarly, the entry of the police in *Les Mâles* and *Normande St-Onge* turns these films briefly into crime films (comic, in the first case); *Bernadette* is a 'religious western' (Carle, 1972: 17); and *La Mort d'un bûcheron* begins as an erotic film but ends as a political film, when Marie moves from naive victim to an awareness of the historical forces shaping her society.

This movement from being exploited to becoming aware is basic to all of Carle's films—often for the characters, but always for the audience. Yet, given the contradictory nature of their environments, his characters cannot be the complete and fully rounded individuals of 'psychological' cinema. There is no such thing as a 'true nature' in Carle's films, since the character embodies the contradictions of society, and personality is not fixed but dynamic and fluid. He insisted that 'only impossible characters are possible today' (1972: 17). Julie, in *Le Viol*, invites our sympathy as the victim of her brothers' aggression, but we also have to watch her sit calmly by as they rape a hitchhiker. Bernadette, as Carle describes her, is 'simultaneously a saint and a prostitute, a generous woman and an egoist' (Tadros, 1972b: 19). The spectator is confronted with characters who are 'simultaneously antipathetic, sympathetic, violent, gentle, evil' and is thus prevented from achieving a secure relationship with the 'world' on the screen (Tadros, 1973a: 20).

While the characters may arrive at a new awareness, the endings of the films rarely provide a sense of release. In *Red*, the Métis hero solves the mystery of his half-sister's murder but is gunned down before he can expose her husband's facade of respectability. Léopold Z goes to midnight Mass with his family; the runaway lovers return to the brothel in *Les Corps célestes*; and Normande St-Onge withdraws into a world of sexual fantasy. But the key factor is that the audience's desire for an ending that resolves the issues is frustrated. The audience is denied the satisfaction of a vicarious revolution. Carle's films work to 'destroy the patterns of what's going on', and he wants 'people to feel frustrated at the end' as long as they also 'feel like doing something about their lives' (Tierney, 1981: 44).

During the 1980s, Carle weathered the crisis in Quebec cinema with two popular adaptations of classic Quebec novels, Roger Lemelin's *Les Plouffe* (1981) and Louis Hémon's *Maria Chapdelaine* (1983). The latter had already provided him with the name of his modern-day heroine in *La Mort d'un bûcheron* and, while these adaptations were set in the past, Carle was concerned to rescue the novels from the conservative myths that had sprung up around them. He continued to make films, documentary and fiction, but it was not until *Pudding chômeur* (1996) that he was again able to arouse the same kind of reaction that the films of the 1970s provoked.

This film reaffirmed and updated Carle's 'belief in the present and its diversity' (Gajan, 1996: 12). Described by the director as 'a eulogy to multiple ethnicities living together', *Pudding chômeur* is set in centre-south Montreal, a poor district that has changed greatly in recent years (Gajan and Loiselle, 1996: 6). It opens with a bizarre sequence in which a truck carrying pigs collides with a school bus full of visually handicapped children. The accident releases the pigs into the city and severs the hand of Mohammed (Michel Laprise), who runs through the street carrying the bloody hand, which is then reattached at a ceremony presided over by Yo-yo (Chloé Sainte-Marie). The community is home to many pseudo-religious sects and a carnival atmosphere reigns, despite the brutality of corrupt police officers and the violence of comic Italian gangsters.

As in the earlier films, the potential of diversity is countered by the conformist tendencies of religion and the media. While Carle insists that this film is 'in direct continuity' with *La Mort d'un bûcheron* (Gajan and Loiselle, 1996: 6), Yo-yo's miracle, and the media sensation it causes, link it rather to *Bernadette*. It is typical of Carle that, despite the satire on bogus religion and the desire to conform, the miracle here, more certainly than in the earlier film, is a 'real' one; consequently, the question of belief is shifted to the spectator. The film celebrates the 'people', even as it shows their fears and vulnerability; and the future of the 'nation' is implied in the ending when Yo-yo buys a convent from a Catholic order of nuns.

The Challenge of David Cronenberg

The camera tracks along a wire fence through which it is possible to read a sign on the building inside: DELAMBRE FRERES ELECTRONICS MONTREAL LTD. A man, who appears to be a night watchman, emerges and speaks to a passing cat in a mixture of French and heavily accented English. Inside the building, he investigates the source of a noise and finds a well-dressed woman standing beside a piece of equipment covered in blood.

Such is the opening sequence of *The Fly*—not the David Cronenberg remake, filmed in Canada in 1986, but the original Hollywood version, directed by Kurt Neumann in 1958. The tension between French and English, suggested by the sign and the bilingual watchman, is not taken up in the rest of the film, which is studio-bound and in which the main characters (even if their names are French) are played by Hollywood actors with American English accents. As Adam Knee suggests in his examination of the ideological meanings of the two versions, it also seems strange that 'the national differences between the United States and its neighbor are repressed in a film dealing with various kinds of alien encroachments' (1992: 33).

The decision to set this film in Montreal may have been motivated by the French setting in the short story that provided its source, but it was also probably a relic of the

Canadian Cooperation Agreement that quietly expired at about the time *The Fly* was made. By the time of Cronenberg's remake, the commercial failure of most of the direct cinema films had prompted pressures to remove specifically Canadian elements (see Chapter 3). In this context, Cronenberg's horror films became key texts in working through the relations between commerce and culture, genre and national cinema.

One of the most profitable investments ever made by the CFDC was in Cronenberg's first commercial feature film, *Shivers* (1975).[2] However, the tension between popular and national cinema became vividly apparent when the agency came under attack for using public money to support a horror film about sexually transmitted parasites in a Montreal apartment building. In the following years, Cronenberg established himself as a major director of 'body horror' films and, despite widespread critical opposition, became a 'full-blown Canadian cultural institution' (Pevere, 1993a: 6). Although he operated within the framework of the American genres, he continued to work in Canada, with the support of the CFDC and the CCA.

Cronenberg's remake of *The Fly* opens with the credits superimposed on what appears to be living tissue observed through a microscope. The image, however, gradually comes into focus revealing a high-angle long shot of a large hall full of people. At the top of the screen, the names of two Indian nations can just be discerned: ALGONKIN and OJIBWA. Down below, in the distance, there is a flashing neon sign on which the word ART can be glimpsed. A conversation then introduces the film's two American stars (Jeff Goldblum and Geena Davis) and reveals that this is a gathering of 'half the scientific community of North America'. Although the sequence was shot on location in Toronto, it lacks the specific identification of national setting found in the Hollywood original. Knee accurately comments that the differences between the United States and Canada are 'even further repressed, as the text designates the setting as a generic North American metropolis' (1992: 34n).

In Cronenberg's previous film, *The Dead Zone* (1983), Canadian locations stand in for various named American places, in keeping with the requirements of the Stephen King novel from which it was adapted. His earlier films are all set, unobtrusively, in Canada, but only in *Videodrome* (1982) does the Canadian setting become thematically central, through the plot's concern with cross-border television signals and its play with the theories of Marshall McLuhan. Critical analysis of these films would thus seem to be more fruitfully situated within a generic rather than a national cinema context. Indeed, many discussions of Cronenberg's work do not mention Canada or do so only in passing.[3]

In a highly influential reassessment of the horror genre, originally published in conjunction with the 1979 Toronto Festival of Festivals, Robin Wood notoriously objected to the 'sexual disgust' that he found in *Shivers* (1984: 194). He later reaffirmed his view that Cronenberg's films generate strong feelings of 'revulsion' through their 'treatment of human physicality' (1983: 135). Other critics, however, have been more appreciative of their 'thematic linking of physical and psychical states' (O'Pray, 1984: 48). Cronenberg himself objected that Wood's ideological analysis misses his focus on fears and needs that arise from the basic human experience of embodiment and that are not amenable to political solutions. Thus, he argued, *The Fly* is 'a metaphor for ageing' and its genre is 'metaphysical horror' (Rodley, 1992: 125, 134). Although he resisted the notion of the Devil or 'a purely evil being', he described himself as embarked on a 'cinematic voyage' concerned to 'discover the connection between the physical and the spiritual' (Rodley, 1992: 118, 128–9).

The 'metaphysical' dimension is vital to the effect of these films, but they do not exist in a cultural vacuum and, at least on the surface, their cultural reference points are 'North American' rather than Canadian. Cronenberg suggested that Wood attacked his films because they do not promote the total rejection of the values of 'middle-class America' (Rodley, 1992: 68). Yet the films are, to say the least, highly ambivalent in their treatment of these values, which function most often as a defence mechanism against the violence and disorder that take over when human beings are released from cultural constraints.

Whereas the original version of *The Fly* plunges the spectator into the horrifying consequences of the scientist's experiments, the remake begins with the banality of cocktail conversation. Although the scientist tells the journalist that he has a secret invention that will 'change the world as we know it', this sounds like a clumsy attempt to seduce her. Only the Indian names high up on the wall allude to earlier 'North American' cultural traditions, which have been replaced by the 'middle-class' and scientific values represented by this gathering. The erotic subtext, cloaked in polite language, links the scientist's experiments to a middle-class culture that suppresses bodily functions and depends on technology that increasingly controls the natural world.

In Cronenberg's horror films, scientific experiments lead to bodily mutations and the breakdown of social order, and the 'scandal' of these films stems largely from their assault on the myth of the hygienic and self-contained body, which is so prevalent in the culture of 'middle-class America'. The series of accidents in *The Fly* that bring about the fusion first of Seth Brundle with a fly, and then of Brundlefly with a piece of equipment, thus testifies to deep-rooted cultural anxieties regarding the definition of the human in relation to the natural and the technological (see Haraway, 1991). For critics sympathetic to the horror genre, then, Cronenberg's films should be judged in terms of how they treat those aspects of human experience with which the genre typically engages, and their national origins are largely irrelevant to their purpose.

More frequently, especially at the beginning of his career, Canadian critics tended to regard horror films as culturally insignificant and Cronenberg as an embarrassment to the national cinema. Nevertheless, a number of attempts were made to read his films within a Canadian cultural context. Piers Handling (1983b) argued the case for 'a Canadian Cronenberg' by pointing to thematic similarities between his films and the direct cinema films. This case was developed and extended by Gaile McGregor, who claimed that it was 'facile' to assume that 'Cronenberg can be explained in terms of American conventions' (1992: 47). Although she does acknowledge 'his very considerable and obviously deliberate use of those conventions', McGregor objects that discussions placing the films' generic affinities in the foreground assimilate them to 'universal categories or processes' (47, 45). For McGregor, *The Fly* is best interpreted in a Canadian context, within which Cronenberg's fear of 'the breaking down of the barriers between Self . . . and Other' can be related to similar fears in the poetry of Margaret Atwood (55).

Despite the strategies in his films that render Canada visually absent or marginal, Cronenberg encouraged such readings by describing himself as 'in exile from American culture' (Jaehne, 1992: 3). His own account of his development as a film-maker stressed his Canadian roots and his early goal, as a member of the Toronto Film Co-op, 'to by-pass the Hollywood system because it wasn't ours' (Rodley, 1992: 15). However, he was equally adamant in his opposition to what he called 'the heavy hand of John Grierson' (Rodley, 1992: 35) that had produced what he called 'a very strong resistance to illusion in Canadian film' (Chesley, 1975: 25). On the other hand, he insisted that 'my films are Canadian because I'm Canadian—therefore my sensibilities are Canadian' (Hookey, 1977: 16).

Yet the attempts to situate Cronenberg's films in a national rather than generic context often seem to obscure how the films are constructed and received. Thus, McGregor's claim that the 'sense of vulnerability, of horrified fascination with the vicissitudes of embodiment' in Cronenberg's films also 'permeates the whole of Canadian literature' is hardly less 'universal' in its scope than the generic readings to which she objects (1992: 53). It is, however, echoed in Geoff Pevere's suggestion that the horror genre may reflect 'a "Canadian" world view' because of its emphasis on 'vulnerability and isolation' (1993a: 9). This attempt to insert the genre into the national culture tends to conjure away the problems posed by Cronenberg's films, generically and culturally.

In an attempt to give a more nuanced account of the Canadian 'sensibilities' in Cronenberg's films, Harkness contrasts the 'sterile modern apartment buildings and hospitals, clean Canadian shopping centres and subways' in these films with the 'deranged environments, decaying and corrupt' of American horror films (1983: 91–2). This distinction needs to be questioned in view of the centrality of the shopping mall in George Romero's *Dawn of the Dead* (1978), a key example of the modern American horror film; but it does point to the complex relations between generic and national attitudes to order and disorder in Cronenberg's work. His concern with scientific and institutional projects to control nature, and with the chaos generated when these projects get out of control, illustrates both Cronenberg's own sense of his 'very Canadian' tendency 'to come down on all sides at once or none at all' (Rodley, 1992: 118) and Michael Silverman's view of 'a post-modern Cronenberg' whose films 'operate entropically by attenuating' the binary oppositions on which genre films have traditionally depended (1984: 33).[4]

As we have seen (Chapter 4), binary oppositions rarely function in Canadian cinema as clearly as they do (at least in theory) in the American genres. The post-modern tendencies noted by Silverman and others have also been linked to changes in Hollywood that occurred at about the time Canada began to produce genre films. Although the emergence of what has been called New Hollywood cinema can be traced further back, its impact became fully apparent in the 1970s. The collapse of the studio system (or rather, its absorption into media conglomerates) was accompanied by the decline of classical narrative cinema (or rather, the emergence of filmmakers who question many of its premises). Along with an emphasis on blockbusters, another feature was the development of an 'American art cinema' by filmmakers such as Robert Altman and Martin Scorsese, who often use genre conventions in highly personal ways. As a result, 'the status of genre as a category [became] one of the most problematic in contemporary cinema' (Tasker, 1996: 223).

Cronenberg's later films illustrate this tendency as they move (at least apparently) away from the horror genre, and they are often discussed as 'art films' or as part of a trend towards 'weird' subject matter in Canadian cinema (see Chapter 11). Indeed, far from being outside the pale of the national cinema, Cronenberg's films can now be seen as important precursors, but by no means the only ones, of the stress on fantasy and subjective vision now central to Canadian cinema. His recent films may not fit comfortably within the horror genre, but, in retrospect, it is possible to agree with Adam Lowenstein's argument that Cronenberg's work is a 'conversation with the horror film, but his contributions to that conversation constantly renegotiate its very parameters' (1999: 44). The experience of embodiment remains central to films that, while they may not be as obviously 'popular' as the earlier films, still pose critical questions regarding the conversation between popular, art, and national cinema in a postmodern age.

For some critics, *Naked Lunch* (1992), *M. Butterfly* (1993), and *Crash* (1996) represent a dilution of Cronenberg's vision because they are all adaptations of literary works by authors with their own distinctive way of seeing. Of these, *M. Butterfly*—based on David Hwang's successful Broadway play—seems furthest removed from the director's usual interests. However, George Melnyk's claim that '*M. Butterfly* was originally a play about a female impersonator, and Cronenberg simply directed the film version' is extremely reductive (2004: 153). In fact, the play and the film are about a French diplomat who falls in love with a Chinese opera singer, unaware that female roles in Chinese opera are performed by men. The major change from the play, one to which many critics objected, is that Cronenberg does not conceal the singer's real gender from the audience.

Rather than a sign of the director's incompetence, this effect raises unsettling questions about the relations of mind and body that relate to his earlier work. As Asuman Suner suggests, René Gallimard (Jeremy Irons) pursues his passion rather like the scientists who seek to 'assert full control over nature' with the result that 'the desire to transcend the limits of the body results in getting stuck even deeper in the flesh' (1998: 50). He has a long affair with Song (John Lone) before returning to France, where he learns that his lover was a male used as a spy by the Chinese government. Although he seems stunned by the revelation, the idea that he did not know, at some level, is so unlikely that we must wonder whether he was repressing his awareness of his true sexual orientation and whether it is possible to separate the mental from the physical in human desire.

The casting of an unmistakably English actor as a French diplomat—in a film by a Canadian director based on the work of an American playwright set in China alluding to an opera set in Japan by an Italian composer—only serves to heighten the sense of unreality in the situation and the setting. Just as René does not (or will not) see who Song really is, the film presents China as 'an eroticized Oriental culture', reproducing his viewpoint even as it distances us from it (Suner, 1998: 55). The entanglement of inside and outside in the body horror films is replicated here by the meshing of subjective and objective vision.[5]

This principle is carried even further in *Crash* and *eXistenZ* (1999). Based on a novel by the well-known science-fiction writer J.G. Ballard, *Crash* caused even more controversy (although mainly outside Canada) than *Shivers* through its conjunction of violent car crashes and explicit sexuality.[6] According to Beard, *Crash* is 'a real art movie', but it is not so easy to pin it down (2002: 155). Lowenstein describes it more aptly as 'a film which resolutely evades audience attempts to define its generic, authorial, or national identity' (1999: 44). The question of authorship is perversely complicated by naming the protagonist (played by James Spader), a television commercial director, James Ballard, and this also feeds into the uncertainty about the film's national allegiances. Two US critics have commented that 'Ballard is British and Cronenberg Canadian, but *Crash* seems peculiarly American since its narrative deals with the exhaustion of the civilizing process' (Brottman and Sharrett, 2002: 126).

Crash is set in 'a Canada that seems to comprise totally of motorways and tower blocks' (Botting and Wilson, 1998: 186), but, while those who know Toronto will recognize the city, the film never clearly identifies it. This sense of an anonymous urban environment reinforces the sense that 'there is no "normal" world; the characters are already damaged beyond repair' (Costello, 2000: 80). Cronenberg's dystopian vision of everyday life thus has much in common with Carle's rather more genial treatment of the idea that 'nature no longer exists' and suggests a link between their films, the 'obliterated environments' of Northrop Frye (see Chapter 3), and Jean Baudrillard's 'hyperreality' (see Chapter 12).

The film centres on the seduction of James and his wife Catherine (Deborah Kara Unger) by the charismatic figure of Vaughan (Elias Koteas). Vaughan conducts research on car crashes and stages re-enactments of famous accidents in which celebrities, such as James Dean and Jayne Mansfield, died. He recalls the scientists in the earlier films when he announces that his 'project' has to do with 'the reshaping of the human body by modern technology', but he later describes this as 'a crude sci-fi concept' that disturbs nobody and which he uses to disguise his real concern with the creation of a 'benevolent psychopathology'. Car crashes become an evolutionary force that, as anticipated in *The Fly* and *Videodrome*, works like a virus through human sexuality to fuse mind, body, and technology.

The contact between flesh and metal is a recurring motif in *Crash*. It is established in the opening sequences in which Catherine places her breast against an aircraft as a man takes her from behind and James has sex with the script girl on a photocopy machine. It is taken up in the metal splint on James's leg at the hospital and in the metal contraption in which Gabrielle (Rosanna Arquette) is encased. Helen (Holly Hunter) jokes that making love in a car is like being in a crash, and Catherine has marks on her body as if from a crash after making love with Vaughan in a car wash. These characters need violence and shock in order to feel anything, and the many shots of traffic speeding along the urban highways suggest that they are indeed the forerunners of an emerging psychopathology.

In contrast to the modern urban setting in *Crash*, *eXistenZ* is apparently set in the near future, but the virtual reality game in which most of the action takes place provides a landscape 'littered with old buildings now being used for something other than their original function' (Rodley, 1999: 10). The game is played with the aid of a 'pod' connected to a 'bioport' installed into the player's body; and, the film depicts the journey of Allegra (Jennifer Jason Leigh), the game designer, and her reluctant body-guard Ted (Jude Law) through the game, which is apparently under attack by a rival manufacturer. Ted's efforts to learn the rules of the game initially point to the differences between virtual and everyday reality, but it gradually becomes clear that there is no significant difference.

Allegra and Ted must also deal with a group called the Realist Underground, whose battle cry is 'Long live realism!' While the goals of these rebels are not entirely clear, they represent not only the cultural forces (like Canadian film critics) opposed to Cronenberg's cinema but also those unwilling to accept the idea that reality is constructed (or virtual).[7] Their inclusion in the game world (and in the film) is a playful reminder that Cronenberg has long anticipated the emergence of cyborg culture, a central motif in science-fiction films such as *The Matrix* (Andy and Larry Wachowski, 1999), the Hollywood film whose near simultaneous release rather over-shadowed *eXistenZ*.[8]

While the film's playful tone was not always recognized or was interpreted as a sign that Cronenberg was not seriously engaged, *eXistenZ* extends and updates the concerns of his earlier work and, among other things, illustrates the complexly evolving relations between the popular and the national in a Canadian context increasingly defined by global economic and technological developments. Although one critic has referred to 'the near complete absence of humour in all his early films' (Crane, 2000: 63), an element of black humour has always been part of their unsettling power. Like the very different films of Gilles Carle, Cronenberg's films use popular forms to entertain but also to raise awkward questions about more 'official' and complacent discourses of cultural identity. Their challenge to the canonical account of Canadian cinema is not just a matter of the use of generic formulas but also their validation of fantasy over more realistic approaches. Fantasy is an important aspect of popular cinema, but other Canadian filmmakers have also worked in the domain of the fantastic in forms that disturb the expectations of viewers in more radical ways. We will turn to their work in the next chapter.

The Canadian Fantastic

The only real themes that matter to me are how humans love each other or hate each other or are envious of each other. All the timeless stuff.

—Guy Maddin (Vatnsdal, 2000: 81)

The imaginary is not an escape. It is not to flee reality that one takes refuge in the imaginary. The imaginary borders reality, completes it.

—André Forcier (Loiselle and Racine, 1988–9: 9)

There can be no doubt that the realist tradition has been a major force in Canadian cinema or that the idea of realism has been especially important in thinking about Canadian cinema. The influence of documentary realism is also apparent in many Canadian films whose allegiances may seem to lie elsewhere. Yet this view of Canadian cinema tends to deflect attention from the many currents that have little to do with the realist tradition. It downplays the extensive output of genre films (see Chapter 4), but what also tends to disappear from view is the rich vein of Canadian films more attuned to the processes of the imagination than to external reality. These films have assumed a much more prominent, perhaps dominant, position in the last decade or so.

No single term can encompass the wide range of films that challenge the centrality of realism in Canadian cinema. These films belong to what is often called the Méliès tradition, after the French magician who pioneered the use of cinema to create an imaginary world of illusions and spectacular effects. The realist tradition is also often defined in opposition to 'expressionism', a term specifically referring to German film-makers in the years after World War I, who used distorted images to express the inner states of their characters as well as the pressures of life in post-war society. As we shall see, Canadian filmmakers draw on many different styles, including surrealism and the Gothic tradition; but I have opted for the term fantastic cinema, for reasons that will become apparent in the next section, although this runs the risk of blurring important distinctions.

Paul Almond's Fantastic Trilogy

As the Canadian film industry gradually evolved from the initiatives of the direct cinema filmmakers, the first major break with the documentary tradition occurred in three films directed by Paul Almond and starring his then wife, Geneviève Bujold: *Isabel* (1968), *The Act of the Heart* (1970), and *Journey* (1972). The first two were produced with the support of Hollywood studios, but critics were not sure what to make of them. They clearly did not belong to the realist tradition identified as distinctively Canadian, but they were also too dark and disturbing to qualify as mainstream commercial cinema. While their most obvious affinity was with European 'art cinema', and they clearly owed much to the films of Ingmar Bergman, the idea of a Canadian auteur seemed both premature and presumptuous to most critics. *Journey*, in particular, was often dismissed as pretentious, and Almond's subsequent career did not fulfill the promise of his early films.

These films belong to the genre of the 'fantastic' that, according to Tzvetan Todorov, depends on the 'hesitation experienced by a person who knows only the laws of nature, confronting an apparently supernatural event'. The effect is to undermine the notion of secure genre boundaries since the fantastic constantly merges into the 'uncanny' (the apparently supernatural event is given a natural explanation) or the 'marvellous' (the presence of the supernatural is confirmed) (1973: 25, 41). In films like Almond's, one of the most important consequences of the fantastic 'hesitation' is to disrupt the screen/spectator relationship.

All three films filter the experience of 'hesitation' through the consciousness of the central character played by Bujold, who, as a francophone actress in English-language films, links the disturbance of the characters' peace of mind to Canada's cultural insecurities.[1] In *Isabel*, the death of her mother forces the title character to return from Montreal to the family farm on the Gaspé Peninsula, where she begins to see ghosts that, according to local superstition, derive from the family's violent and incestuous past. When the film was released, the US reviewer Hollis Alpert complained that it does not reveal whether the ghosts are actual or imagined and insisted that 'movies that deal with the supernatural had best be clear whether we are to believe in the damned things or whether it's all in the character's imagination' (Edsforth, 1972: 22). The film does not fit comfortably into the horror genre (or, in Todorov's terms, the marvellous) or into that of the psychological thriller (Todorov's uncanny), and so it remains in the precarious domain of the fantastic, much to the dismay of critics who police genre boundaries.

In *The Act of the Heart*, Martha comes from the country to Montreal with the intention of becoming a professional singer, but she is troubled by religious doubts and sexual fears. These are intensified when she falls in love with a Catholic priest (Donald Sutherland), and, in the shocking final sequence, she burns herself alive to provide an example for a world that has forgotten Christ. The 'hesitation' here stems less from doubts about the status of the images than from the problem of interpreting Martha's actions. As Janet Edsforth points out, the film leaves unanswered the question of 'whether Martha was in fact a saint or a psychotic' (1972: 26). If she is a saint, her self-immolation takes on a mythic resonance (and the film enters the realm of the marvellous); if she is a psychotic, her death simply confirms her fear that life is meaningless (and the film becomes uncanny). The film does not allow the certainty of either resolution, and even the difficulty of convincingly representing her final act (which led Robert Fulford to ask, 'if a commercial film isn't illusion, what's the point?') adds to the central dilemma of how to give physical expression to spiritual desires (1974: 24).

In *Journey*, Bujold plays a woman found floating down a river on a log and rescued by Boulder (John Vernon), the leader of an isolated commune. The 'hesitation' experienced by this woman (who has no memory of her past life and whom Boulder names Saguenay after the river in which he found her) reflects her inability to decide what the Undersky commune represents. The clothes and way of life suggest that they are early settlers: but is this because the film is set in the past, because the commune is based on a rejection of the modern world, or because it is a product of her imagination? The last option runs counter to the film's emphasis on the physical reality of the life of the commune and its natural surroundings, but it gains some support from the oblique way in which the narrative is presented. Robert Fothergill was driven to object that the film is constructed 'with an elusive indirectness, with the result that for much of the time the spectator is not quite sure what is going on, or what the characters are talking about' (1972: 35).

The opening image is an extreme close-up of a woman's face. We hear indistinctly the sounds of a car braking, footsteps, and a door opening (or perhaps a rifle being loaded). The woman speaks the name 'Damien' and says, 'you've come back.' As she calls his name again, the camera pulls back to reveal that she is adrift on a log in the middle of a river. After her rescue, a series of brief sequences, separated by fades, involves us in her gradual recovery of consciousness; but we also share the point of view of the commune members as they examine the nameless woman who has mysteriously appeared in their midst.

This double perspective—Saguenay's look at the commune, their looking at her—draws the spectator into the tension between self and other that is central both to the trilogy and to Todorov's theory of the fantastic. The 'themes of the self' deal with 'the fragility of the limit between matter and mind', while the 'themes of the other' form a chain that leads from desire through cruelty to death (1973: 120, 135). Each of Almond's protagonists undergoes an experience that exposes the fragile relations between 'matter and mind' and that stems from her association of sexual desire with male aggression and with death. The crisis caused by this experience generates the fantastic hesitation and disrupts the character's relation to her social and natural environment as well as the spectator's relation to the film. The interaction of themes of self (the problem of consciousness) with themes of the other (desire, cruelty, death) creates the structuring tensions of the films.

Almond himself has described *Journey* as 'a visionary allegory' (Fothergill, 1972: 35), and it is tempting to try to explain away the obscurities in these films by an allegorical interpretation. Yet attempts to pin down the meaning of the allegory usually lead to frustration. Thus Guy Morris felt that *Isabel* is 'a simple story that can be made complex if you want to play the game of looking for hidden messages' (1968: 18), and Jean-René Ethier complained that 'the allegory in *Journey* constantly hides its keys' (1973: 27). As Michel Euvrard remarked in an article on *Journey*, allegory presupposes that 'the public has the key to the system of signs used by the author', but he suggested that the necessary communal myths do not exist 'in an urban, individualist, pluralist society in which only the memory remains, unequally preserved, of the different religions and mythologies to which the population has subscribed in the course of history' (1972: 11).

Despite the obstacles to modern allegory, Euvrard argues that the 'allegorical elements' in *Isabel* and *The Act of the Heart* enable Almond to dispense with 'traditional psychological analyses and motivations' and that 'the (partial) allegory makes it possible to move directly from the concrete—from existence and physical presence—to the *typical*.' He then adds that the '(complete) allegory' in *Journey* involves a further leap over 'historical and sociological determinations' to bring about a movement 'from the concrete to the *abstract*' and 'to establish directly the bond between physical and material realities and that spiritual reality which socio-historical obstacles prevent from being attained in Montreal (or any other large city of the consumer society)' (1972: 12). Martha's experiences in Montreal in *The Act of the Heart* confirm the difficulty of contacting 'spiritual reality' in a modern urban setting, but the fact remains that *Journey*'s spectators are also products of the consumer society. Its allegory is complete only in the sense that the images consistently resist literal interpretation and not because they refer to communally accessible keys.

According to Todorov, the availability of an allegorical interpretation would eliminate the fantastic hesitation (1973: 32). Saguenay's presence sets off tensions in a community that seemed united in a common purpose, and she is eventually sent back down the river. In the final images, industrial installations are visible on the riverbank, confirming that the film is indeed set in the present and that the commune is an attempt to create a community its members could not find in the outside world. Their problems in coping with the disturbance caused by Saguenay's arrival parallel the spectator's difficulty in resolving the film's enigmas. Although *Journey* goes further than either *Isabel* or *The Act of the Heart* in demanding a more-than-literal reading, all three films work by evoking and then frustrating the need for keys. If the films are viewed as fantastic rather than allegorical, the trilogy emerges as a disturbing exploration of the difficulty of relating the material and the spiritual in modern society.

Canadian Gothic

A strong 'Gothic' strain runs through Canadian literature. The term dates back to the eighteenth century and originally referred to works that sought to tap into the dark and irrational forces associated with Medieval Europe (known as the 'Dark Ages') as opposed to the 'civilized' restraint of contemporary society. It came to stand, more generally, for 'a certain mood of terror or horror, in which the dark mysteries of life were brought to the fore'; and, as a style, the Gothic was closely associated with the 'grotesque', which 'emphasizes incongruity, disorder, and deformity, and arises from the juxtaposition or clash of the ideal with the real, the psychic with the physical, or the concrete with the symbolic' (Northey, 1976: 4, 7). The Gothic is a central feature in many works in the horror genre—and the term has been applied to the films of David Cronenberg—but it also designates a literary tradition of dark romances, of which the most famous examples are the novels of the Brontë sisters (*Jane Eyre, Wuthering Heights*).[2]

This branch of the Gothic is already apparent in Almond's *Isabel*, but several important films of the 1970s confirmed its position in Canadian cinema. Gordon Sheppard's *Eliza's Horoscope* (1974) draws mainly on the grotesque in its depiction of a young woman (Elizabeth Moorman) seeking astrological and religious guidance in her search for a perfect man. *Kamouraska* (Claude Jutra, 1973) and *The Far Shore* (Joyce Wieland, 1976) are more specifically Gothic fictions: both are historical films, based on actual events, but both focus on the subjective and emotional experience of women who become trapped in traditional marriages and break out through acts of passionate excess.

Kamouraska, Jutra's follow-up to *Mon oncle Antoine* (see Chapter 3), proved controversial on a number of grounds. Based on a highly poetic novel by Anne Hébert (who collaborated with the director on the screenplay), it was the most expensive film yet made in Canada and required the investment of a French co-producer. Jean Pierre Lefebvre objected that the production encouraged a 'climate of inflation' that threatened the survival of Quebec cinema; although, with a budget reported to be around

$750,000, it was hardly an expensive film by Hollywood standards (1976: 44). Indeed, its intimate and claustrophobic style was partly dictated by budgetary constraints, and cinematographer Michel Brault explained that 'there are very few long shots because we didn't have enough money to reconstruct entire streets' (Evanchuk, 1975: 22). Audiences expecting a *Gone with the Wind*-style epic were inevitably disappointed and, to compound matters, the film was released in a truncated print after the producers rejected Jutra's three-hour version.[3]

The style was not just a question of economics, however, since it also corresponds to how the narrative is filtered through the consciousness of Elisabeth d'Aulnières, who is in a state of nervous exhaustion at the deathbed of her second husband. As Elisabeth, Geneviève Bujold may have been cast partly because she had become 'the Canadian cinema's only international star' (Shuster, 1973: 28), but the film also benefits from the ability to combine intensity and vulnerability that she demonstrated in Almond's trilogy. Flashbacks depict her involuntary memories of her first unhappy marriage to the squire of Kamouraska (Philippe Léotard), her love affair with an American doctor (Richard Jordan), and the bloody murder of her husband by her lover. As Jutra himself suggested, it becomes 'a film-mosaic which leaps continually from one place to another'(Perreault, 1972), an effect intensified by the cuts in the release print and hardly calculated to appeal to critics, like Robert Fulford, who thought that audiences were 'entitled to simple stories' (1974: 74).

Although the adaptation follows the novel closely, some critics felt that the film 'sacrifices much of the psychological complexity' of the novel in favour of its 'gothic elements' (Russell, 1983: 135n). Jutra certainly made no secret of his own attraction to this aspect of the novel, noting that 'on the back cover of the book it says it is the story of snow, love, and blood' (Bujold et al., 1973: 49), and one reviewer thought he had succeeded in making a sort of '*Wuthering Heights* on the St Lawrence' (Shuster, 1973: 28). The murder is presented in complex intercutting between the doctor's journey through the snow to Kamouraska, Elisabeth at home but apparently sensing his experiences, and Elisabeth in the present remembering an event that she did not witness. By such devices, the film constantly reminds us that it is depicting events through Elisabeth's subjective memory and thus involves us in her desperate attempt to make reality conform to her inner needs.

In *The Far Shore*, Wieland takes an apparently more detached perspective on her central character and tells her story in a simpler, linear fashion. She nevertheless creates an intense involvement with Eulalie (Céline Lomez), a woman from Quebec who finds herself trapped in her marriage to Ross (Lawrence Benedict), an English-Canadian engineer. Set in the period following World War I, the film links the human cost of the war to the idea of progress, represented by Ross's work in rural Quebec and the Ontario northlands; but the prime focus is on Eulalie's relationship with Tom McLeod (Frank Moore), a painter modelled on Tom Thomson. Historically, Thomson's disappearance is an unsolved mystery, but the film proposes a fictional solution: on a trip to the north, Eulalie escapes with her lover in his canoe, leading to a pursuit, at the end of which Ross's friend (Sean McCann) shoots the couple from the shore.

In her only feature film, Wieland, best known as an artist and avant-garde film-maker (see Chapter 7), unsettled the critics by drawing heavily on popular generic conventions.[4] As Brenda Longfellow puts it, 'Wieland's debt to the melodramatic tradition extends far beyond the gothic proportions of her narrative' (1992: 50). Although Wieland described her characters as 'archetypal Canadian personalities' and insisted that it could not be mistaken for an American film (Moses, 1975: 41), one critic dismissed the film as 'our Canadian *Love Story*' (Leroux, 1976: 42), and there were many complaints about its melodramatic excesses. However, its style is deliberately naive—with many long takes, an iris effect, silent film music during the chase—to evoke the filmmaking of the period and to invite the spectator to view the film as 'an emotional history' (Wieland, quoted in Charent et al., 1976: 32).

Many critics resisted this invitation. Douglas Ord objected to the unrealistic depiction of the north (1977: 42), and André Leroux was shocked that the film 'deforms reality for the sake of the fiction' by showing a fictional character painting the canvases of Tom Thomson (1976: 41–2).[5] There was also concern for the lack of realism when Eulalie dives fully dressed into a lake to swim to her lover and when they make love passionately in the lake. One unsympathetic critic called the latter 'the most far-fetched coupling ever dreamed up for the screen' (Wedman, 1976: 30), although it has also been celebrated as 'the most sublime depiction of lovemaking in a Canadian film' (Longfellow, 1999: 169).

Both Elisabeth and Eulalie are women whose desires drive them to what their societies condemn as acts of madness. Jutra, who trained as a doctor, was especially interested in how society uses the diagnosis of madness to label those who refuse to conform. The conjunction of sex and death in Bênoit's perception of life around the asbestos mine pushes *Mon oncle Antoine* into Gothic territory; and a distressed child is a central figure in two other Quebec films that make fuller use of Gothic themes and imagery: *Les Bons Débarras* (Francis Mankiewicz, 1979) and *Léolo* (Jean-Claude Lauzon, 1992). Both of these films are deeply invested in the vision of Réjean Ducharme, who wrote the screenplay for *Les Bons Débarras* and whose novel *L'Avalée des avalés* (1966) figures prominently in *Léolo*. Ducharme's highly poetic novels often depict the adult world through the eyes of disturbed children.

A child's consciousness was already at the centre of *Le Temps d'une chasse*, Mankiewicz's first feature film (see Chapter 3); but in *Les Bons Débarras*, Manon (Charlotte Laurier) is both an observer of a grotesque adult world and a disturbing figure of excess. Her intense attachment to her mother Michelle (Marie Tifo) makes her extremely jealous of Maurice (Roger Lebel), her mother's policeman boyfriend, and of Ti-Guy (Germain Houde), her brain-damaged uncle, who lives with them and whom she repeatedly addresses as 'mongol'. Although she is not interested in school, she reads *Wuthering Heights* with great enthusiasm and refuses to accept the gulf between its heightened passions and the impoverished reality of life in small-town Quebec.

It is possible to read the film as a political allegory, depicting 'the extreme conse-quences of the alienation to which Quebec has submitted in the form of poverty and social isolation' (Lockerbie, 1995: 37), but Bill Marshall insists that 'the dominant *mise en scène* of the film is that of realism' (2001: 111). While also stressing the film's 'gritty realism' in his review, Robert Fulford added that a plot summary makes it 'sound like one of those Gothic monstrosities' (1984: 10–11). Fulford thought that Mankiewicz had avoided this possibility, but Peter Morris has recently praised the film's 'gothic structure' and its concern with 'the irruption of the monstrous, irrational id into rational society' (2002: 102).

As Morris acknowledges, the opening sequence depicts 'the landscape of social victims so typical of the Canadian realist tradition' (2002: 103). After this opening, however, the constant tight framing and lack of establishing shots suggest the intensity of the emotional conflict and the constricted vision on which it is based. Pointing out that, 'though the film looks realistic, the characters often express themselves through a kind of poetry' (Irving, 1980: 13), Mankiewicz suggested the way Ducharme's screenplay acts in counterpoint to the images, investing the apparently ordinary setting with a mythic quality.

The boundary between everyday reality and myth becomes even more uncertain in Lauzon's delirious rendering of his own childhood in *Léolo*. Léo Lozeau (Maxime Collin) disavows his working-class Montreal family and constructs an elaborate fiction in which he is actually Léolo Lozone, the son of a Sicilian agricultural worker who masturbated on a tomato that then accidentally impregnated the boy's mother (Ginette Reno). While critics attacked *Un Zoo la nuit*, Lauzon's first feature, for combining two very different genres (see Chapter 4), *Léolo* goes much further in constructing a rich blend of fantasy and reality in which images and sounds from a variety of classical and modern sources collide and flow into each other. The style of the film has been variously described as 'surrealism', 'baroque', and 'an exaggerated grotesque realism' (Beaulieu, 1992: 52; Ramsay, 1995a: 35; Marshall, 2001: 116).

A few allusions to Quebec culture occur in a multinational array of quotations that range from Tibetan monks to Tom Waits, but the film studiously avoids explicitly naming its setting as Quebec. In the opening sequence, Léo sits on the steps of his house wearing a cowboy outfit, while the narrator describes his working-class neighbourhood as 'Mile End, Montreal, Canada'; and the Sicilian peasant points out that the tomatoes are going to 'America', a destination confirmed by a caption that sets the following sequence 'a few days later in America'. Although Lauzon denied any political intentions, Léo's fantasy of being Italian clearly alludes to contemporary fears of the disappearance of a distinctive Quebec culture, already suggested in the expansion of the Italian restaurant in *Un Zoo la nuit*.

However, the film's 'mosaic' style works against the negativity of the narrative, which depicts Léo's descent into the catatonic state that afflicts the rest of his family. In the final sequence, he lies naked in a bath of ice cubes, and we see the imaginary Italian landscape of his dreams. Lauzon argued that this ending is a 'liberation' that affirms 'the power of the imagination', insisting that what is important is not 'the body of this boy, it is not his temporal death, but what he leaves in his writings' (Racine, 1992: 10). These have been rescued from the garbage by an old man (Pierre Bourgault) whom Léo calls the 'worm tamer'; and the narrator, who initially seems to be the older Léo, is presumably reading from them.[6] While some critics objected that the extensive use of voice-over narration betrayed a 'lack of confidence in the images', the poetic language provides a grounding for the film's rich fabric of multi-cultural allusions (Larue, 1992: 53).

Lauzon was a flamboyant and abrasive personality whose antics antagonized the Quebec media. He died in 1997 without making another film, when the small plane he was piloting crashed in northern Quebec. The myths surrounding his life and films are explored in Yves Bélanger's documentary *Lauzon/Lauzone* (2001), and he can now be seen as an important filmmaker in the development by which the Gothic tradition became part of what critics often call the 'weirdness' (perhaps just an alternative name for the grotesque) of contemporary Canadian cinema, a development that will be discussed more fully later (see Chapter 11).

Lost and Delirious: The Films of André Forcier and Guy Maddin

Surrealism originated in France during the 1920s as a provocative movement in the arts under the leadership of André Breton. Its main goal was to liberate 'all those forces . . . which personal inhibition and social circumstances prevent from becoming realized' (Cardinal and Short, 1970: 32). In keeping with this goal, surrealist films are an assault on the audience, a refusal to obey the rules of continuity and the cause-and-effect relations they construct in favour of a dream logic that activates the unconscious mind and repressed desires. Although the term 'surrealist' is often used loosely to describe many of the Canadian films that do not belong to the realist tradition, the two filmmakers to whom it has been applied most consistently are André Forcier and Guy Maddin.

While Forcier draws on a long and rich surrealist tradition in Quebec culture, Maddin's surrealist credentials are rather less secure; but a comparison of their films in the context of their ties to surrealism reveals significant affinities. Like many earlier surrealists, both have constructed a personal mystique that is difficult to separate from their works, and both identify themselves with specific local milieux. Forcier, like many of his characters, grew up in the east end of Montreal, and his lack of respect for the cultural establishment earned him a reputation as the '*enfant terrible*' of Quebec cinema, until Lauzon succeeded to that title. Maddin was an early member of the legendary Winnipeg Film Group and has built up an image of himself as eccentric and obsessive, like many of the characters in his films.

There is no evidence that they know each other's work, although Maddin's films have aroused considerable interest in Quebec, and both Maddin and his frequent collaborator George Toles are great admirers of *Léolo*.[7] Both acknowledge the influence of Jean Vigo, the French anarchist filmmaker, who died young after making two enormously influential films, *Zéro de conduite* (1933) and *L'Atalante* (1934). Maddin has also said that 'if anyone inspired me to make movies it was Bunuel' (Monk, 2001: 42), the great surrealist filmmaker who remained faithful to the spirit of the movement through a long and varied career. Whereas Maddin is most indebted to Luis Bunuel's experimental early films, *Un Chien Andalou* (1928) and *L'Age d'or* (1930), Forcier's early work is closer to the Mexican films of the 1950s and his later films can be compared with Bunuel's final films, from *Belle de jour* (1967) to *Cet Obscur objet du désire* (1977), although, oddly, Bunuel's name is rarely mentioned in discussions of Forcier.

Forcier's early films were made on extremely low budgets over long periods of time and set in working-class districts of Montreal. The characters live marginal existences, seeking what pleasure they can in their impoverished environment. They are admirable in their simplicity and refusal to conform but also function as a 'metaphor for a suffering Quebec, closed in on itself and deprived of a collective ideal' (Grugeau, 1989: 29). In these early films by Forcier—*Le retour de l'immaculée conception* (1971), *Bar Salon* (1973), and *L'Eau chaude, l'eau frette* (1976)—the surreal breaks through only in odd images here and there, but it is also apparent in the way the characters create their own fantasies and rituals to make their lives bearable. *Au clair de la lune* (1982), in which Albert (Guy L'Ecuyer), an arthritic former bowling champion, befriends François (Michel Côté), a strange albino man who says he comes from 'Albinia', marks 'a turning point . . . towards films oriented more to the imaginary . . . , representing odd characters and extreme situations' (Beaulieu, 1997: 18).

Some critics prefer the early films because of their rootedness in the actuality of life in Montreal, but Forcier insists that all his films have 'solid roots in Quebec society' (Loiselle and Racine, 1988–9: 8). He describes his approach as 'magic naturalism' but adds that he hates realism and considers himself 'simply as a surrealist' (Bonneville, 1994: 12–13). He seeks to anchor his films in the real because 'before metaphors or surrealism can exist, the real must exist first' (Gajan and Loiselle, 1997: 10), and insists that 'the elements of the fantastic' come from the imagination of his characters (Loiselle and Racine, 1988–9: 8).

The visual style in Forcier's films thus rarely calls attention to itself but rather offers an undistorted view of their skewed narratives. In *Une Histoire inventée* (1990), the idea that Florence (Louise Marleau) is so beautiful that all men adore her is embodied in the pack of former lovers who follow her wherever she goes. When Manon (Céline Bonnier) in *Le Vent du Wyoming* (1994) levitates in her grief at losing the man she loves, this miracle is treated as a literal fact, even though a priest (Marcel Sabourin) immediately tries to convince the nuns who have witnessed the event that they are victims of a 'collective illusion'. Similarly, in *La Comtesse de Baton Rouge* (1997), the Great Zénon (Frédéric Desager), a cyclops, who uses his one eye as a film camera and projector, is neither a fantasy nor a freak but simply one character in the story of Rex Prince (Robin Aubert), a film director who falls madly in love with a bearded lady named Paula Paul de Nerval (Geneviève Brouillet).

The directness and clarity of Forcier's shooting style is far removed from what Maddin calls his 'love affair with degraded imagery, or imagery with veils or mists or blizzards of decomposition in front of them' (Vatnsdal, 2000: 27–8). He often films through filters, gauze, vaseline, and other obstacles to vision, creating the impression of watching an unrestored movie from the past, and his stories are bizarre reworkings of old genres.[8] In his first feature, *Tales From the Gimli Hospital* (1988), he created a mock-saga about the rivalry of two men confined to a hospital during a smallpox epidemic in what is presumably Manitoba but is constantly described as if it were Iceland, where all the characters come from (like Maddin's own family). As he suggests, the film 'eschews sharp focus in favour of oneiric portraiture and dismisses the literal mindedness of continuity as inimical to dreaming' (Maddin, 2003: 92).

Archangel (1990) draws on the montage style of Soviet silent cinema and the hybrid form of the early sound film or 'part-talkie' (Vatnsdal, 2000: 64–5). It depicts the experiences of John Boles (Kyle McCulloch), a Canadian soldier searching for his lost love in Russia at the end of World War I. He has also lost his memory, like, it seems, almost everybody else he encounters. As Johanne Larue suggests, the film 'remembers the cinematic past but presents only characters who suffer from problems of memory' (1991: 45). The improbable characters and situations are linked by a disjointed narrative in which important details seem to have been omitted or forgotten.

This typical refusal of clarity perhaps explains the disappointment of many viewers, and Maddin himself, with *Twilight of the Ice Nymphs* (1997), his only film to date shot in 35mm and full colour, even though the plot of this film is as tangled as his earlier efforts. For his next feature, *The Saddest Music in the World* (2003), Maddin reverted to black and white, shooting with multiple cameras on Super-8 and 16mm film. This film originated from an idea by the British novelist Kazuo Ishiguro, but Maddin and Toles moved the action from contemporary London to Winnipeg in the 1930s, which Maddin recreated in a large warehouse. With the help of an international star (Isabella Rossellini), Maddin moves closer to the mainstream, and he sees the film as a departure from his 'semi-surrealistic' style towards a new 'clarity' (McBride, 2003: 10). However, it still offers a demented story, about a radio contest to find which nation can produce the saddest music, in which a Canadian father competes against his two estranged sons (representing the United States and Serbia).

The plot also incorporates Maddin's favourite motif of amnesia and is, like all the earlier films, constructed around the surrealist theme of 'mad love'. Similarly, in Forcier's films, 'love remains inexorably marked with the stamp of the impossible' and 'accommodates itself badly to the real' (Grugeau, 1990: 28). Their films are filled with characters driven to excess by love for someone who does not return that love or is otherwise inaccessible. In Maddin's *Careful* (1992), the precarious stability of an Alpine community is disturbed by a complex web of incestuous desires, culminating in a cat-astrophic avalanche. In Forcier's *Une Histoire inventée*, much-loved Florence is herself desperately in love with Gaston (Jean Lapointe), the one man who can resist her charms but who proceeds to falls in love with her daughter, Soledad (Charlotte Laurier).

There is an apparent difference in how the filmmakers handle the emotions generated by these complex entanglements. Forcier is suspicious of melodrama, which, he argues, 'implies a certain superficiality of emotions' (Bonneville, 1994: 12). Maddin, on the other hand, embraces melodrama as the hyperbolic 'narrative of our dreams with all the nocturnal terrors and desires given the respect they deserve' (2003: 76). Their films, however, suggest that their approaches may not be as divergent as they seem. Marie-Claude Loiselle describes Forcier's 'ability to make us swing . . . from the verge of melodrama to an irrepressible state of laughter, or again to make the tragic and the ludicrous flow into each other' (1994: 17). Similarly, Steven Shaviro argues that 'Maddin's films are driven by a tension between romantic excess . . . and absurdist humour' and that 'ludicrousness is the mask under whose cover . . . extreme feelings become possible' (2002: 216–17).

Their strategies may be different but both create a child-like vision that resists the constraints and complications of 'normal' adult life. Forcier's characters are 'big children' (the working title for *Le Retour de l'immaculée conception* was *Les Grands Enfants*), but he has a very unsentimental view of childhood, as exemplified in several determined young women played by Louise Gagnon. In *Bar Salon*, Amélie rounds up stray cats and sells them to a Chinese restaurant; in *L'Eau chaude, l'eau frette*, Francine has a heart condition and uses her pacemaker to jump start a friend's motorcycle; and in *Au clair de la lune*, Linda slashes the tires of cars parked near the bowling alley to provide customers for her father's garage. In Maddin's case, the adult characters are also child-like and the children are viewed equally unsentimentally, but the films also strive to return to the childhood of the medium. The result may be impaired vision, but the images have a simplicity that has been lost with the development of more sophisticated technology.

Forcier also questions the impact of new developments in visual media. In *Le Comtesse de Baton Rouge*, Rex, who has made a film telling the same story and with the same title as Forcier's, warns Julie (Michèle-Barbara Pelletier), a hopeful young director, that 'pellicule est passé.' Later, he admits to using 'virtual editing' on his new movie because it allows him to see 'all the possibilities' more quickly; but he agrees with Edouard (Gaston Lepage), his former editor, that a film acquires its character from the 'time that passes' during the editing process. Maddin also likes to take his time in creating his films and has complained that 'the Canadian filmmaking industry makes films on the same shooting schedules . . . as the American one' (Vatnsdal, 2000: 51).

'For me, cinema is what concentrates life', says Forcier (Loiselle and Racine, 1994: 24). He insists that 'surrealism is an explosion of the real, not an escape from it' (Gajan and Loiselle, 1997: 10). Maddin would agree, but his constant allusions to earlier films and styles encourage critics to describe his work, not inaccurately, as postmodern rather than surrealist. Will Straw, for example, argues that Maddin is not a surrealist because his films are 'texts wilfully weighed down by the accessories of rigidly codified schools and genres rather than uncontrolled eruptions of the fantastic and oneiric' (2002: 309). On these grounds, Forcier would not be a surrealist either; yet, while some surrealists (Antonin Artaud, for example) did seek to break completely with conventional codes and conventions, others (such as René Magritte) tried to destroy them from within. Despite their major differences, Forcier and Maddin both belong in the latter camp. They are important contributors to a major, but often overlooked, tendency in Canadian cinema, challenging both the canonical and commercial pressures that seek to define the 'mainstream'. As we shall see in the next chapter, other filmmakers have worked even more precariously in the margins to produce films that disrupt conventional expectations.

Shifting Centres and Margins

If you want to break with what I call the 'normal' product, you must get out of the normality of production. And in this sense, Jean Pierre Lefebvre is more clear-sighted than me.

—Gilles Carle (Conseil québécois, 1976: 75)

In the world of the silicon chip, there are no centres and no margins.

—Arthur Kroker (1984: 129)

The history of film in Canada has been shaped by the conditions of production, distribution, and exhibition. As we have seen, economic and geographical factors ensured that Canada would not develop a commercial film industry to rival the Hollywood studio system. These same factors also meant that the institutions that eventually led to the sustained, if highly precarious, production of feature films in Canada would be located mainly in the centre of the nation. Ottawa, as the federal capital, became the headquarters of the CFDC (and, later, Telefilm Canada), adding proximity to decision-makers to the other advantages that filmmakers in Montreal and Toronto had over their counterparts elsewhere.

This question of centres and margins is not simply a geographical one but also involves the relation between the mainstream film industry and other forms of production. In Canada's case, of course, the problems of distribution and exhibition make the term 'mainstream' problematic even when applied to the production of feature films under (more or less) industrial conditions. One effect of this situation is that practices that might otherwise be considered marginal tend to become more central in the discussion of Canadian cinema and its relations to national identity. These practices include regional filmmaking but also various kinds of avant-garde and artisanal production. The filmmakers working in these conditions do not usually aspire to the mainstream, but they do seek to change the relations between margin and centre, to open the eyes of audiences to different ways of seeing.

The Cinema We Need?

In an article published in 1982, Seth Feldman surveyed the development of 'experimental film' in Canada and argued that it consisted of 'two distinct sensibilities' that had emerged successively. The first stage began with Norman McLaren's innovative animated films at the NFB, such as *Neighbours* (1952), which won an Academy Award,[1] and culminated in the installations at the Montreal Expo in 1967. Feldman dubbed this stage 'public service experimentation' and suggested that it had been displaced by 'a wave of new talent' from the filmmaking co-operatives that had sprung up around the country (1982: 22). Although inspired by the works of Michael Snow and Joyce Wieland, who had come to prominence as avant-garde artists while living in New York, these young filmmakers sought to develop a distinctively Canadian approach.

A few years later, Bruce Elder, a filmmaker singled out by Feldman as a leader of the new movement, published a manifesto entitled 'The Cinema We Need'. Appearing in the February 1985 issue of *Canadian Forum*, Elder's passionate attack on the state of film production and criticism in Canada set off a debate that, among other things, exposed the problem of defining a national cinema, especially in the Canadian context. Elder denounced the critics who had supported the direct cinema feature films and were now supposedly promoting the idea of 'New Narrative' as the basis for a distinctive Canadian cinema. He did not specify which films he had in mind, but he did attribute the term to Peter Harcourt and Piers Handling, who apparently used it to refer to narrative films that incorporated avant-garde techniques, thereby 'hijacking . . . the hard-won, unrewarded achievements of vanguard cinema' (1985a: 34).

Elder's approach was unabashedly prescriptive and called for a national cinema that would be neither realist nor narrative. For him, there was no significant difference between the Canadian films praised by critics like Harcourt and Handling and mainstream Hollywood feature films. His argument had much in common with the critique of realism that grew out of the political movements of the 1960s and 1970s (see Chapter 1), but I will focus here on his claim that narrative cinema is complicit with 'the will to mastery' that uses technology as a means to 'subject nature and other people to our will'. According to Elder, 'narrative is the artistic structure of technocracy' because it 'first creates and then reconciles discord' and thus 'eliminates the unmanageable ambiguities and the painful contradictions inherent in experience' (1985a: 32–3).[2]

Even if we accept that mastery is the goal of narrative filmmaking, however, it is open to question whether it always achieves this goal. Indeed, 10 years earlier, the direct cinema fiction films came under attack precisely for their failure in this regard: 'Think of *Goin' Down the Road*, *Wedding in White*, *Mon Oncle Antoine*, *The Rowdyman*, *Paperback Hero*,' wrote John Hofsess, 'good stories, fine acting, profoundly poignant moments, but nowhere a character with the brains, balls, will or gall to master life as it must be lived in the twentieth century' (1975a: 67–9). The implicit comparison here is with Hollywood films whose heroes usually succeed in overcoming all obstacles, while their Canadian counterparts, seen from the perspective of mastery, are abject losers. They have often been viewed in these terms, thus conveniently explaining the failure of Canadian films at the box office; but a case can be made that these films call into question the ideology of mastery against which they themselves were judged (see Leach, 1999a: 33).

As Elder's critics pointed out, it is impossible to imagine that the kind of avant-garde cinema he advocated could ever become the basis of a national cinema. Whatever its merits, its formal and intellectual challenges ensure that it will remain a minority taste, and its distrust of 'representational thinking' (which leads, according to Elder, to 'modern universities . . . and Auschwitz') ensures that most avant-garde films will not directly represent any specific social situations (1985b: 34). Accordingly, surveys of national cinemas usually present avant-garde filmmaking as, at best, a marginal activity (which Elder clearly resents). In the Canadian context, however, the realist/narrative films that Elder rejected were themselves quite marginal to most Canadian filmgoers, and his manifesto thus raised awkward questions about how to define the 'national' in Canadian cinema.

Elder went on to develop his vision in a lengthy book, in which he examined Canadian history, art, and philosophy to identify 'those features of the Canadian sensibility that have given rise to a realist style' (1989: 1). In this book, he discusses several NFB documentaries and devotes a chapter to *Goin' Down the Road*, with the aim of demonstrating the 'limitations of the reality principle' (151). The entire second half of the book consists of seven chapters on avant-garde film, with especially close attention to the films of Michael Snow and Jack Chambers. Elder thus constructs a national cinema in the image of 'the cinema we need', a project that involves rejecting not only the direct cinema tradition, whose films he admits have a certain 'integrity', but also what he sees as a film industry that produces only '*schlock* commercial vehicles . . . which are constructed on the model of the American B-Movie' (420, n6).[3]

Avant-garde filmmakers usually work in the context of art schools rather than the film industry, and they disregard most of the conventions that have come to dominate commercial film production. Their films are usually shorter or, often, considerably longer than the usual feature film, and they are more concerned with the processes of perception and cognition than with what is seen. One of the seminal modern avant-garde films, Snow's *Wavelength* (1967), was filmed in a loft in New York and has been described as a 'critique of spatial representation . . . based on an intricate composition of variations and interruptions within the optical illusion of spatial transversal in a zoom' (Turim, 1985: 113).[4] Elder's *Illuminated Texts* (1982) is, according to the director, a three-hour meditation on 'the way the meaning of the words "from", "to", and "and" are conceived and the implications that follow from these conceptions' (Morris, 1984: 151).[5]

If the emphasis on form and structure means that these films do not overtly address questions of national identity, it has been argued that they do so in a more fundamental way than more mainstream films. For example, according to Michael Dorland, Elder 'anchors the Canadian cultural project in the concept of the nation itself' (1985: 36). Bart Testa suggests much the same thing when he points out that 'Elder's use of "technology" as his central critical idea' derives from George Grant's *Technology and Empire* and is thus deeply immersed in a distinctively Canadian tradition of philosophy and cultural theory (1985: 27). Teasing out these links is not my concern in this book, however, partly because my evaluation of the cinema we have is very different from Elder's and also because I do not share his view that the effects of narrative—or of the commercial film industry—are necessarily 'deleterious' (a favourite term of his).

Canada *is* represented in some important avant-garde films. Jack Chambers's *The Hart of London* (1970) takes off from newsreel footage of a deer trapped in the city of London, Ontario, to create a complex text that 'documents the reconciliation of one man and one place over time' (Feldman, 1977: 334). In *La Région centrale* (1971), Snow used a computer to program the movements of a camera on a mountain in Sept-Îles, Quebec, to produce a three-hour, constantly moving vision of the snow-covered landscape seen from the perspective of what he called a 'bodiless eye' (Morris, 1984: 252). While these films integrate the Canadian environment into their modernist explorations of cinematic perception, Rick Hancox's *Moose Jaw: There's a Future in Our Past* (1992) is a more irreverent, postmodernist study of the relations between personal and collective memory generated by the filmmaker's return to the Saskatchewan city where he grew up.[6]

Perhaps the avant-garde filmmaker whose work was most bound up with the Canadian experience was Joyce Wieland, whose films combine a feminist view of gender relations with a nationalist critique of Canada's domination by the United States. In a move that was unusual in the Canadian context, Wieland's exploration of these themes in avant-garde films like *Rat Life and Diet in North America* (1968) and *La Raison avant la passion* (1969) was continued in a commercial feature film, *The Far Shore* (see Chapter 6).[7] Unlike British filmmakers such as Derek Jarman, Peter Greenaway, and Sally Potter, however, who also crossed over from the avant-garde to more mainstream production, Wieland's feature did not obviously incorporate 'experimental' techniques, and it was neither well accepted by general audiences nor by the avant-garde.

Since the time of this debate, the distinction between mainstream and avant-garde filmmaking in Canada, while still clearly apparent, has become more difficult to define. The British avant-garde filmmakers just mentioned took advantage of the innovative policies of Channel 4 television, founded in 1982 with a mandate to serve minority interests, and a similar situation developed in Canada with the gradual recognition, at Telefilm Canada and elsewhere, of a market for films that challenge social and aesthetic conventions. In this context, the involvement of provincial arts councils in the funding of feature films and the emergence of digital video also increase the possibilities for exchange between the two modes of production.[8]

Examples of this development include the work of the Winnipeg Film Group, most notably the films of Guy Maddin (see Chapter 6), the film work of the Quebec avant-garde theatre artist Robert Lepage (see Chapter 12), and the films of Peter Mettler (who directed the 1992 film version of Lepage's stage production *Tectonic Plates*). In *Picture of Light* (1994), about his journey to northern Manitoba to film the northern lights, and *Gambling, Gods and LSD* (2001), a three-hour record of his travels in Canada, the US, Switzerland, and India, Mettler combines avant-garde techniques with the documentary tradition.

Mettler studied with Elder at Ryerson College in Toronto, and these are avant-garde films in the sense that 'the process of watching is more crucial than what is actually being seen' (Lan, 2002: 15). They are also closely related to the Canadian documentary tradition through their concern with the interaction between subjective perception and the objectivity to which documentary aspires. *Gambling, Gods and LSD* is a demanding work, made over several years and distilled from a first cut that was 55 hours long; but it received support from mainstream producers and a wider release than most avant-garde films. Its rambling structure allows the filmmaker to investigate a number of manifestations of the desire for transcendence within different cultures. Despite the often exotic images of geographical and cultural difference, the journey gradually brought Mettler to realize that 'everything I looked at contained the things I had seen before' (McBride, 2002: 29).

The question of whether this discovery is attributable to the reality with which the film engages or to the way in which the filmmaker looks at it returns us to the debate on realism. In its multinational—or perhaps post-national—perspective, the film also offers a challenge to the idea of national cinema, to which we will return at the end of this book. The proliferation of avant-garde film and, increasingly since the 1980s, video continues the exploration of how we perceive the world around us; and many Canadian filmmakers have gained international recognition.[9] In this book, however, my main focus is on the cinema we have, even if we hardly know it, on the feature films that have emerged from the often uncomfortable and complicated environment of film production in Canada.

Dirty Movies and Aerial Views

The films of Jack Darcus and William D. McGillivray are marginal in both the geographical sense of the term, in that they come from the west and east coast respectively, and in the sense of exploring the possibilities of film language outside the constraints of industrial production. These films are not really avant-garde, since they tell stories set in recognizable Canadian locations, but both directors are also visual artists, like many avant-garde filmmakers. Both have expressed frustration at the limited resources with which they must work, and their films sometimes show the signs of this pressure. Neither has been especially prolific (Darcus has made eight features since 1969, MacGillivray five since 1983), but both value their relative freedom to make films in accord with their own artistic visions, which often prove difficult or uncomfortable for some viewers.

Darcus started making films in British Columbia in the late 1960s, and he credits the example of Larry Kent, whose early films demonstrated the possibilities of small-budget production (see Chapter 2). However, just as Kent moved to Montreal to pursue his career, Darcus decided, after his first three films, to work in Toronto, although he continued to live in Vancouver and was able to make films there again when the situation in British Columbia improved in the 1990s. His films have received little theatrical distribution, but he has been able to take advantage of the demand for Canadian content on television. He admits that he is 'essentially very much on the periphery of everything' (Spaner, 2003: 71) but insists that this precarious situation has its benefits: 'In a sense, if you're very small you're free, or if you're big you're free. It's when you get in the middle that the compromises start' (Allison, 1986: 12).

MacGillivray was born in Newfoundland and was a founding member of the Atlantic Filmmakers Co-operative in Halifax, Nova Scotia, in 1974. His first film was the medium-length *Aerial View* (1979), and, soon after, he set up Picture Plant, his own production company. Like Darcus, he is committed to 'the cinema that grows out of need rather than out of dollars' and has acknowledged that 'it would terrify me to make a large film because I think the battles to maintain control would be greater than the battles to get your ideas out' (Henderson, 1987: 19). In words that could also be applied to Darcus, Peter Harcourt argues that MacGillivray's films 'embody the political struggle of the regions against the centre and of the personalized cinematic utterance against the homogenized language of the cinematic machine' (1987: 15).

Although Darcus is a visual artist, language is an important element in his films, and some critics find his dialogue obtrusive and pretentious. Yet the films also make extensive use of silence, and Seth Feldman has situated them among 'a small body of English Canadian films which seem to celebrate the conscious renunciation of language as central to their protagonists' triumph' (1984b: 54). In *Proxyhawks* (1971), an artist (played by Darcus) and his lover (Susan Spencer) live out a stormy relationship in which she associates his treatment of the birds of prey with which they live to the atrocities of the Vietnam War. In *Wolfpen Principle* (1973), a Czech concentration camp survivor (Vladimir Valenta) and a city Indian (Lawrence Brown) share a desire to release the wolves from a local zoo. These characters may desperately try to articulate their feelings but, as Feldman (1984b: 55) suggests, their words are 'finally of less worth than the howls and screeches of the various animals with whom his characters are obsessed'.

For Darcus, language is an attempt to communicate that usually fails and, in intimate relationships, words become a weapon to protect each partner's sense of self. The sexual bond may link them to nature, but they erect barriers between themselves and the outside world and between each other. This is especially apparent in two claustrophobic films in which the intense emotions constantly verge on theatricality and melodrama. *Deserters* (1983) deals with the exchanges that occur when a Canadian couple take in an American deserter and the sergeant who is pursuing him. In *Kingsgate* (1989), three couples become entangled on a visit to the farm of the writer Daniel Kingsgate (Alan Scarfe). A large amount of alcohol is consumed as the darkly comic plot works through the tensions between the characters' personal obsessions and their need for mutual support, the former expressed in frequent threats to leave and the latter in the compulsion to stay.

One sympathetic critic suggested that this film has 'a fascinating way of alternating between high-pitched melodrama, black comedy and the edges of psychological horror' (Zeldin, 1989: 24). Other critics find this lack of consistency irritating, as demonstrated by José Arroyo's complaint that in *Overnight* (1985), 'the various elements . . . simply explode in different directions' with the result that 'the humour is never quite funny and the satire is itself worthy of being satirized' (1986: 24). In this film, later retitled *Not Another Dirty Little Movie*, Victor (Scott Lavel) is an actor who reluctantly takes a part in a pornographic movie that Vladimir (Scarfe), an émigré Czech director, wants to turn into a work of art. On the one hand, the situation is a satiric metaphor for the Canadian film industry, summed up by an old porn star's affirmation that 'we may be little and dirty, but we're Canadian'; on the other, it offers a philosophical argument that, as Vladimir puts it, life is a 'dirty movie' and we just have to make the best of it in an attempt to realize our 'ideals'.

In *The Portrait* (1992), the narrative is punctuated by lectures on the history of portrait painting given by David (Scarfe), who himself paints portraits. The genre, he argues, emerged along with modern cultural attitudes that emphasize the individual as well as economic exchange, requiring both a personal relationship and a commercial contract with the sitter. David feels that portrait painting has been in decline since the invention of photography, and he tells a student that he only paints portraits to seduce beautiful women. The story deals with his tangled economic and personal relations with three women: his estranged wife, Lillian (Gabrielle Rose), his model and lover, Helen (Gwynyth Walsh), and Marguerite (Barbara March), an attractive new client.

David asks his students what is wrong with wanting to be popular and then raises questions about why artists should not simply 'seek to please'; but he (like the film) seems to agree with the students' idealistic insistence on the demands of art. The implication is that the artist must occupy an uncomfortable position on the margins if he (and Darcus's artists all are male) wants to remain true to his vision; but he must also remain in contact with the 'dirty' reality of public life, not only for economic reasons, but to keep the vision alive.

MacGillivray also explores the tensions between personal artistic ideals and economic and commercial pressures in a wide variety of media: architecture in *Aerial View*, television in *Stations* (1983), painting in *Life Classes* (1987), music in *The Vacant Lot* (1989), and storytelling in *Understanding Bliss* (1990). He is more interested than Darcus in the specific properties of each medium, but he also explores how these media work to construct centres and margins in relation to which his artists (male and female) must situate themselves.

MacGillivray has argued that 'structured stories . . . don't leave you any room to move' (Henderson, 1987: 17). This implies that narrative is a force for ideological control, first of the filmmaker, then of the spectator, paralleling the relation of region to centre and artist to technology. The slow pacing, long shots, and long takes in his films literally give the actors room to move, while also giving the spectator time to reflect on the possible meanings embodied in the characters and their stories. This detachment is also a way of respecting what Robin Wood, in his discussion of *Life Classes*, calls 'the not-quite-knowability of a "real" human being' (1989: 31).

As a way of seeing that is simultaneously precise and hesitant, it is most fully developed in *Stations* and *Life Classes*. In the earlier film, Tom (Mike Jones) is a television journalist in Vancouver who takes stock of his life when an old friend commits suicide after an interview in which Tom asked him about the abuse he suffered as a child. During a train journey across Canada, he interviews the passengers and thinks over his own past, which is evoked by family photographs and shaky 'home movie' images. He finally decides to quit his job and return to his home in Newfoundland. As Tom McSorley puts it, the film 'explores the time and the space that is Canada; . . . how Canada is imagined by those who populate it and by those who control its media systems' (2002b: 44). In so doing, it places itself on the margins of that system through its structure: according to MacGillivray, 'the joke in *Stations* was that we went on a single line from Vancouver to St John's by rail, but the story goes all over the place' (Henderson, 1987: 17).

In *Life Classes*, MacGillivray deliberately set out to make a more linear (and perhaps less marginal) film, but he gave it a prologue that makes the spectator aware of the film as a film and foregrounds its themes. The camera tracks through a shopping mall towards a store advertising a 'Liquidation Sale', in front of which is a bank of televisions on which we see Jacinta Cormier, the actress who plays Mary Cameron in the film, at what purports to be its Halifax premiere, responding to questions from an interviewer in the studio. Her description of the crowd streaming in seems like MacGillivray's wishful anticipation of his film's future premiere; but, although we never learn where the mall is, the relay from Halifax to the studio to the mall introduces the film's concern with how technology links margins and centres.

After Cormier describes Mary as, like herself, a product of a culture and a victim of the changes it was going through, there is a cut to a truck carrying a satellite dish. This cut takes us to Cape Breton, where the dish, which belongs to Earl (Leon

Dubinsky), Mary's boyfriend, will (illegally) link the small town to the modern world of global communications. Mary is still attached to local traditions, represented by the Gaelic songs she has learned from her grandmother, yet when she finds she is pregnant, she decides not to marry the unreliable Earl but to move to Halifax.

In the city, she comes into contact with the arts community. At the employment office, she meets a woman who collects modern paintings and explains that she is interested in the 'conceptual underpinnings' of art; a lecturer in an art history class uses the same phrase. After a presentation at the local art college, Mary asks some awkward questions and is surprised to learn that the German conceptual artist neither carves nor paints her objects but just 'thinks of them'. Mary's 'naive' outlook has already been made apparent when she explains that the conceptual underpinnings in her paintings are 'numbers, I guess'. While MacGillivray suggests that 'the paint-by-numbers thing . . . represents a kind of unquestioning acceptance of what's around you' (Henderson, 1987: 15), the film offers Mary's enjoyment of her paintings as a sign of a need for self-expression that is not encouraged by the abstract concepts of art theory or by the established canons of taste.

Her decision to pose as a nude model is a sign of Mary's willingness to sacrifice her own feelings to support her child (by presenting her body as an object) but also of her own discovery of herself, a process that reaches its climax when she persuades Earl to pose in the nude and is acclaimed for her drawings. She is reunited with Earl when she takes part in a conceptual art performance in which naked people improvise to music that reminds them of their past. This event, the work of a New York artist and broad-cast live to New York, is picked up by Earl's satellite dish so that Mary's friends and family see and hear her. When the video artist sees the feedback from New York, she comments that 'it looks like it was right next door' (which it actually is!), reiterating the confusion of distance and immediacy introduced in the opening sequence. The film leaves us to explore the personal and cultural implications of its treatment of art and technology.

Jean Pierre Lefebvre and the Quebec Imaginary

Both Darcus and MacGillivray acknowledge Jean Pierre Lefebvre as an important inspiration for their own work.[10] As a major figure in Quebec cinema, Lefebvre is certainly not marginal in a geographical sense, but his approach was very different from that of Gilles Carle, who sought to create a national-popular cinema from within the established film industry (see Chapter 5). Yet their careers did share a similar trajectory: like Carle, Lefebvre formed his own production company (Cinak), was very prolific for many years, but then ran into difficulties beginning in the 1980s.

In terms that anticipate his later comment on MacGillivray, Peter Harcourt described Lefebvre's films as 'part of a cinema of contestation, of a cinema that contests simultaneously the values both of conventional cinema and of the society that so passively consumes it' (1981: 101). Lefebvre also saw his work as contesting a media-saturated culture characterized by 'a flood of images, words, and sounds' that seeks to '*neutralize* the spectator' (1975: 29). From a theoretical perspective, as Bill Marshall points out, this position is 'profoundly undialectical', since it regards spectators as 'passive objects of manipulation' and allows no room for resistance (2001: 62). Yet, the practice of making films on the margins of the industry is itself an act of resistance, and Lefebvre's films usually depict characters caught up in a complex tension between resistance and complicity.

These characters are presented in such a way as to involve the spectator in this tension. Referring to his first feature film, *Le Révolutionnaire* (1965), Lefebvre explained that he wanted an actor who had 'no "physical presence" in the sense that one expects of an actor' and who 'would not give the spectator the possibility of putting himself in his place . . ., because above all I did not want to make a psychological drama' (Delahaye and Straram, 1967: 58). This strategy governs the acting style in all his later films, in which, as André Leroux puts it, 'the actors refuse to act "naturally"' and 'seek less to transmit a feeling of cinematic reality (the famous fusion of actor with character) than to bear witness to a situation' (1971: 23).

In keeping with Quebec's economic reality, Lefebvre insisted that 'our cinema is a poor cinema' and was highly critical of moves towards larger budget productions (see Chapter 6). His films are shaped by this requirement, but poverty becomes both an aesthetic and ethical factor that binds form to meaning. According to Lefebvre, it was the lack of resources that led Quebec filmmakers 'to adopt—despite ourselves— the shot-sequence rather than cutting' (Pageau, 1971: 102), but his own sequence shots and long takes make us aware of real time as well as the alienation from real time involved in conventional cinematic structures.[11]

It is clear that Lefebvre wanted nothing to do with what he called 'the trap of realism' (Barrowclough, 1982: 25). He distanced himself from the documentary tradition because 'drama allows us to play more with *l'Imaginaire*, with the formation of images within the subconscious' (Harcourt, 1981: 120). Michèle Favreau thus argues that his films should be characterized as a 'poetic cinema' that stresses its artifice but, through its 'depersonalized characters and dedramatized situations', requires the spectator 'to go "right to the heart" of things, right to the structure, to see how they are articulated and to disengage the meaning' (1971: 86).[12]

The 'poetic' dimension makes the spectator aware of the processes of signification that Lefebvre felt had been effaced by the speed of modern communications. He declared that his goal was 'to augment the number and form of signs', while remaining himself '"on the margin" of these signs, not to interpret them but to organize them' (Lefebvre, 1968: 109). This marginal position is transmitted to the spectator by a number of strategies, including an emphasis on off-screen space: 'I am much more interested in what cannot be shown, in what is off the screen and in what the viewer has to find for him/herself' (Barrowclough, 1982: 26).

The signs in Lefebvre's films are primarily those of Quebec culture, and the freedom he seeks for the spectator is part of his desire to contribute to a new collective awareness of the need for change. He suggested that because of the difficulty of 'defining ourselves internally, it is normal that we are incapable of expressing ourselves' (Lefebvre, 1965: 27). His efforts to relate inner experience to outer reality, to link the personal and the political, placed him in a marginal position with regard to established political thinking. According to Michel Brûlé, Lefebvre's cinema 'rejects with a serene magnanimity the left and the right, the terrorists and the priests, traditionalism and the great consumer society, nationalism and planetarism' (1971: 18). For Lefebvre, this uncertain position tied him to Quebec's 'outcast culture' because 'we are much more American than we are French—but we are neither' (Barrowclough, 1982: 25). The goal was to develop a sense of Québécois identity based on a freedom denied both by the US-dominated consumer society and the chauvinist outlook of the ideology of *conservation*.

These principles underlie the 24 feature films directed by Lefebvre in a period between 1965 and 1998. They give a remarkable consistency to a body of work that includes a wide variety of films, ranging from a crime thriller, *On n'engraisse pas les cochons à l'eau claire* (1973), to a gentle story of the last days of an old couple, *Les Dernières Fiançailles* (1973), to a satire on sex films, *Q-Bec My Love* (1969). Another unifying thread is found in a trilogy—*Il ne faut pas mourir pour ça* (1967), *Le Vieux Pays où Rimbaud est mort* (1977), and *Aujourd'hui ou jamais* (1998)—in which Abel (Marcel Sabourin) functions both as Lefebvre's alter ego and as an allegorical figure representing, over a period of 30 years, Quebec's search for cultural identity.

It is also possible to divide his output roughly into two periods (although with much overlap) of more directly political/satirical films and gentler films concerned with individual identity and personal experience. As we shall see, each group contains elements of the other; but, in order to bring out the richness of Lefebvre's work, I will focus on two films, *Les Maudits sauvages* (1971) and *Les Fleurs sauvages* (1982), that illustrate these tendencies. The word 'sauvages' in the title of both films also points to Lefebvre's concern (with different connotations in each case) to relate political and cultural issues to the natural origins and context of human life.

Les Maudits sauvages is based on the conceit of yoking together the seventeenth and twentieth centuries, the acted and the real, the civilized and the savage. It is described in the credits as 'an almost historical film', and the meaning of this phrase becomes clear from the gradual intrusion of modern objects into action apparently taking place in 1670. When Thomas Hébert (Pierre Dufresne) leads his pack horse into an Indian camp, he presents the chief with a transistor radio and, while the 'savages' are examining it, a black man appears in the background, wanders up, takes a look, and passes casually on. In return for his gifts, Thomas receives a beautiful Indian maiden, Tékacouita (Rachel Cailhier), and he leads her back to the modern city. Later, there are photos of Trudeau and Bourassa on the wall when Thomas is beaten by police, who refuse to accept that he was born in 1630 but who use an encyclopedia of history rather than the proverbial telephone directory to avoid leaving marks on his body.

The play with anachronisms is a distancing device that brings out the implications of the opening title: 'No one is responsible in the face of history. We all are.' This effect is reinforced by the long takes that force the actors into static and uncomfortable tableaux, and give the audience time to take in the discrepancies and to think about their meaning. The audience becomes aware of the presence of the camera, which is even reflected in lighted store windows as it tracks along beside Thomas when he walks through the city streets. These devices serve to universalize the problem of oppression, seeing the oppression of French Canadians, Indians, women, consumers, and believers in other gods as parallel aspects of a system that sees non-conformists as 'savages' and converts its victims into helpless masochists who perpetuate the system that enslaves them.

The effect is not to place the blame simply on colonialism or male chauvinism but to see oppression as the result of society's lack of respect for the individual. Thomas is responsible for the degradation of the Indians (by selling alcohol) and the woman (by exploiting her body), but he is also the victim of police brutality. His wife (Nicole Filion) rejects him when he returns with his Indian mistress (while she is slaving over a stove); the priest (Luc Granger) fails to understand her and is uncomfortable with his vocation (to sell religion to the Indians). The parallels with the present are brought out when Thomas watches Jean Talon (Marcel Sabourin), the governor, on television, speaking on 'free enterprise' and his plans to give Louis Riel and his 'terrorists' safe passage to the US in a canoe. At the end of the film, Thomas returns to the Indian camp, where he finds the priest blessing dead bodies after a massacre. Thomas shoots the priest, thus fulfilling his desire to become a martyr, and then joins a circle of hippies smoking pot in the ruins of the Indian camp.

The film is punctuated by a recurring still shot of Tékacouita on horseback, which gradually comes closer as she recites a poem about her oppression as a woman and as an Indian. As Lefebvre has explained, Tékacouita was 'the first Iroquois to have embraced the Catholic faith' and was represented in Quebec schools as 'a kind of Indian goddess . . . , the image of total purity, resignation, and so on' (Harcourt, 1981: 123). Thomas desecrates this image by taking her as his mistress and making her work as a topless dancer in a bar, and she is able to express herself only in an inner monologue because they do not know each other's language. Thomas finally comes to realize that she must think of him as a 'damned savage'.

The ending of Les Maudits sauvages exposes the hypocrisy of a religious and political ideology that claims to represent civilization but, in fact, projects its own repressed savagery onto those with different values. While Lefebvre acknowledged that he had 'no right to speak for the Indians', he added that he felt 'deeply related to their mentality, their way of living, and to their way of relating to time and space' (Harcourt, 1981: 124). Through his marginal practices, he thus destabilizes the idea of the 'savage' as 'other' and opens up questions about the attitudes to nature on which the so-called civilized society is based.

Les Fleurs sauvages returns to many of these issues, although the title refers to 'wild' flowers rather than more dangerous 'savages'. This is appropriate since the film belongs to a movement towards 'intimist' films in Quebec, often seen as a withdrawal from the social and political arena after the 'No' vote in the 1980 referendum (although Lefebvre had worked in this vein before). Its leisurely narrative depicts a few days in the life of a family during the annual visit of Simone (Marthe Nadeau) to the country home of her daughter Michèle (Michèle Magni) and her husband Pierre (Pierre Curzi).[13]

The couple has left the city to live a relatively frugal life, he working as a photographer and she as a potter. The film also chooses an aesthetic poverty aimed at an openness that will break through the sexual and generational barriers lurking behind the apparently unruffled surface.

The film thus combines the 'realism' of Pierre's photography with the 'naive' vision of his daughter Claudia's paintings. This child-like perspective is a way of breaking out of the trap of realism, but the film points out the limitations of this perspective through its appropriation of the radio programs Simone listens to, in which male announcers address the 'ladies' as if they were children. The main distancing effect is the frequent use of black-and-white shots in a predominantly colour film, which point to a desire (expressed in the title song) to communicate an inner reality, while they express the characters' inability to communicate their feelings. The black-and-white sequences represent the imaginary as opposed to the real, but they are also linked to Pierre's photographs of people (as opposed to those of rocks and flowers, which are in colour).

Often unclear is whether the imaginary shots originate with the bearer of the look or with the object of the gaze, thus creating a shared 'mindscreen' suggesting that the thoughts that remain unspoken are nonetheless communicated. They often represent Simone's unspoken disapproval of the informality and openness of the younger family, but they also register Michèle's desire to get closer to her mother. She picks a bunch of wildflowers for her mother's room, reminding her that she used to do the same in the past; but Simone deflates this gesture by pointing out that other flowers were not available at that time. The generation gap becomes a way of exploring changes in Quebec society, and the motif of 'wildflowers' points to the desire to break down barriers and create a more 'natural' life.

The film works to renew the Quebec myth of closeness to the land, but through the younger generation (who do not farm). When Michèle asks her mother how she coped with eight children, Simone replies that in those days they did not ask questions and it was 'natural'; she also comments that it is 'natural' that Pierre should be interested in sex because he is a man. The word 'natural' here refers to what is 'normal' according to her inherited values, but when her grandson Eric (Eric Beauséjour) insists that it is 'natural' to eat wildflowers, he uses the word as a way to challenge accepted conventions. While Lefebvre does not present the return to nature as a perfect solution to society's problems, it does connect with the utopian impulse in all his films.

Les Fleurs sauvages confirms André Leroux's claim that 'the greatness of Lefebvre's cinema lies in the presentation of the weight of the past and uncertainty of the present so that we can learn to overcome them' (1971: 23). Although Lefebvre has had great trouble finding support for his film projects since the early 1980s, he has remained productive in the medium of video (see Harcourt, 2001). In this way, he has retained his freedom of expression, but in the present conditions of production and exhibition the use of video confirms his marginal situation. His achievement is probably the greatest of Canada's marginal filmmakers, but his work, like that of Darcus and McGillivray, is an intensification of the possibilities and limits already present in a national cinema whose 'mainstream' constantly struggles for recognition.

Engendering the Nation

What, then, is the version of *la condition canadienne* reflected to us by our feature films? It is the depiction . . . of the radical inadequacy of the male protagonist.

—Robert Fothergill (1977a: 235)

Are gender and nation equal categories of identity and forms of culture, mutually determining and relational? Or is gender subsumed by nation?

—Kay Armatage et al. (1999b: 12)

In a 1992 article on 'Women in French-Quebec cinema', Chantal Nadeau argues that, 'far from proposing new relations to alterity, Quebec films produced in the last few years have consolidated the centrality of the male subject in the construction of a national identity.'[1] She goes on to assert that the men in these films, 'even in the anguish of their being, never question the order of traditional power in which they live' (1992: 8). This sweeping judgement downplays the complexity of both gender and national identity. The representation of women (and men) in Canadian cinema, the emergence of major women filmmakers, and the questioning of patriarchal and heterosexual norms are topics that demand a careful attention to the cinematic language and cultural contexts of the films that engage with them.

The family was a central element in the cultural traditions of Quebec, in which the absent father and strong mother were dominant motifs; and the idea of the nation as a family was (and continues to be) a favourite metaphor for politicians in general. When the institution of the family came under attack in the 1960s, the frameworks that shaped the experience of personal and national identity, and the relations between them, began to disintegrate, bringing a new sense of individual rights and freedoms. This process may have moved slower in Canada than in many other nations because of the puritan traditions of the original settlers. According to Ronald Sutherland, 'Canadian Puritanism has taken much the same form of expression in Protestant English Canada as in Roman Catholic Québec', and 'sex relations have been more greatly distorted than has any other area of human activity' (Sutherland, 1971: 61, 70). However, the effects of the 'sexual revolution' did manifest themselves in ways that are often ambiguous and contradictory in Canadian cinema from the 1960s on.

Sex in a Cold Climate

In the direct cinema fiction films, the figure of the male adolescent functions as a metaphor for the search for national identity, famously characterized by Robert Fothergill as 'the psychological history of a younger brother' seeking (and usually failing) to define himself against the more assured males of US popular culture (1977a: 243). The main exception to this rule is Clarke Mackey's *The Only Thing You Know* (1971), in which a young woman leaves home to find herself. Ann (Ann Knox) overhears her parents arguing about her future much as Peter does in *Nobody Waved Good-bye* (see Chapter 2); but her sexual affairs, with a Canadian teacher and a US draft dodger, are depicted more explicitly than in any of the earlier films. Her search for identity is central to the film; but it is the teacher who tells his Canadian history class, 'I guess we all have to understand ourselves before we understand other people—probably.'

A much more confident assertion of identity, which links the national and the sexual, occurs in the 'maple syrup porno' movies (a term coined by *Variety*) produced in Quebec in the late 1960s. These films exploited the loosening of moral constraints that accompanied the Quiet Revolution, and resulted in a confrontation between the still powerful traditions of the past and the much louder 'sexual revolution' that transformed Western culture at this time. The first and most successful directors associated with this development were Denis Héroux and Claude Fournier, whose films offer quite different perspectives on the new society.

As a student at the University of Montreal, Héroux co-directed *Seul ou avec d'autres* (1962), a feature film that applied the techniques of direct cinema to a love story set amid the cultural ferment of campus life.[2] With *Valérie* (1968), he established himself, along with producers John Dunning and André Link, as a major figure in the film industry. The film has been aptly described as 'a fairy story in which the fairies undress, . . . in which taboos fall as quickly as the clothes, but in which morality is preserved' (Belzile, 1995: 10). It opens with a close-up of an eye as Valérie (Danielle Ouimet) puts on makeup, an image that aligns us with her vision but also defines her as the willing object of the gaze. After she is rescued from her convent school by a youth on a motorcycle, a modern version of the gallant knight on his charger, she works as a topless dancer, then as a prostitute; she then falls in love with an artist, who has a young son; and the film ends with the reconstitution of the family.

Fournier had an even closer relationship with direct cinema than Héroux, having worked at the NFB for many years. He emulated the commercial success of *Valérie* with *Deux Femmes en or* (1970), a genial mixture of slapstick and satire in which two suburban housewives (Monique Mercure and Louise Turcot) decide to relieve their boredom by seducing the men who work in their neighbourhood. Whereas *Valérie* ends with an endorsement of married love, however, this film ends with a sardonic irony that does not negate its satire. The two wives seem about to be punished for their transgressions, but they are found not guilty by an all-male jury and then become stars on Broadway. Unlike Valérie's, their rebellion is not directed against the rigidity of traditional values (the convent), but against the conformism of the new materialistic society.

The difference between the sensibilities of the two directors can be seen by comparison with the contemporary work of Paul Almond (see Chapter 6). *Valérie* appeared in the same year as *Isabel*, and its heroine is both more confident and more objectified than Almond's sensitive and insecure character. However, in Héroux's *L'Amour humaine* (1970), made in the same year as Almond's *The Act of the Heart*, Constance (Louise Marleau) shares Martha's spiritual and sexual anguish when she renounces her vows as a nun to marry a former priest. Whereas Martha commits suicide by burning herself to death, Héroux's film ends happily with the reunited couple making love accompanied by a lush romantic score. Fournier's *Les Chats bottés* (1971) similarly rejects Almond's bleak vision but also Héroux's romanticism: when Louise Latendresse (Louise Turcot) tries to set fire to herself, she carries a can of gasoline and pours it over herself next to a fire hydrant, but the sequence comes to an abrupt end when the matches will not light. These two tendencies—the romantic and the cynical—interact in various ways throughout recurring attempts to build a commercial film industry in Canada.

The maple syrup porno phenomenon spread to English Canada but without anything like the same impact. In any case, these were not really porn films, and they were scandalous only because on-screen nudity was still a relatively new experience. They gradually faded away in the 1970s when real porn became more easily available and (mainly female) nudity became more common in films with greater cultural respectability. In Quebec, the liberalism of the Quiet Revolution transformed the traditional Catholic culture, and by the 1970s Ontario's system of film censorship had become the most restrictive in Canada.

Two films by women filmmakers, working in the realist tradition, tested the censors in Ontario and elsewhere, while addressing questions of sexual representation in the context of feminist theory. Bonnie Sherr Klein's *Not a Love Story* (1981), a documentary about pornography and its impact on women's lives, combines graphic examples of its topic with a therapeutic discourse, like that in Allan King's *A Married Couple*, but made more explicit through its focus on the personal responses of the director and her on-screen companion, stripper Linda Lee Tracy.[3] Anne Claire Poirier's *Mourir à tue-tête* (1979), a fiction film that incorporates documentary sequences, opens with a brutal rape and then uses a variety of Brechtian devices to examine the issue of rape, following, but expanding on, the example of Michel Brault's treatment of the October Crisis in *Les Ordres* (see Chapter 1).[4]

Sexuality remained a major concern in many Canadian films of various kinds, as the discussions in other chapters of this book demonstrate. Its commercial possibilities were exploited in films such as *In Praise of Older Women* (George Kaczender, 1978), which helped to launch producer Robert Lantos on his highly successful career; but it was through more artful explorations of bizarre or disturbing aspects of sexual experience that Canadian cinema gained its reputation for 'kinky, dark, quirky and obsessive sex' (Monk, 2001: 119).

Katherine Monk's attempts to explain this development seem rather contradictory. She cites Pierre Trudeau's concern to keep the state out of the bedrooms of the nation but argues that, nevertheless, 'sex = Guilt in Canadian society.' Apparently, 'the Canadian psyche simply revels in sexual imagery on screen', but what really distinguishes Canadians is that they are 'sexual realists'. Thus they do not buy into the 'manufactured nonsense' represented by 'the sexually omnipotent James Bond, who can rescue a rich heiress from an avalanche one minute and have sex with her the next' (2001: 120, 123, 142). Unfortunately for this argument, James Bond films are as popular in Canada as elsewhere, and the more 'realistic' Canadian films remain confined to a limited (but perhaps growing) niche market. It is certainly true, however, that sexual themes now permeate Canadian cinema.

Dream Lives: The Rise of Women's Cinema in Canada

The feminist analysis of gender representations in film began in the 1960s and was in full swing during the 1970s. Along with a concern with how women were depicted on screen, efforts were made to acknowledge the work of women filmmakers and there were calls for more opportunities for women in the film industry. In Canada, as elsewhere, there had been very few women directors. Historians have celebrated the pioneering work of Nell Shipman, who wrote and starred in *Back to God's Country*

(1919) and then produced and directed films in the US (see Armatage, 2003). There were also several women directors in the documentary field, notably Evelyn Spice Cherry, Judith Crawley, and Jane Marsh.[5]

The first Canadian feature film directed by a woman was *Madeleine Is . . .* (Sylvia Spring, 1970), followed shortly after in Quebec by *La Vie rêvée* (Mireille Dansereau, 1972), and both films raised awkward questions in the context of the emergence of feminist film theory. 'Dream Life' could easily have been the title of Spring's film as well, and the emphasis on fantasy and subjective experience in both films rubbed against the realist tradition as well as against the dominant forms of political and feminist theory of the time. Although it generated some publicity because of its pioneering status, *Madeleine Is . . .* received mixed reviews and, as Kay Armatage pointed out, 'died after exactly one week' at the same Toronto cinema where *Goin' Down the Road* played for 19 weeks (1971: 27). Dansereau expressed frustration with the reception of her film in Quebec, where 'no one liked it', although it was 'much better recognized outside of Quebec' (Longfellow, 1987: 11).

Both films deal with women who compensate for the frustrations of their everyday lives by creating an alternative dream life, and both involve an abortive trip to the country, the refusal of 'male' political strategies, and the use of laughter to undercut masculine pretensions. Dansereau, whose film was produced by ACPAV (a co-operative that has been a major force in Quebec cinema), complained that the men in the group 'thought that if I made a film on women, it should be militant.' But she saw this as 'a *man's* idea of what is revolutionary about women', contrary to her 'intuitive, very emotional and personal approach' (Ibrányi-Kiss, 1977: 253). She addresses this difference in the film through an argument between Virginie (Véronique Le Flaguais) and her brother, and it is a recurring issue in *Madeleine Is . . .*, in which Madeleine (Nicola Lipman) grows increasingly disillusioned with the radical politics of her boyfriend Toro (John Juliani).

While the city of Vancouver, to which Madeleine has come from Quebec, figures as prominently as Toronto does in *Goin' Down the Road, Madeleine Is . . .* fits less easily into the direct cinema tradition because of its focus on her inner life. In its most extreme form, this is represented by fantasy sequences in which Madeleine escapes to an island where she plays with a clown, whom she identifies with David (Wayne Specht), a businessman she meets in 'reality'. As Fothergill noted, the men in the film perfectly embody the types of coward, bully, and clown that he found everywhere in Canadian cinema (1977a: 240); but in the final sequence Madeleine rejects all these men and discovers that she is her own clown. However, her self-discovery is not simply a retreat into subjective vision, since she has also developed as an artist through her drawings of homeless street people.[6]

In *La Vie rêvée*, Isabelle (Liliane Lemaitre-Auger) and Virginie meet while working for a film company that produces advertising and pornography. The film's style stresses the interpenetration of dream and reality, and it depicts the efforts of the women to free themselves from their dreams of the father as authority figure (the basis of the old ideology of the family) and of the macho male associated with the new view of sex as a consumer commodity. Both of these perspectives are embodied in their colleague

Jean-Jacques (Jean-François Guité), suggesting that the new is merely a reworking of the old. Like David in *Madeleine Is . . .*, J.J. proves to be impotent, and the final sequence shows the two women tearing down the posters from the walls of their room, revealing the names of the filmmakers behind them.

The film thus plays on the way in which 'dream life' creates a utopian 'imaginary space' (as an escape from a 'symbolic' order that denies power to women and to Quebec) but is itself invaded by the commodified images of the dominant ideology. As Dansereau put it, 'what I'm saying is stop identifying with the images in *Vogue* and *Elle*, stop making ideal images of what should be happiness' (Betancourt, 1974: 47). Yet the film was criticized by some feminists, not only because the women's 'retreat from all social life' brings them 'closer to the world of childhood than to that of independence' but also because 'the author oscillates between a critique of mythic images and her desire to transform everyday life into a game' (Carrière, 1983: 164–5). However, in its playful refusal to distinguish clearly between fantasy and reality the film develops its vision of the need to integrate the personal and the political.

The friendship between Isabelle and Virginie, which carries lesbian overtones for many critics, gives their struggle a more collective dimension than Madeleine's isolated efforts to prove that she exists.[7] Dansereau was especially concerned about the reception of her film because of her conviction that 'the same problems exist for women as exist for Quebec in relation to the rest of Canada' (Ibrányi-Kiss, 1977: 251). This idea of female solidarity and its difficult relations to the national context would later become a principal feature of the work of women filmmakers in Canada.

The Real and the Visionary: Léa Pool and Patricia Rozema

Spring's career as a feature filmmaker began and ended with *Madeleine Is . . .* and, while Dansereau did make two more features and several documentaries, none had as much impact as *La Vie rêvée*. Their work did pave the way for women filmmakers who, while still constituting a minority, have become a major force in Canadian cinema. Many films by women directors are discussed elsewhere in this book, but in the 1980s several significant films appeared from different parts of the nation. In Quebec, Micheline Lanctôt moved from acting to directing with *L'Homme à tout faire* (1980) and *Sonatine* (1984); in British Columbia, Sandy Wilson drew on her memories of her own adolescence to create *My American Cousin* (1985); and, in Alberta, Anne Wheeler began her productive career with a powerful melodrama, *Loyalties* (1986).[8]

The most prominent women filmmakers who emerged at this time were Léa Pool and Patricia Rozema. Both are undoubtedly Canadian auteurs (see Chapter 9), but they occupy a slightly anomalous position in the context of the national cinema, since Pool was born in Switzerland and moved to Quebec as a student, and Rozema was born in Canada but to Dutch parents who brought her up within strict Calvinist traditions. While their films are very different in many ways, both are lesbians, and their sexual orientation is an important factor, although they both resist interpretations that pigeonhole them as lesbian filmmakers. I will focus here on their remarkable first features,

Pool's *La Femme de l'hôtel* (1984) and Rozema's *I've Heard the Mermaids Singing* (1987).

La Femme de l'hôtel deals with the intersecting lives of three women: film director Andréa (Paule Baillergeon), an unnamed actress (Marthe Turgeon) who plays the leading role in her film, and Estelle (Louise Marleau), a woman who leaves home and moves into the hotel where Andréa is making her film. When she first sees her, Andréa realizes that Estelle embodies the qualities that she wants to bring out in her main character, a singer who breaks down in the middle of a performance. The women gradually merge into one composite figure with Estelle representing the 'unconscious' and 'spiritual dimension', Andréa 'the conscious, intelligent, practical', and the actress 'the body' (Pool, quoted in Bonneville, 1985: 12).[9] We learn little about their pasts because Pool felt that they should not be too defined or 'the whole structure of slidings would not have worked' (Gaulin, 1984: 8).

In the opening sequence, the camera pans slowly across the Montreal cityscape, as an off-screen woman speaks of the film she is to make. She says that she has just returned after a long absence, and we then see Andréa explaining to her (male) lover that her film will be set in 'lieux de passage'. Pool insists that 'the place is as important as the characters' in her films, since it enables her to express feelings that neither she nor they can put into words (Loiselle and Racine, 1991: 47); but Brenda Longfellow points out that 'location is rarely given any . . . concrete specification', and Montreal becomes 'a kind of anonymous postmodern urban space' (1999: 176–7). In actuality, the hotel used in the film is in Quebec City, and Pool wished she could have created a composite city to match the permeability of the characters (Bonneville, 1985: 12).

The blurring of the boundaries between inner and outer space was nicely captured by critics who referred to the city as the site of 'an immobile journey' and the characters as undergoing 'an internal exile' (Gingras, 1991: 68; Loiselle, 1991: 56). Yet their poetic imprecision ensured that Pool's films would come under attack both from nationalist and feminist positions; Chantal Nadeau thus complained that 'Pool's work . . . does not address the issues of difference and identity in Quebec society' (1992: 13). However, *La Femme de l'hôtel*, like many of Pool's films, seeks to go beyond the prevailing ideological discourses by creating characters who are 'always on the edge' and for whom 'madness is not far away' (Pool, quoted in Bor, 1989–90: 68). Madness represents a desire to get 'outside the world of "discourse"' (Pool, quoted in Gaulin, 1984: 7), which is, of course, not possible in reality—hence the impossible situations in which her characters find themselves; but it speaks to the utopian desire to unite the different aspects of the woman in *La Femme de l'hôtel* into a whole being.

Mary Jean Green argues that 'the object of the quest' in Pool's film is not 'to pin down the identity of one mysterious personality, as in the Hollywood model', but rather to raise questions about female experience whose answers are 'not suddenly unveiled at the end but, instead, gradually revealed in the process of its development' (1989–90: 56). *I've Heard the Mermaids Singing* adopts a similar strategy, and received similar criticisms, but its more playful approach ensured it reached a much larger audience. Both films were made on very small budgets, but *Mermaids* was a breakthrough film for Canadian cinema; it was acclaimed at the Cannes Film Festival and went on to earn revenues of more than $6 million (on a budget of $350,000) (see Posner, 1993: 1–21).

Like *La Femme de l'hôtel*, *Mermaids* centres on three female characters, and Rozema says that she sees something of herself in each of these women (Delisle, 1987: 22). Polly (Sheila McCarthy) narrates the story in direct address to a video camera (that we later discover she has stolen). The film deals with her attraction to Gabrielle (Paule Baillergeon, again), the curator of the art gallery where Polly finds work, and with her disturbance at the arrival of Mary (Anne-Marie McDonald), Gabrielle's lover. The role of the curator was originally intended for a male actor, but Rozema says that she wanted to make an 'anti-authority' rather than an 'anti-masculine statement' and to depict Polly as 'a rather nonsexual, universal character' to whom men as well as women could relate (Jaehne, 1988: 23).

Polly is impressed by Gabrielle's French accent, with its associations of sophistica-tion and taste, and by her ability to use a critical vocabulary associated with the New York art scene. In comparison, Polly is defined by her naiveté and clumsiness. She repeatedly drifts into fantasies that are rudely interrupted by her everyday reality. Her ineptness led to comparisons with the weak males in the direct cinema films, and Rozema saw her as 'in some ways, representative of Canada, a country that isn't always the centre of international news' (Pevere and Wise, 2004b: 16). In her own video, Polly sits slightly off-centre; but, despite her constant self-deprecation, it is she who controls the narrative, as she reminds us when she suggests that 'you just want to know what happened next.' As Cindy Fuchs puts it, Polly confesses to 'the audience of her mind' and, since 'we are that audience, we and Polly construct each other' (1988: 54).

Despite these strategies to 'make conscious the mechanism of cinematic looking' (Goodwin, 1988: 23), the film came under attack for its gender politics. One critic even argued that it 'only *fools* us into thinking it is a feminist film' and that it 'captures the look of a documentary' in an effort to make the audience 'believe that it is seeing something *real*, something *true*' (Harrison, 1989: 25–6). Similarly, in an article in *Screen*, Teresa de Lauretis argued that the film appropriated feminism and lesbianism but they were 'preempted of their sociopolitical and subjective power' (1990: 20). These criticisms, like those directed towards Dansereau and Pool, amount to a demand for a more directly political film. Although Rozema claimed she was trying to 'reflect the complexity of a female story' (Jaehne, 1988: 23), she also insisted that 'gender is a category that doesn't interest me' (Brunette, 1990-1: 57).

Polly's attraction to Gabrielle is less a sign of lesbian desire (the thought does not occur to her) than an aspect of the film's concern with 'the notion of universal or objec-tive standards of value in art' (Austin-Smith, 2002: 229). The art gallery is in a converted church, and Rozema points to the parallels between 'organized art and organized religion', both of which depend on 'authority': the moral of both the film and its production processes is, she says, 'don't listen to authorities. Trust yourself' (Jaehne, 1988: 23). In one of Polly's fantasies, when she acquires the powers of articulation she so sadly lacks in reality, she endorses the 'relativist mentality' which holds that there is no 'right way'. Yet the film also bears witness to a desire for the absolute through Gabrielle's desire to 'make something breathtakingly beautiful that will last forever and for all time'.

The conflict between these perspectives culminates in two actions that provoke the film's climax. Polly, who takes photographs of everyday life in the city, sends her work to Gabrielle under an assumed name and is distraught when the curator dismisses them as worthless.[10] When she discovers Gabrielle's secret desire to be recognized as an artist, Polly steals and displays one of her paintings, which is represented in the film only as a pure white light, and it is acclaimed as a masterpiece by a (male) art critic. Polly later discovers that it actually was painted by Mary, but its representation as a glowing light associates it with Polly's dream life and leaves us to imagine its perfection. For Rozema, this strategy solves 'the age-old problem of how to discuss art without having to evaluate it' (Pevere and Wise, 2004b: 19). Although Polly reports that the critic was 'speechless' when he saw it, his written review refers eloquently to a 'fusion of the real and the visionary' that comes close to the condition of music. The tension between fantasy and reality thus mirrors the tension between the various experiences of art and the discourses that try to describe them.

The film ends with the reconciliation of the three women. Gabrielle and Mary find Polly making her video and realize that she was the photographer. Mary asks why the photographs have to be judged—'what's good?'—and Polly leads them through a door that opens magically onto a wooded landscape. This is the first of what Wyndham Wise calls Rozema's 'miracle endings' (Pevere and Wise, 2004b: 23), and she acknowledges her belief that 'fiction answers our need for utopias' (Pevere and Wise, 2004b: 23) and that the fairy tale is 'the ultimate story form' (Cagle, 1999: 189). Yet these endings are literally incredible, and they make us aware of the discrepancy between our own desires for universal and absolute truths and the subjectivity and relativity of the complex and complicated reality in which we live.

Thom Fitzgerald's Alien Bodies

As Christine Ramsay demonstrated in an essay on *Goin' Down the Road* originally published in 1993, the focus on a 'flawed masculine "Canadian essence"' in the canonical account of Canadian cinema distracts attention from other aspects of the films, such as their concern with 'real regional, class, cultural, and gender differences in the structure of "the democratic nation" called Canada' (2002a: 11). More recently, Thomas Waugh launched an even more radical attack on this approach by proposing 'an alternative queer Canadian canon of voices, visions, and images of alternative male sexuality' that 'must be situated not as margins but as a troubling core that transforms the corpus around it, that queers it' (1999: 11, 41).

Waugh's queering of the canon begins by excavating the hints and tensions that disturb the ostensible projects of films that depict same-sex relationships within officially heterosexual frameworks. These subterranean pressures came to the surface in *Outrageous!* (Richard Benner, 1977). This film hyperbolizes the instability of Canadian identity through its depiction of the relationship between a gay female impersonator (Craig Russell) and a schizophrenic (Hollis McLaren) and through its 'happy' ending made possible by the impersonator's success as a performer in New York.[11] Gay and lesbian characters were already beginning to appear with increasing frequency in films that, like Pool's and Rozema's, proposed a more fluid sense of sexuality than that allowed by the prohibitions and taboos that had previously surrounded the subject. The films and videos of John Greyson explored the pleasures and problems of gay male sexuality even more directly, most notably in *Zero Patience* (1993), his musical about the myths surrounding AIDS.[12]

I will focus here on the films of Thom Fitzgerald, another openly gay filmmaker, whose work uses representations of the male body to challenge aesthetic and cultural norms and the ideologies they sustain. Fitzgerald was born in the US and, of his four major feature films to date, only one is set in Canada. He moved to Nova Scotia when he was 18, and all these films are officially Canadian productions even though they push the limits of the conception of national cinema. After achieving critical acclaim, and an unusually wide release for his first feature, *The Hanging Garden* (1997), he encountered strong critical resistance to his subsequent films, and they received little or no theatrical distribution.

The Hanging Garden is set in Nova Scotia, and critics were ready to view it as a contribution to the tradition of regional filmmaking in Canada. In his review, Glenn Walton pointed out that 'there are lots of gothic touches' but quoted the director to the effect that the film is basically 'a kitchen-sink drama . . . about everyone's need to find their place in the family' (1997: 37). This makes it sound more like *Les Bons débarras* than *Léolo* (see Chapter 6), but the realist surface is radically disturbed by a narrative structure that blurs the boundaries between past, present, and the imaginary.

The film depicts three stages in the life of 'Sweet William': a young boy (Ian Parsons) dominated by his father, an obese adolescent (Troy Veinotte), and the (thin) prodigal (Chris Leavins) who returns after a long absence during which he has made a new life for himself in a 'big city'. Coming home for the wedding of his sister Rosemary (Kerry Fox), the older William finds that his earlier selves keep reappearing; and the film's hold on reality is most startlingly disturbed when the adolescent, unable to cope with the pressures of being gay, hangs himself in the garden of the family home. The narrative thus hinges on the undecidability as to whether his suicide (and perhaps his obesity) is an imaginary projection of William's feelings about his homosexuality or whether he actually committed suicide and his return home is imaginary.

Although they do not correspond to the developments in William's life, the three chapters into which the film is divided are named after flowers, and most of the characters also bear the names of flowers. The garden represents the potential harmony between nature and culture, but it also stands for the mark left on William by Whiskey Mac (Peter MacNeill), his alcoholic father, who drills him as a child into memorizing the names of the plants and the seasons in which they bloom. William is closer to his long-suffering mother, Iris (Seana McKenna), but even she adds to his troubles as a teenager when she pays for him to visit a prostitute in an attempt to 'cure' his homosexuality.

This visit provides another enigma that gives the film a linear movement in its 'present' and eventually leads to a break with the oppressive past. On his return, William meets Violet (Christine Dunsworth), whom he initially takes for a boy, and who turns out to be not his younger sister (as the family claims) nor his sister's illegitimate child (as he comes to suspect) but his own daughter, the offspring of his one heterosexual experience. When the truth emerges, Iris disappears and William decides to take Violet to live with him and his male lover in Toronto.

In a sympathetic review, José Arroyo acknowledged that *The Hanging Garden* 'could easily have been stultifying and pretentious', but he added that, while 'each element in it risks ridicule, . . . the end result is a moving and rich film' (1998: 46). Fitzgerald's subsequent films—*Beefcake* (1998), *The Wild Dogs* (2002), and *The Event* (2003)—were even riskier, and critics were not slow to label them as pretentious or to greet them with ridicule. These films all are more difficult to watch than *The Hanging Garden*, but they build on that film's use of William's bodily transformations to create powerful metaphors for the destructive effect on gender and sexuality of oppressive social attitudes.

In *Beefcake*, the bodies are those of the nude male models in the popular magazines that provided an outlet for gay men in the US after World War II. The juxtaposition of interviews and re-enactments of beefcake culture, as well as the comic pastiche of period style, recalls the treatment of the lesbian pulp fiction of the same period in the NFB's *Forbidden Love: The Unashamed Stories of Lesbian Lives* (Aerlyn Weissman and Lynne Fernie, 1993).[13] In Fitzgerald's film, the narrative centres on the arrival of Neil (Joshua Peace) at the mansion of Bob Mizer (Daniel MacIvor), the founder of the Athletic Model Guild in Los Angeles in 1945, but the main interest lies in the many photographs and modelling sessions. The bodybuilding culture is celebrated for offering pleasure to men at a time when homosexuality was virtually outlawed; but the film also explores the tension between the aesthetic ideal of the male body and its commercial exploitation.

In absolute contrast to these idealized bodies from the past, *The Wild Dogs* was shot on digital video in present-day Bucharest and is filled with the broken and deformed bodies of the people on the streets that Fitzgerald witnessed when he went there to make a horror film for the USA cable television network.[14] In that film, he felt, these people were treated as freaks, and Fitzgerald registers his discomfort in *The Wild Dogs* by casting himself as Geordie, a pornographer sent to find 'teenage Lolita girls' for his boss's Web site. The title refers to the plague of stray dogs that has infested Bucharest since the fall of the Ceauşescu regime in the mid-1980s, and Geordie's visit is intercut with the story of Bogdan (Mihai Calota), a dog-catcher employed by the government who takes pity on the animals and tries to save them. When he is arrested, his wife Varvara (Simona Popescu), who works as a maid at the Canadian embassy, gives up their child for adoption, and Geordie's attempts to help the victims of his exploitative job also serve only to make things worse.

The link between *Beefcake* and *The Wild Dogs* may be found in Jean Baudrillard's observation that 'idealization always goes with abjection, just as charity always goes with destitution' (1994: 79). In the latter film, the bodies on display—including those of a midget, a legless boy, and a youth who crawls on legs that grow backwards—bear witness to the abject misery of the city. While Fitzgerald came under attack for exploiting these people, he wanted to avoid making them objects of pity. Through the compromised figure of Geordie, the film exposes what he calls the fine line between 'exploitation and charity' and tries to 'let the real world in'.[15] The sexual fantasies to which the brothels of Bucharest minister are now also catered to in the virtual realm of the Internet, and the film struggles to overcome the absorption of suffering into the same realm. Its location shooting gives it an authenticity equal to, but more perverse than, that which critics had recently celebrated in another film also shot on digital video, *Atanarjuat: The Fast Runner* (see Chapter 10).

The Event also deals with an extreme situation and exposes the difficulty of finding an adequate response. It depicts the last months of Matt (Don McKellar), a New York musician, who decides to commit suicide when he realizes that the drugs he is taking for AIDS are no longer working. The title refers to a party held to celebrate his life and assist him to die, and the story is told in flashbacks as Nick (Parker Posey) a police officer, investigates the suspicious circumstances of his death. However, another 'event' occurred in New York during the filming, and, when the flashbacks reach September 2001, a long shot of the New York skyline includes the World Trade Center towers, which then disappear, followed by shots of balconies draped with flags. This major public catastrophe is thus incorporated into the film, again risking charges of exploitation, but also provoking questions about the relations between the two events.

One of the effects is that the arrests of those who were at the party occur in streets full of flags. After the prosecution breaks down because all of the guests at the party confess to administering the fatal dose, Matt's mother, Lila (Olympia Dukakis), and sister, Dana (Sarah Polley), are shown (using a hidden camera) handing out leaflets on AIDS beside 'Ground Zero'. Yet the film is not so much about AIDS as about the question of assisted suicide, also addressed in Denys Arcand's *Les Invasions barbares*, released (much more widely) in the same year, in which the attack on the World Trade Center is one of the 'invasions' that parallel the dying man's disease (see Chapter 9).

At the end, Nick explains to Brian (Brent Carver), the doctor she has investigated because of his involvement in a number of suspicious deaths, that her own father had asked her to help him die; and, she ends with the ambiguous reflection, 'I hope I did the right thing.' Brian then reveals that it was Lila who prevented her son from coughing up the pills; and, after we see her doing so in a flashback, she also says, 'I hope I did the right thing.' The need to strive for 'the right thing' is central to Fitzgerald's vision, along with the difficulty of breaking with the rigid and entrenched categories of traditional political and sexual morality.

Pour la suite du monde (Directed by Michel Brault, Pierre Perrault. Produced by Fernand Dansereau. ©1962 National Film Board of Canada. All rights reserved. Photo used with permission of the National Film Board of Canada.)

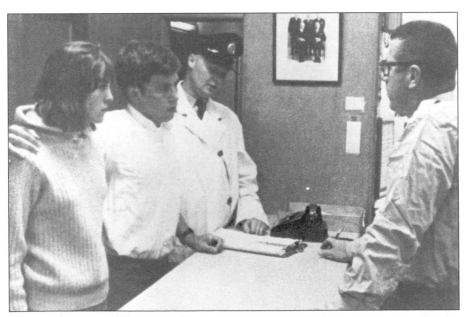

Nobody Waved Good-bye (Directed by Don Owen. Produced by Roman Kroitor, Don Women. © 1964 National Film Board of Canada. All rights reserved. Photo used with permission of the National Film Board of Canada.)

Le Chat dans le sac (Directed by Gilles Groulx. Produced by Jacques Bobet. © 1964 National Film Board of Canada. All rights reserved. Photo used with permission of the National Film Board of Canada.)

Mon oncle Antoine (Directed by Claude Jutra. Produced by Marc Beaudet. © 1970 National Film Board of Canada. All rights reserved. Photo used with permission of the National Film Board of Canada.)

waydowntown (2002. Directed by Gary Burns, with Fab Filippo. Used with permission. Courtesy of Burns Film.)

Pouvoir intime (1986. Directed by Yves Simoneau, with Marie Tifo and Pierre Curzi. Used with permission.)

I Love a Man in Uniform (1993. Directed by David Wellington, with Tom McManus. Used with permission.)

La Mort d'un bûcheron (1972. Directed by Gilles Carle, with Carole Laure. Used with permission by Les Films de Ma Vie. Image from La Cinémathèque, Québecoise.)

Careful (1992. Directed by Guy Madin, with Jackie Burroughs, Kyle McCulloch, and Brent Neale. Used with permission.)

Le Vent du Wyoming (1994. Directed by Marc-André Forcier. Used with permission. Courtesy of Transfilm Inc., © 1994.)

Picture of Light (1994. Directed by Peter Mettler. Used with permssion. © Peter Mettler.)

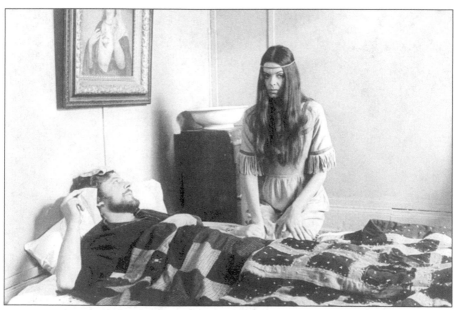

Les Maudits sauvages (1971. Directed by Jean Pierre Lefebvre, with Pierre Dufresne and Rachel Cailhier. Used by permission by Cinak ltée.)

La Femme de l'hôtel (1984. Directed by Léa Pool, with Marthe Turgeon and Paul Baillargeon. Used with permission from ACPAV. Photo by Martine Waltzer.)

The Hanging Garden (1997. Directed by Thom Fitzgerald, with Chris Leavins, Seana McKenna, and Ian Parsons. Used by permission of Triptych Media Inc. Photo by C. Reardon.)

Gina (1974. Directed by Denys Arcand, with Céline Lomez, Gabriel Arcand, and André Gagnon. Used with permission by Les Films de Ma Vie. Image from La Cinémathèque Québecoise.)

Ararat (© 2002. Serendipity Point Films Inc., All rights reserved.)

Rude (1995. Directed by Clement Virgo, with Sharon M. Lewis. Used with permission of Conquering Lion Pictures and the Feature Film Project.)

Atanarjuat (2001. Directed by Zacharias Kunuk, with Natar Ungalaaq. Used with permission. Norman Cohn © Igloolik Isuma Productions.)

Maelström (2002. Directed by Denis Villeneuve, with Marie-Josée Croze. Photo by Michel Tremblay. Used with permission. Courtesy of Max Films.)

Men With Brooms (© 2002. Serendipity Point Films Inc., All rights reserved.)

Two Canadian Auteurs:
Arcand and Egoyan

I make films for Ingmar Bergman, and he will
no doubt never see them.

—Denys Arcand (Gural and Patar, 1982: 53)

It's the difficulty of representing the self in a
society completely obsessed with representation
that interests me.

—Atom Egoyan (Taubin, 1992: 19)

The idea of the filmmaker as an artist with a personal vision is usually associated with the *politique des auteurs* developed by critics writing for *Cahiers du cinéma* in the 1950s. These critics would go on to become the filmmakers of the French New Wave, whose work revitalized the idea of 'art cinema' as an alternative to the commercial production of the Hollywood studios. In Canada, there has been a tendency on the part of critics to limit auteur cinema to the work of directors who write their own screenplays, but it is important to note that the *Cahiers* critics championed such directors as John Ford, Howard Hawks, and many others who worked within the Hollywood studio system. What was important to these critics was that the filmmaker used film language in a distinctive and consistent manner, in the same way that a literary author develops a personal style using the resources of written language. These auteurs were true film artists, unlike *metteurs-en-scène*, directors who relied on the written word of the screenplay.

The art cinema circuits that developed in North America and elsewhere were closely associated with the growth of film festivals throughout the world. Exposure at festivals is often important for Canadian filmmakers, and the establishment of major international festivals in Montreal and Toronto has boosted their profile. Yet the repertory cinemas in many Canadian cities tend to privilege 'foreign' art films. Canadian films usually lack the assured treatment of complex psychological or social situations found in European art films, as well as the exotic appeal of films from less familiar parts of the world. Not quite popular, Canadian films are not quite art cinema, either.

The auteur theory came under attack in the 1970s from theorists who saw it as an outmoded relic of the romantic glorification of the artist as a lonely individual, ignoring both the collective nature of filmmaking and the social and political contexts that shape films and their reception. However, while these criticisms have been widely accepted, the idea of the director as author remains a central principle in film studies, in the practices of art cinema, and, increasingly, in the publicity discourses around even Hollywood productions.

This situation in Canada changed, to some degree, in the 1990s with the new funding policies of Telefilm Canada and the establishment of provincial film development offices and arts councils. It now became possible for filmmakers in both languages to develop a significant body of work in relative artistic freedom, although the process of raising the budget for a feature film is now extremely complicated and the situation of even established auteurs remains highly precarious. Indeed, Jean Pierre Lefebvre, among others, has recently lamented the decline of 'the *cinéma d'auteur*' in Quebec, because the funding bodies insist on dealing with producers rather than directors (Harcourt, 2001: 63).

Many of the directors discussed elsewhere in this book have been or can be regarded as auteurs, and I have approached many of them from this perspective (while also acknowledging the social, cultural, and industrial factors that help shape even the most personal vision). In this chapter I will focus on Denys Arcand and Atom Egoyan, two filmmakers who have achieved international recognition with a substantial body of films that reward analysis in terms of their distinctive personal visions. As we shall see, despite the evident differences between their films and the contexts in which they make them, they share a commitment to ambiguity and uncertainty that is characteristic of 'art cinema' but that also seems to reflect a distinctively Canadian sense of cultural instability.

Ups and Downs: Denys Arcand's History Lessons

Many critics acclaimed Arcand's *Les Invasions barbares* (2003) as a mature work by a major filmmaker and celebrated its Academy Award as best foreign-language film as a major accomplishment for Canadian cinema. There were dissenting voices, especially in Quebec where Arcand has always been a controversial figure, but there seemed little doubt that he had confirmed his status as an auteur.[1] The film itself encourages this view since it is a belated sequel to *Le Déclin de l'empire américain* (1986), which established Arcand's international reputation, and includes characters from *Jésus de Montréal* (1989), in which he successfully built on that reputation. Arcand seemed to be reflecting on his past work and reassessing it in the context of the new millennium.

Yet, the long gap between the earlier films and this reflection is typical of Arcand's career, which may appear to lack the consistency required of a genuine auteur. He had made films in the meantime, but these were generally regarded as minor works—although true adherents to the concept of the director as auteur would insist that even minor works by an auteur are more rewarding than any film by a *metteur-en-scène*. A similar gap appeared in the late 1970s and early 1980s when Arcand, like many other Quebec filmmakers, was unable to work on his own projects. In any case, even his more important films before 1985 did not correspond to the usual definitions of 'art cinema'. Arcand's status as an auteur rests on finding links between three different modes of filmmaking: the three 'art films' already mentioned, three feature-length documentaries—*On est au coton* (1970), *Québec: Duplessis et après* (1972), and *Le Confort et l'indifférence* (1981)—and three genre films—*La Maudite Galette* (1971), *Réjeanne Padovani* (1973), and *Gina* (1975).

The key underlying feature that runs through this disparate body of work and shapes his personal vision stems from Arcand's training as a historian. He studied history at the Université de Montréal and, after co-directing the student film *Seul ou avec d'autres* with Denis Héroux, he joined the NFB in 1964 to work on historical documentaries. His historical perspective persists in his later films, but he noted that his training convinced him that 'we know so little about the past that to me it would be absolutely inconceivable to do a period film' (Barker, 1990: 4).[2] Apart from the specific historical references, always used to judge the present, the films betray Arcand's roots as a historian in their ingrained pessimism about the possibility of changing the course of events and the detached perspective they take on human endeavours, both highly controversial aspects of his work.

At the beginning of *Québec: Duplessis et après*, Lord Durham (played by film director Robin Spry) reads from his report to the British government after the 1837–8 rebellions, describing the inhabitants of Lower Canada (Quebec) as 'a people without history or literature'. Arcand then cuts to newsreel shots of Maurice Duplessis invoking 'our ancestors' in a political speech. The appeal to history is an attempt to counter Durham's denial of a cultural heritage, but Arcand's documentary on the 1970 provincial election shows not only that all the political parties echo Duplessis's rhetoric but also the persistence of Quebec's problems despite the much-vaunted changes wrought by the Quiet Revolution. At the end of *Le Confort et l'indifférence*, dealing with the 1980 referendum campaign, a final caption, taken from Alexander Solzhenitsyn, reads 'our lives are so short compared with the slow unrolling of history.'

For Arcand, this unrolling involves 'a kind of blind force that advances like a glacier and . . . it will continue to advance' (Dorland, 1986: 18). His version of history is thus one that has little appeal to those committed to bringing about political change in Quebec, especially since his films combine this pessimistic outlook with a dark sense of humour. In *La Maudite Galette*, a heist film that depicts a morally bankrupt society, the voice of Pierre Trudeau, justifying the invocation of the War Measures Act 'last October', is heard on the radio as Berthe (Luce Guilbeault) sits impassively drinking in the kitchen. When the stripper (Céline Lomez) is gang-raped in her motel room in *Gina*, 'O Canada' is playing on the television. However, despite such satiric moments, Arcand insists that his films have 'never defended a cause' and that he does not know whether he is 'for or against independence' (Loiselle, 1995: 149).

Arcand is thus, as Pierre Véronneau suggests, 'the filmmaker of uncertainty: he doubts the certainties of others, he scorns the complacent possessors of truth, he does not believe in the existence of a unique version' (1987–8: 24). He most fully demonstrates his openness to contradictions in *Le Déclin de l'empire américain*, in which he incorporates his thesis that 'the key to our history is to be on the margins of the American Empire' (Jutras et al., 1987–8: 6). In the pre-credit sequence, Rémy (Rémy Girard) lectures on the power of 'numbers' in history, arguing that the blacks will prevail in South Africa but not in North America. He does not mention Quebec, but Arcand inserts a close-up of a female Vietnamese student intently listening, foreshadowing Rémy's admission of his sexual attraction to his female students but also alluding to the changing demographics in Quebec.

Quebec history becomes a structuring absence in a film in which most of the characters are historians. In a reversal of gender stereotypes, the opening sequences show the women working out in a gym while the men prepare the meal that will bring them together in the second half of the film. Throughout, they engage in highly articulate conversations, mainly about sex, but also on the political thesis suggested by its title, without once addressing Quebec's past or future. The only allusion to this topic occurs when Mario (Gabriel Arcand), the working-class lover of Diane (Louise Portal), briefly interrupts the proceedings and gives her a book by the historian Michel Brunet, which he certainly has not read. While the film's appeal derives from their lively conversations and their evident enjoyment of each other's company, the inbred relationships within the group produce a constant state of tension and break down when Rémy's wife Louise (Dorothée Berryman) overhears Dominique (Dominique Michel), the head of the department, casually mentioning that she once slept with Rémy.

The film, like Arcand himself, is 'ambivalent' towards these characters who can 'express great insight into their own condition' and then 'prove incapable of seeing the blatantly obvious' (Loiselle, 1995: 152). For Bill Marshall, 'the convenience of its irony' makes the film 'complicit with the very forces of cultural commodification' that it claims to denounce (2001: 293). Yet Arcand is very much aware of this tension between criticism and complicity. He makes this clear in *Gina*, in which a film crew tries to make a documentary critical of working conditions in the textile industry, as Arcand himself had done with *On est au coton*. Arcand finished his film, which was then banned by the NFB, but the fictional crew members are stopped even before they finish. They abandon their social conscience and are last seen working on a crime film rather like *La Maudite Galette*, which Arcand made after leaving the NFB. *Gina* itself is, of course, a commercial genre film in the same vein.

Arcand felt that his turn to genre did involve an element of 'complicity', but this was also true, in a different way, of his working conditions at the NFB. His approach to the crime film involved a strong 'critical' element, through the use of such strategies as long takes and a static camera that undermine the drive to resolution through action and violence. 'Instead of asking yourself what is happening to the hero,' he claimed 'you ask yourself why it is happening' and 'why this society produces this kind of individual' (Tadros, 1972a: 29).

Marshall also complains that *Le Déclin* is uncritical because it 'refuses to comment on its own construction through a severing of the realist illusion' (2001: 293). This is a rather odd argument to make about a film in which, as Denise Pérusse points out, 'the editing introduces a distance from the action and words of the characters' and, in general, 'the narrator . . . is far from effacing himself' (1987–8: 49). The cross-cutting between the male and female groups is highly self-conscious, and the credit sequence asserts a strong sense of a controlling narrator: the camera tracks along spacious university corridors to come to rest on Diane doing a radio interview with Dominique on her new book about 'the frantic drive for personal pleasure' in modern society caused by 'the decline of the American empire'.

Near the end, however, the authority of the narration is called into question by an argument about the nature and extent of a friend's self-proclaimed sexual exploits, raising doubts about the truth of the 'histoires' told, and often visualized, during the film. A similar puncturing of the realist illusion occurs at the end of *Gina* when, after a bloody sequence in which Gina takes revenge on the rapists in accordance with generic expectations, we see her at the airport leaving for Mexico, accompanied by Mexican music. The camera pans away from her to reveal musicians playing, and the next sequence begins with a woman shooting her husband on a city street. This time the camera pulls back to reveal that it is a scene from a film being shot by the former members of the documentary crew. The double exposure of the apparatus undercuts the illusion of the final marriage ceremony as a happy ending that will resolve the problems of Dolorès (Frédérique Collin), the worker whose situation has been compared with the stripper's throughout the film.

In a similar way, the opening of *Jésus de Montréal* plunges us into the heightened emotions of a man committing suicide, which is then revealed as a theatrical performance when the audience begins to applaud. This is an appropriate effect to introduce a film about 'maintaining one's integrity in a world where reality is a problematic concept'

(Harkness, 1989: 238). There is always, however, a bedrock of the real in Arcand's films that frames the artifice and complications of the social world: in *Québec: Duplessis et après*, recurring images of cars abandoned in the snow punctuate the account of the political campaign, and in *Le Déclin*, shots of the natural beauty of the lake act as a counterpoint to the sexual entanglements of the characters. The equivalent shots in *Jésus* are panoramic views of Montreal, whose beauty acts as a counterpoint to 'the commercial city' and 'the suffering city' that Daniel (Lothaire Bluteau) encounters when he takes on the role of Jesus in a new version of the Passion Play (Testa, 1995: 107).

The lake from *Le Déclin* appears again in *Les Invasions barbares*, and the new film picks up on an image from its predecessor that invokes death as a fact of nature and art as a human response to mortality. When Claude (Yves Jacques), who is gay and suffering from a serious illness that appears to be AIDS, lectures to his art history class on the association of dawn with death in painting, the slides are projected on his body, and there is an abrupt cut to the lake at dawn. In the sequel, Claude is alive and gleefully enjoying the generosity of the Canadian government as a cultural ambassador in Rome, and it is Rémy, the inveterate womanizer of the earlier film, whose terminal illness brings the old gang together in a crowded hospital, like the one to which Daniel was taken at the end of *Jésus*.

The film's title and central motif were anticipated in an article on Quebec cinema by Gilles Thérien. Alluding to *Le Déclin*, Thérien argued that, 'if one speaks of empire and decline, there is always at the gates of whatever empire a horde of Barbarians ready to invade the territory' so that 'to think of the empire is also to think of what undermines it, the thought of the Barbarian' (1990: 10). The idea is introduced into the later film when a shot of the second plane crashing into the World Trade Center abrubtly fills the screen, before being identified as an image on television accompanying a commentary by Alain (Daniel Brière), a graduate student in *Le Déclin*, who compares the attack to earlier atrocities and suggests what makes it important is that this time the 'barbarians' struck at 'the heart of the empire'. Later, a policeman (Roy Dupuis) speaks of the impossibility of controlling the drug trade, which he also describes as an 'invasion'.

Arcand himself relates the film to a future in which nations will disappear and 'the notion of borders will be almost irrelevant', because 'there will be American citizens on one side' and everybody else will be considered as 'one and the same thing: barbarians' (Howell, 2003: 30). Yet it is American culture that is colonizing the world more like a virus working internally than a violent assault from the outside world. In the film's use of the metaphor, as Pierre Barrette suggests, 'the individual and the collective come together, reflect each other, interpenetrate' (2003: 5). Not only do barbarians also come from within, as with the disease that consumes Rémy's body, but Quebec is increasingly part of a new global economy.

The film opens in London with Sébastien (Stéphane Rousseau), Rémy's son, receiving a telephone call from his mother in the banking house where he works. Rémy considers his son a materialistic barbarian, but the son's wealth procures a comfortable room in a wing of the hospital that has been closed because of cutbacks and who pays for the heroin that eases his father's final days. The opening credits appear over a long tracking shot behind a woman walking down a hospital corridor, filled with patients waiting for rooms. This shot is a perverse reminder of the one at the beginning of *Déclin*, and the woman (Johanne-Marie Tremblay), who administers communion to the patients, turns out to be Constance, one of the actors/disciples from *Jésus*.

The contrast between global wealth and the state of the health system in Quebec sets up the way in which, as Philip Kemp suggests, Arcand 'frequently . . . teases his audience by switching moods on us, from cynical to affirmative and back' (2004: 37). There are satiric caricatures of hospital administrators and union leaders and comic vignettes by Rémy's former girlfriends. After some of his students visit him in hospital, we discover that the moving scene has been arranged and paid for by Sébastien. Yet the tone can also encompass intensely emotional sequences like the farewell message that Rémy receives on a computer screen from his daughter Sylvaine (Isabelle Blais) from a yacht somewhere in the Pacific.

However, it remains essentially a comedy, and the shifts in tone enforce Arcand's characteristic double vision. When Gaëlle (Marina Hands), Sébastien's partner, who works for an art auction house in London, looks for religious artworks in Montreal, she visits a storage room with Father Raymond (Gilles Pelletier), the disillusioned priest from *Jésus*. The film clearly endorses her judgement that the art has little aesthetic and no market value, but it also raises questions about the shift from the domain of the sacred to that of commerce. Similarly, it supports Rémy's judgement of himself as a professional failure but celebrates the affection he receives from his friends, who all are complicit in his assisted suicide. It ends on a note of tentative hope when Nathalie (Marie-Josée Croze), Louise's daughter, who administers Rémy's dope and his final overdose, tries to overcome her addiction and moves into his apartment, looking with interest at the history books on his shelves.

Dark Mirrors: Reflections on Atom Egoyan

Critical response to *Ararat* (2002), Atom Egoyan's ninth feature film, was deeply divided. As a large-budget film (produced by Robert Lantos's Serendipity Point films) dealing with the Armenian genocide, it seemed a major departure from his earlier, more intimate and personal films. Yet, while *Ararat* does not explicitly refer back to the director's earlier work, as *Les Invasions barbares* does, it includes several of the 'family' of actors who recur from film to film, most notably his wife Arsinée Khanjian, who has appeared in all the features. It also draws on his personal background as the son of Armenian parents, born in Egypt but brought up in Canada.

Although the earlier films usually deal with characters seeking to come to terms with their past, they seem far removed from Arcand's historical sensibility. As well as being set in vaguely defined locations (see Chapter 3), these films unfold with a kind of dream logic, marked by repetitions and coincidences, with the result that, as Ron Burnett notes, 'history is absent' (1993: 10). Egoyan acknowledged that he was 'not particularly interested in giving details or being precise about a particular state of national isolation' but rather used his displaced Armenian Canadians (and others) as 'a metaphor for a certain attitude or a certain perception of existence' (Arroyo, 1987: 17).

That perception grows out of being an exile or simply not feeling at home. In *Next of Kin* (1984), Peter (Patrick Tierney) starts out, much like his namesake in *Nobody Waved Good-bye*, in his bedroom listening to his parents downstairs argue about his future; but this Peter leaves home and constructs an improbable alternative identity as the long-lost son of an Armenian family. Van (Aidan Tierney) in *Family Viewing* (1987) renews contact with his ethnic roots, and eventually rediscovers his Armenian mother, through the family videos his father Stan (David Hemblen) is systematically erasing. In *The Adjuster* (1991), Noah (Elias Koteas) lives in a show home amid the wasteland of an unfinished housing estate with Hera (Khanjian), who may or may not be his wife and who comes from an unspecified war-torn country.

The one partial exception to this rule of imprecision is *Calendar* (1993), a small-budget film shot on 16mm and video that depicts the breakup between a photographer (played by Egoyan himself) and his wife (Khanjian) during a visit to Armenia to photograph churches for a calendar. Their journey through Armenia is intercut with sequences that take place after the photographer returns alone. These are presumably set in Canada but are confined entirely to his apartment, where he entertains a succession of young 'ethnic' women who all perform the same ritual of making a telephone call in their own language. The visual absence of Canada contrasts with the rich presence of the historical sites that are, however, then frozen and fetishized in a calendar for exiles living elsewhere. In Armenia, the photographer tells his wife that 'we're both from here but being here has made me from somewhere else', and, at the end, we hear her voice on his answering machine asking, 'Were you there? Are you there?'

Geoff Pevere suggests that Egoyan's films are 'about the desperate search for something like home in an era when technology threatens to erase the idea altogether', but he also points to how technology seeks to fill the gap when 'media become environments' (1995: 10, 17). One of the distinguishing features in the earlier films is the presence of video cameras and their low-resolution images that contrast with film images that seem more stable and permanent. If *Family Viewing* offers home video as a kind of electronic memory, it is an erasable memory, and Van also discovers that Stan can only make love with Sandra (Gabrielle Rose) if he records the act over tapes of his former wife, and then only when listening to erotic phone calls from sex-worker Aline (Khanjian). This film also included sequences shot with television cameras to suggest that family life corresponds to the formulas of television sitcoms.

The films explore the cultural effects of video as a medium, including its domestic, voyeuristic, and surveillance possibilities, but Egoyan argues that the video images also serve to make the spectator 'conscious of the process of fabricating the image' (Grugeau, 1989: 8). In so doing, they draw attention to the film camera as the 'absent presence of the filmmaker' and thus help to fulfill Egoyan's concern to make the audience 'aware that I am photographing people and to be deeply suspicious of my reasons' (Taubin, 1989: 29). His films thus grow out of a resistance to 'films which have the ability to make people think that what they're seeing is real' (Porton, 1997: 14).

This does not mean that the events depicted in Egoyan's films, like the school bus accident in *The Sweet Hereafter* (1997), are not real. We see the bus skid off the road and slide across the frozen lake from the point of view of Billy (Bruce Greenwood), whose children are on board and who is helpless to intervene. Katherine Monk comments that, 'had this scene been directed by someone like Steven Spielberg or Michael Bay, we would have seen a close-up of the ice on the road intercut with the bus wheels speeding along the pavement' and other devices to create suspense, excitement, and involvement (2001: 94). The effect of Egoyan's approach is not the denial of emotion, of which he has often been accused, but rather his recognition of the traumatic fact of the event and its impact on people who must struggle to come to terms with it. As Egoyan himself puts it, his style is designed to 'elaborate experience over incident' (1997: 23).

His films certainly do not invite easy emotional responses, partly because of the shifting tone and dark humour that they share with Arcand but also because of the mannered acting style that reveals the influence of the Theatre of the Absurd (Samuel Beckett and Harold Pinter, in particular).[3] Because of what he calls his ongoing 'suspicion about what it means to be natural' (Porton, 1997: 12), his films constantly draw attention to the role-playing in which his characters engage and by which they define themselves. They often talk in clichés and their words are often surrounded with 'invisible inverted commas' (Coates, 1997: 24). In *Speaking Parts* (1989), for example, the film producer (Hemblen) repeatedly calls people 'special' even as he exploits them, which makes it difficult to believe him when he tells Lance (Michael McManus), the star of his new film, that he is making 'three of these suckers' at the moment but this one is 'special'. It also undercuts the desperate effort made by Lisa (Khanjian) to express her love for Lance by telling him that he is 'special'.

Most disturbing from the point of view of conventional acting styles, however, is that there is no sense of something hidden beneath the surface that could explain the characters' behaviour. For Egoyan, 'the concept of surface proves to be the most complex and intriguing aspect of any rendering of personality' (1993: 25). Yet he also insists that it is not his films that are lacking in emotion but a society in which 'overt emotional expression is not rewarded' (Pevere and Wise, 2004b: 76), as well as 'all these technological playthings [that] hold us at a distance from one another, while giving us the illusion of communicating' (Racine, 1989: 10).

The desire to communicate and the satisfaction that resonant images provide coexist in Egoyan's films with his sense that the illusion of communication prevents real communication and that images can be used to manipulate. He describes himself as 'torn between these two tendencies: I love making images, yet I'm suspicious of them' (Pevere, 2002: 20). By interweaving different stories, his narratives often create the impression that the characters do communicate, but usually unknown to themselves. In *Exotica* (1994) and *The Sweet Hereafter*, for example, flashbacks that seem to be triggered by the memory of one character end with a return to another character. What also pulls against the apparent coldness of the films is that their central preoccupation, with what Amy Taubin nicely calls 'the relationship between so-called family values and . . . sexual desire' (1992: 18), is the very stuff of melodrama.

Some critics welcomed *The Sweet Hereafter* as a more openly communicative film and suggested that this was because it is not based on an original screenplay but adapted from a novel by the US writer Russell Banks. Yet it works very much like his other films. As well as the bus accident, it deals with the relationship between two fathers and their daughters. Sam (Tom McCamus) has an incestuous relationship with Nicole (Sarah Polley), while Mitchell (Ian Holm) is estranged from Zoe (Caertham Banks). In the film's final image, light shines through the window on Nicole while she is babysitting Billy's children. This is apparently a flashback, but it seems to represent her feelings of release after lying at the inquest, against her father's wishes, and thus foiling Mitchell's attempt to initiate a lawsuit. The fluid time scheme emphasizes the linear succession of sequences rather than their chronological relations (plot time takes precedence over story time), implying that the preceding events are an expression of the tensions experienced by Nicole because of her too-close relations with her father (and perhaps equally by the lawyer's guilt at being too far from his daughter).[4]

The outcome of the tension between the strong materials at the core of Egoyan's films and an awareness of their intricate organizational principles is a moral ambiguity not unlike that in Arcand's work. Tom McSorley refers to how the films generate 'states of epistemological uncertainty for characters and the audience alike' (2002a: 10), while Eleanor Ty suggests that 'it is not easy to find the moral of his films' because 'everything depends upon images; thus, everything lurks in the realm of the ambiguous' (1999: 11). Egoyan indeed insists that 'ambiguity seems to me essential for the credibility of a film', adding that he is not a 'moralist' (Racine, 1989: 11).

His films do, however, set up moral dilemmas that implicate the spectator in the making of value judgements. In *Speaking Parts*, for example, Clara (Gabrielle Rose) feels that the producer has betrayed her screenplay, a personal account of the death of her brother when he donated a kidney to save her life. Since Clara is a fairly sympathetic character and the producer a smug manipulator, it seems that we should side with the artist, but it is hard not to admit that his idea of using the format of a television talk show enlivens an apparently rather conventional, if deeply felt, script.

In *The Adjuster*, Noah describes his job as an insurance adjuster as sorting out what has value from what has not, and Hera, a film censor, replies that hers is the same. The film deals with the relations between 'value' and 'desire' in a society in which both are defined in economic and legal terms. Noah sleeps with his clients to help them overcome their 'shock' but, apparently, without any desire of his own, just as Hera tapes pornographic films for her sister to see while, apparently, not experiencing the arousal to which the other censors admit.

The ambiguity and uncertainty that underlie Egoyan's vision raise some troubling moral questions when applied to a historical atrocity. However, the event with which *Ararat* deals is one that is real (it ends with a caption that adamantly affirms this point) but denied. The effect of this denial is noted in the film when Raffi (David Alpay) points out that Hitler insisted that his plans would work by asking, 'who remembers the extermination of the Armenians?' Even the much better-known events of the Jewish Holocaust have been denied, and Steven Spielberg made *Schindler's List* (1993) to overcome the fading memory of the slaughter of the Jewish people. Egoyan's response is an implicit critique of films like Spielberg's that generate emotional responses based on the power of the image to simulate (and thus substitute for) the real.

At the opposite extreme is an event such as the attack on the World Trade Center, which was rendered highly visible thanks to modern communications technology. Egoyan has said that he does not know if he would have been able to make his film after September 11 (Pevere, 2002: 18), and the frequent comparison of the televised images to Hollywood disaster movies must have reinforced his sense of the merging of reality and illusion in postmodern culture (see Chapter 12). His resistance to this process is reflected in his decision to relegate the spectacle and action to a film within the film, also called *Ararat*, whose production in Toronto is one of the narrative strands that Egoyan weaves together.

This film reconstructs the events that took place in Turkey in 1915 much as Spielberg represented the Holocaust in Poland—or as the persecution of Hungarian Jews was depicted in Robert Lantos's own historical epic, *Sunshine* (István Szabó, 1999). However, Egoyan is not completely contemptuous of this film, which is being made by Edouard Saroyan (Charles Aznavour), a veteran French director of Armenian descent, and which at least (unlike most such epics) uses subtitles rather than requiring all the characters to speak English.[5] As we shall see, images from the film in production become entangled with the memory and imagination of several characters, and Saroyan's film becomes just one layer in a complex exploration of the problem of finding an adequate way of convincingly representing the real horror of the event.

For the American critic Roger Ebert, this way of telling the story produces 'a needlessly confusing film' (Melnyk, 2004: 161), but more sympathetic critics saw it as a film about 'the impossibility of "truth" in storytelling' (Pevere, 2002: 15). Egoyan's story involves not only what happened in Turkey in 1915, and during the making of the film about it, but also the experiences of two troubled families in Toronto whose lives are affected by the production. Ani (Khanjian), an art historian who becomes a consultant on the film, is an expert on Arshile Gorky, the Armenian painter who survived the massacre as a child; her son Raffi, whose father was killed attempting to assassinate a Turkish diplomat, is having an affair with his step-sister Celia (Marie-Josée Croze), who blames Ani for the death of her father. Philip (Brent Carver), an attendant at the art gallery where Celia slashes a Gorky painting, is living with his lover, Ali (Elias Koteas), a half-Turkish actor who plays the governor in Saroyan's film; his disapproving father David (Christopher Plummer) is a customs officer, who questions Saroyan when he arrives to make the film and then interrogates Raffi when he returns from Turkey with cans of undeveloped film that may contain drugs.

What links all these stories is a concern with what Egoyan called, referring to the treatment of incest in *The Sweet Hereafter*, 'the politics of denial' (1997: 23). The personal and public stories are thus interrelated, as are the different layers of storytelling. These include Saroyan's film, Gorky's painting, Ani's lectures, a digital video made by Raffi during his trip to Turkey, and a book by Clarence Ussher, an American doctor who is played in the film by a Hollywood star, Martin (Bruce Greenwood), and whose eyewitness account was a vital resource for Rouben (Eric Bogosian), Saroyan's screenwriter, and for Egoyan in writing his own screenplay.

Egoyan's organization of this complex material can be illustrated by two sequences. After Saroyan's arrival at the airport, a cut takes us to a painter at work, identified by a caption as Gorky (Simon Abkarian) in his New York studio in 1934. His off-screen look cues shots of the young Gorky (Garen Boyajian) and his mother (Lousnak Abdarian) that seem to represent his memory but will later be located in Saroyan's film (it is not clear whether the shots in the artist's studio also come from the film). An apparent voice-over commentary becomes Ani's lecture on the artist, which is attended by Saroyan and Rouben and disrupted by Celia. In a later sequence, Raffi reads David a passage from the script in which a German nurse reports to Ussher about the torture of women, cueing images of her making the report (in German) and then of the events she is describing. As the women are stripped and abused, the camera moves to reveal Saroyan and his crew, followed by a shot of Gorky as a boy watching these events and a cut back to his older self in the studio.

This sequence, and another in which a woman is raped on a cart while her daughter hides beneath, raises questions, not only about the kind of movie Saroyan is making but also about their inclusion in Egoyan's film that apparently critiques that approach. However, looking and visual representation are never simple or innocent acts in Egoyan's films. After Ani objects to the 'poetic licence' that Rouben claims for his screenplay, she tells him that 'it is difficult for me to imagine these things', and there is an immediate cut to a battle scene from the movie, a translation of imagination into vivid images that substitute for her imaginative incapacity. Later, when Ani bursts onto the set to protest a historical inaccuracy, Martin (as Ussher) passionately attacks her as if she were actually interrupting the doctor's efforts to save a wounded boy.

The actor's identification with his character foreshadows the shots of the faces of Saroyan, Rouben, and Martin at the premiere, where they seem genuinely shocked and moved by their own creation. Their response to the emotional power of the images contrasts with Raffi's conclusion, in his comments to his mother on the soundtrack of his video, that 'there is nothing here to prove that anything ever happened.' If Egoyan's films stress experience over incident, *Ararat* makes clear that, as Jonathan Romney points out, there is also a 'need to reshape experience through creative discourse' (2003: 6). A film that protests the denial of a real event thus confirms Pevere's observation that Egoyan's films show that 'the more we yearn for authenticity, the more we seek artifice' (Pevere and Wise, 2004b: 64).

By the time David discovers that Raffi's film cans do indeed contain drugs, the long interrogation has convinced him that, despite his lies about shooting footage for a film that is already finished, Raffi was not unaware of their contents. He does not disillusion him and lets him go. David's story about what he has done then leads to the beginnings of a reconciliation with his own son. Like *Les Invasions barbares*, *Ararat* thus ends on a note of tentative hope that is inevitably ambiguous but that affirms the importance of the 'personal', while fully acknowledging the way personal experience is shaped by public discourses and by the complex interweaving of images and fictions that we take for reality. Perhaps what makes these auteurs Canadian emerges in the tension between the public and the personal.

Possible Worlds: Diasporic Cinema in Canada

Diaspora as a concept . . . offers new
possibilities for understanding identity,
not as something inevitably determined
by place or nationality.

—Paul Gilroy (1997: 304)

It is a coloured, métissé, polymorphous,
urban, and cosmopolitan Quebec in which
Alexis Tremblay, that Québécois of the mythic
stump, the star despite himself of Perrault's films,
appears today as the distant ancestor of another
society and perhaps even of another world.

—Nathalie Petrowski (de Blois, 2001: 27)

The discourses of national identity in Canada have traditionally focused on the tension between an English-Canadian identity crisis and a more secure Québécois identity frustrated by its lack of a national status. While both sides of this opposition are more complicated than they are often made to seem, its terms have come under increasing pressure from a growing awareness of the nation's ethnic diversity and from the associated idea of Canada as a multicultural state.

In 1971, Pierre Trudeau announced 'a policy of multiculturalism within a bilingual framework' based on the principle that, 'although there are two official languages, there is no official culture, nor does any ethnic group take precedence over any other' (Hodgins et al., 1974: 177). The policy was usually interpreted as encouraging immigrants to retain their own cultural traditions, as opposed to the idea of the 'melting pot' associated with the assimilation of immigrants into mainstream culture in the United States. However, its official and unofficial effects were often highly controversial. Despite the premise that there was 'no official culture', the policy generated a large bureaucratic apparatus, and there was a concern that it encouraged the preservation of ethnic cultures in museum conditions, ignoring new developments within the home cultures. It also seemed to imply that the immigrant and the host culture had no effect on each other, but, despite these deficiencies, official multiculturalism did help to open up and to complicate the ongoing debate on national identity.

The films produced by the NFB to promote the official policy also came under attack on similar grounds. These were often 'docudramas', such as John N. Smith's *Sitting in Limbo* (1985) and *Train of Dreams* (1987), depicting the problems faced by immigrants in a sympathetic light but, according to their critics, tending to reinforce ingrained stereotypes and to represent immigrants precisely as a 'problem'. Cameron Bailey has described these kinds of film as a 'cinema of duty' that perpetuated the established 'framework of centre and margin, white and non-white communities' (1992: 38).

For these reasons, the idea of 'multiculturalism' has given way in much recent discussion of migrant cultures to that of 'diaspora'. Originally a term used to describe the dispersal of the Jewish people and then applied to the transportation of Africans to North America as slaves, it is now used by theorists, including Paul Gilroy, more generally to refer to 'the "scattering" of peoples, whether as the result of war, oppression, poverty, enslavement or the search for better economic and social opportunities, with the inevitable opening of their culture to new influences and pressures' (1997: 304).

The diasporic experience thus results in the emergence of hybrid identities rather than the coexistence of distinct cultural identities, as envisaged by official multiculturalism. Hybridity involves its own pressures and negotiations but provides an alternative to complete assimilation, on the one hand, and a fundamentalist adherence to old cultural forms, on the other. It also offers new possibilities for members of the host culture, especially for younger people, and the effects are likely to be felt most intensely and complexly in a relatively new country that is uncertain of its own values.

As Gilroy points out, the diasporic effect is not just a matter of the physical movement of peoples but also of media technologies that circulate images from one culture into another. He argues that 'technological acceleration, arising from digital processing and computer-mediated communications, means that individual identity is no longer limited to forms of immediate physical presence established by the body' (1997: 314). The elimination of the need for physical presence produces a kind of temporal diaspora in which messages and images from different historical sources are recycled and combined in contemporary culture. Such practices encourage us to think of identity not primarily as a genetic inheritance but as a construction or performance drawing on the resources offered by our contemporary media environment.

In this context, diasporic experience is highly ambivalent and unsettles traditional notions of identity not only within migrant communities but also for all those open to the possibilities. This is not to imply that all such experiences are equal: clearly, there are more pressures on people from outside the home culture, especially for those who belong to visible minorities. However, the unsettling effect extends well beyond the racial and ethnic issues that are its primary reference and resonates with, for example, the contemporary questioning of traditional ideas of gender relations and sexual orientation. Accordingly, the films produced by members of the Canadian diasporic communities are often organized around three *interrelated* themes: the literal experience of diaspora, the impact of new media technologies, and the effects of both on bodily experience.

Where Is Home?

During the 1990s, English-Canadian cinema was enriched, and complicated, by the work of young filmmakers from the diasporic communities that had established themselves in many cities, most notably Toronto and Vancouver. In films such as Srinivas Krishna's *Masala* (1991), Mina Shum's *Double Happiness* (1994), and Clement Virgo's *Rude* (1995), the characters must negotiate between the cultural traditions of their original communities and the demands of life in a new country that is uncertain of its own values. The balance of sympathies between old and new is different in each film, but all involve not only a sense of the problems but also an attempt to develop new cinematic pleasures that would correspond to cultural identities that are both hybrid and provisional.

Each of these films disturbs the flow of its narrative with devices that call attention to the process of representing the diasporic experience. In *Masala*, the main such device is the musical numbers, in the style of popular Indian cinema, that interrupt the narrative and express the characters' fantasies. Another is the casting of the actor Saeed Jaffrey in three different roles: Lallu Bhai, a wealthy sari merchant; his brother Tikkoo, who earns a modest living as a mailman; and the god Krishna. In the latter role, he first appears on the in-flight movie screen of an Air India jet just before it blows up, after which he is mainly seen on a video, through which he communicates with Tikkoo's mother (Zohra Sehgal).[1] She persuades him to help Tikkoo, and he does so by arranging a series of coincidences that leave the mailman in possession of an extremely rare Canadian stamp.

As the whimsical appearance of the god on the doomed airliner suggests, the film also unsettles the spectator by the rapid shifts of tone between its serious and playful components. The plot centres on Krishna (named after the god and played by the director himself), a young rebel who missed the flight on which his parents and brother died, but the film embeds this plot in what Christopher Gittings aptly calls a rich array of 'ironized samplings from a diverse field of cultural texts' (2002: 246). It is a *masala*, which in Indian cookery is a mixture of 'a bunch of different things to create a taste that doesn't exist in any one of the things' (Krishna, quoted in Bailey, 1992: 47), and the film constantly undermines those cultural forces that seek to fix things and keep them separate. It uses stereotypes but repeatedly undermines them; it pokes fun at official multiculturalism and the idea of the nation that it serves.

The pompous Minister of Multiculturalism (Les Porter) tells an audience of wealthy Indo-Canadians that Canada is 'a home large enough for all faiths, all communities and all individuals'. In the middle of his speech, he is disturbed by the arrival of Krishna, the disaffected nephew of Lallu Bhai, in whose home the gathering is taking place. Just released from prison, Krishna is clearly not at home in these surroundings, although his uncle does reluctantly agree to let him stay. The luxurious modern house reveals the material benefits to those who play along with official multiculturalism but also exposes the emptiness of their claim to be preserving their traditional culture. At the end of the film, Krishna is stabbed by a white racist, but the effect of his death is undercut by the final sequence, the ironic resolution of the dispute caused by Tikkoo's obstinate refusal to give up his stamp: the Minister of Multiculturalism presides over another ceremony opening the Canadian Museum of Philately, with Tikkoo as its first director.

Several reviewers complained that it was difficult to identify with the main character, and, from within the Indo-Canadian community, Yasmin Jiwani accused the film of being 'a masala that combined the ingredients of an internalized racism mixed with a postmodernist discourse of identity, sexuality and race' (Waugh, 2002: 265). However, the disorienting formal effects work to implicate the spectator in the diasporic situation and to address the loss of feeling often associated with the post-modern condition. Krishna is disturbed at not being able to feel anything about the deaths of his family, although the many aircraft that appear in the film frequently remind him of the disaster. After Krishna's death, he 'sees' yet another plane flying over, and then Rita (Sakina Jaffrey), Tikkoo's daughter, with whom he has become involved, expresses guilt that she can feel nothing about his death.

Krishna revealed his own 'postmodern' stance by suggesting that 'to think that we can tell stories that make sense is a lie about the world' (Bailey, 1992: 45), but this is also a refusal of the fundamentalist assertion of fixed and absolute meanings. As Imre Szeman points out, however, the film does try 'to make sense of the hybridity of its characters in the context of their place in the first "officially" multicultural society', and its formal structure opens up the utopian possibility that 'the confusion of space and time, such as in the patterns of flight undertaken by immigrant communities', will produce a new acceptance of hybrid and unofficial forms of identity (1994: 14, 17).[2]

In *Double Happiness*, the device that most overtly breaks the narrative flow is direct address to the camera. The film begins with Jade (Sandra Oh) holding a clapperboard and describing her family, and later her parents and sister also describe their feelings to the camera. As Jade points out, her family is not quite the Brady Bunch, but her allusion invites us to consider the similarities as well as the differences. Mina Shum says that she hoped her film would 'transcend cultural barriers' because 'the difficulty of leaving home is something everyone has gone through' (Banning, 1999: 291). The film superimposes this map of common experience onto the diasporic one of not knowing where home is, and Jade's narration and her ingratiating personality make it much easier to identify with her than with Krishna in *Masala*.

The main emphasis is on Jade's strategies to thwart her parents' attempts to find an eligible Chinese male for her to marry. Her father (Stephen Chang) insists that his children follow Chinese traditions, and he has already disowned her older brother. For the most part, however, the tone remains comic, as when Jade discovers that one of the suitors recommended by her parents is gay. Her need to conceal her affair with Mark (Callum Keith Rennie), an insecure white Canadian youth, also generates several amusingly awkward situations.

As Edward O'Neill suggests, 'whatever questions about cultural identity Shum's film poses are played out as questions about sex and marriage' (1997: 54–5), but this is a common feature of Canadian diasporic cinema. The emergent hybrid cultural forms not only unsettle traditional notions of ethnic and national identity but also create situations in which, as Thomas Waugh says of *Masala*, 'gender and sexuality are troubled and in flux' (2002: 264).

Jade's ability to cope with the demands of her family is related to her ambitions as an actress. When she rehearses in her room, she loses her real-life self in the part and appears in costume amid appropriate sets. She repeatedly has to snap out of these performances to resume her domestic duties, much as mundane reality interrupts Polly's fantasies in *I've Heard the Mermaids Singing* (see Chapter 8). Her aspirations also conflict with the limited roles available to Chinese Canadians: when she auditions for a small role as a waitress in a television show, she is asked to speak with an accent and tries a French accent, before realizing that what is wanted is a stereotypical Chinese one. Despite the constraints, however, Jade enjoys role-playing and turning stereotypes against themselves. Just as in *Masala*, according to Lysandra Woods, 'stereotypes send up identity as performative rather than essential' (2002: 213), so O'Neill argues that, in *Double Happiness*, 'identity is figured not only as a performance, but as a strategic one' (1997: 58).

In *Rude* the ideas of hybrid identities and role-playing are complicated by the film's Rastafarian imagery. The main device that disrupts the narrative flow is the pirate radio broadcasts of the title character (Sharon M. Lewis) during an Easter weekend. However, Rude's poetic monologues do not so much interrupt the narrative as engender the three stories that interweave but never connect, three examples of what she calls the 'ten million Nubian tales in the Projects'. She functions much like a voice-of-God commentator, even though she is visible (but mainly hidden in the shadows of her studio), female, and black. Her authority is contested by the voice of a police officer who calls to say that he will close her station down, but she claims to represent the 'disenfranchised diasporic voice' and identifies herself with 'the conquering lion of Judah' (which is periodically seen prowling through the spaces of the stories).

Rude does not narrate these stories but rather provides a poetic monologue that brings out the underlying meanings that link them. In the most fully developed story, Luke (Maurice Dean Wint) returns home from prison to find that his wife (Melanie Nichols-King) has become a police officer and that he must rebuild his relationship with his young son. His place as the boy's father has been taken by his brother Reece (Clark Johnson), who has also replaced him as a drug dealer for a gangster called Yankee (Stephen Shellen), so that Luke struggles, also, to avoid being pulled back into a life of crime. In a second story, Maxine (Rachael Crawford) lives in an empty apartment after the departure of her boyfriend and is troubled by the voyeuristic videos he made of her and by her visions of the daughter she did not have because of an abortion. The third story focuses on Jordan (Richard Chevolleau), a boxer who joins his friends in beating up a gay man but then must come to terms with the realization of his own gay desires.

Rude has been described as 'a trickster figure', a term that links her to First Nations legends (Gittings, 2002: 257), and she indeed refers to the 'Ojibway sacred soil' on which African Canadians must live out their struggles. In her 'SOS from the land of the Mohawk and the Ojibway', Native spirituality is coupled with Rastafarianism to commemorate a shared experience of oppression and to suggest a possible source of renewal. The same connection is made on the mural that Luke paints on a wall in the neighbourhood, which remarkably remains undefiled while he is in prison, and in front of which the film reaches its violent climax when his wife shoots Yankee, who is holding their son hostage.

This final confrontation, like many other moments in the film, evokes the "hood movies' of popular American cinema, while the reggae and gospel music, with which Rude's voice shares the soundtrack, grounds the film in black cultural forms that have become part of contemporary youth culture. Set in a city that is actually Toronto but which Rude calls Babylon, and in a neighbourhood that looks like the New York projects of the 'hood movies, the film received some criticism for not addressing the specifics of African-Canadian experience. The most outspoken critic was Rinaldo Walcott, who, as summarized by Erin Manning, 'argues that the politics of place are not adequately addressed in *Rude*, and thus the politics of blackness in Canada are not theorized' (2003: 69).

This kind of argument, like Jiwani's critique of *Masala*, tends to impose what Kobena Mercer calls a 'burden of representation' on the diasporic filmmaker, who is expected to speak for the entire community, whose interests are rarely addressed in films (1994: 81).[3] From a rather different perspective, John McCullough takes Virgo to task, partly because *Rude* does not measure up to 'the standards of realism' but also because it fails to use its distancing devices in the political manner of Bertolt Brecht and remains 'wholly mute on the concept of revolution' (1999: 23). It is certainly true that the diasporic films discussed here do not seek to destroy the spectator's pleasure in the film, in the spirit of certain avant-garde and political critiques of popular cinema, but rather they set out to produce new hybrid forms of pleasure that have a broad appeal for audiences from different cultural backgrounds.

These diasporic voices have unquestionably made a major difference to English-Canadian cinema, and there are many more films than the three I have discussed here.[4] One problem is that critics tend to ghettoize the filmmakers by assuming that they will make only films dealing with the diasporic groups to which they belong. Thus Deepa Mehta's first feature, *Sam and Me* (1990), a comedy about the friendship between an Indian immigrant (Ranjit Chowdrey) and the elderly Hungarian Jew (Peter Boretski) he is hired to care for, received a generally positive response. *Camilla* (1994), her second film, also dealt with an unlikely friendship, but this time it involved two white characters—a young woman (Bridget Fonda) and an eccentric old lady (Jessica Tandy)—travelling from Georgia to Toronto. The stars were American, yet the screenplay was a typically quirky story by Canadian writer Paul Quarrington. It even included cameos by Chowdrey as an unlikely southern sheriff and Graham Greene as a smooth con man, but the critics seemed to think that Mehta was out of her depth. One recent writer even claims that she directed the film in Hollywood (Melnyk, 2004: 178).[5]

Quebec: Métissage and the Politics of Identity

The situation in Quebec is rather different. Although there are many diasporic communities, mainly in the Montreal area, they have had less of an impact on film production. Since Quebec has a much stronger sense of a collective identity, it is more difficult to develop and express the kind of hybrid identities that have developed in Toronto and Vancouver. Such identities are found in the films of Robert Lepage (see Chapter 12), and he deplores the extent to which 'mistrust of the foreigner is engrained in the Quebec identity' (Coulombe, 1995a: 23). The ideology of *conservation* (see Chapter 3) stressed an idea of 'home' based on a deep suspicion of outside influences, and a long literary tradition depicts close-knit communities disturbed by the arrival of an 'outlander', to use the title of the English translation of Germaine Guèvremont's novel *Le Survenant* (1945).

Such encounters occur in several of the Quebec feature films of the 1940s (see Chapter 3), most notably in *Le Gros Bill* (René Delacroix, 1949). The outsider is Bill Fortin (Yves Henry), who arrives, from Texas, in a small Quebec village. The effect is initially comic: 'western' music accompanies his train as it pulls into the snowbound station, and he must overcome problems of communication because he speaks no French. He becomes an outcast when Alphonse (Maurice Gauvin) and other village youths, who resent the handsome Texan for attracting their girlfriends, frame him as a thief. By rescuing Alphonse from the river after a logging accident, Bill redeems himself, and he is finally integrated into the community through his engagement to Clarina (Ginette Letondal), the one villager who can speak English.

Bill is not really a foreigner but the son of a villager who emigrated, and he returns because he has inherited his uncle's farm. The film speaks rather to the idea of *américanité* and the need to protect and define Quebec culture in relation to the powerful influence of 'America' (a term that often seems to encompass English Canada). Since the collectivity defines itself by its French linguistic and cultural roots, it must protect itself not only from outside influences but also from the presence of immigrants, especially those from non-French backgrounds.

While the Quiet Revolution opened Quebec to broader cultural influences, the rejection of the term 'French Canadian' in favour of 'Québécois' also encouraged a tendency to regard hyphenated categories of identity as a sign of weakness rather than of potential and complexity. The term often used to describe the new cultural forms emerging from the diasporic experience is *métissage*, previously used—mostly disparagingly—to describe the interbreeding of whites and Indians. It now may carry more positive connotations, but Marco de Blois has denounced it as 'a fashionable word' that conceals the true complexity of Quebec's cultural heritage (2001: 27).

Italian Canadians are the diasporic group most prominent in Quebec cinema, partly because their European background and Catholic heritage render them less different than is the case with other ethnic groups. Yet their growing numbers and cultural confidence are perceived as a threat to the survival of a strong francophone culture. As we have seen, the Italian presence is a key issue in Jean-Claude Lauzon's *Un Zoo la nuit* and *Léolo* (see Chapters 4 and 6, respectively), and the ending of Denys Arcand's *Jésus de Montréal* also generates tensions around this question. The donation of Daniel's heart to an American man and his eyes to an Italian woman, the film's parallel to Christ's resurrection, can be viewed as an ironic comment on the neglect of the fran-cophone majority or as a call for the Québécois to 'let go of their myth of the unitary, historical subject that is at the basis of their nationalism' (Alemany-Galway, 2002: 131).

The experience of the Italians in Quebec is addressed from within in the films of Paul Tana, who came to Quebec at the age of 11. His first feature, *Les Grands Enfants* (1979), initially seems like a genial version of Forcier's *Le Retour d'immaculée conception* (whose working title it appropriates), with its depiction of a group of young Montrealers seeking direction in their lives. Yet the film gradually opens up to encompass people from a wide variety of cultural backgrounds. The main character is François (Gilbert Sicotte), a Québécois who refers to his 'marginal existence' but wonders what it is marginal to. He thinks that his English-Canadian neighbour Gary (Bryan Doubt) represents the Quebec dream because he speaks French and lives in a French neighbourhood, but Gary insists that his grandmother was Polish and that, in any case, the neighbourhood is largely populated by Portuguese immigrants.

It is François's relationship with Jeanne (Julie Vincent) that offers a tentative possibility of resolving the alienation he feels and developing a new sense of Quebec culture. After he meets her in the home of one his friends, they slowly get to know each other, and she tells him that she came from Italy as a child and has been in Quebec for 19 years. She resents constantly being asked where she comes from, even though she has lost all trace of an accent and has adopted a French name (she was originally called Giovanna). However, she does not reject her background and takes François on a tour of the Italian district before they decide to live together.

In *Caffè Italia Montréal* (1985) and *La Sarrasine* (1992), both made in collaboration with the historian Bruno Ramirez, Tana explores the history of the Italian presence in

Quebec, thereby revising the 'official' history that portrays the Québécois identity as purely French. *La Sarrasine*, set at the beginning of the twentieth century, is a virtually bilingual film, in which the lives of a French-Canadian family and an Italian immigrant family become entangled in a series of cultural misunderstandings. These come to a climax when Giuseppe (Tony Nardi), an Italian tailor, tries to break up a brawl and kills the son-in-law of his friend Alphonse (Jean Lapointe). This catastrophe becomes the prelude to the story of the emerging independence of two women.

Through her struggle to get justice for her husband, Ninetta (Enrica Maria Modugno) resists the patriarchal restraints of traditional Sicilian culture and refuses to return 'home', even after he commits suicide in prison. At the same time, Félicité, (Johanne-Marie Tremblay), Alphonse's daughter, rejects the idea of retiring into widowhood under the dubious protection of a priest who denounces the effect on Quebec society of 'foreigners' who act as if they were 'at home', and instead takes over the family store in Montreal.

Since the film shows Ninetta learning to write under her husband's guidance and because her journal helps Félicité realize what they have in common, Bill Marshall argues that *La Sarrasine* fits into a liberal 'post-Quiet Revolution narrative' in which education is seen as way of promoting 'intercultural exchange' (2001: 281). However, while Ninetta does grow in confidence as a result of her new command of language, the main exchange that occurs is with a woman who recognizes the feeling expressed in a journal she cannot read. The final sequence, in which Ninetta visits Alphonse in his country home, shows her squatting to urinate beside a large tree in a snow-covered landscape, affirming her sense of belonging through an image that draws on the ties to the land in French-Canadian cultural traditions.

Another diasporic filmmaker in Quebec is Arto Paragamian, who is, like Atom Egoyan, of Armenian descent, and his films offer a similar 'cool, ironic perspective' on the culture in which he lives (Alioff, 2001b: 21). His two feature films to date, *Because Why* (1993) and *Two Thousand and None* (2000), were made in English, but he did participate in *Cosmos* (1996), a French-language project made up of episodes directed by a group of promising young filmmakers and put together by producer Roger Frappier. The title character is a Greek-Canadian cab driver, who sleeps in his cab and links the different stories in which all the main characters are white and francophone. Paragamian directed these linking sequences as well as the final episode, in which Cosmos and a black colleague pursue bank robbers who have stolen his cab.

There are other diasporic filmmakers in Quebec, and they are likely to become an increasing factor in the future. So far, however, the impact of the new cultural diversity has been explored mainly in films by Québécois directors, such as Gilles Carle's *Pudding chômeur* (see Chapter 5). *L'Ange de goudron* (Denis Chouinard, 2001) interweaves a thriller plot involving terrorism with the efforts of an Algerian immigrant to obtain Canadian citizenship for his family. The Italian presence is still the most acknowledged and becomes the source of broad comedy in *Mambo Italiano* (Émile Gaudreault, 2003) when an Italian-Canadian family tries to cope with the discovery that their son is gay.

New Worlds/Old Stories

The relativism and hybridity of postmodern, post-colonial societies are often expe-rienced as disorienting and destabilizing. A longing for old certainties has produced a resurgence of fundamentalism in many of the world's religions, which is itself a key aspect of postmodernism. Deepa Mehta came under attack from fundamentalist groups when she returned to India to make *Fire* (1997), the story of two oppressed women in a Hindu family who have a lesbian affair. Her depiction in *Earth* (1998) of the bloody events during the partition of India also provoked protests, and the production of an intended third film was halted by riots.[6] She returned to Canada to make *Bollywood/Hollywood* (2002), a film in which Canada becomes the slash between two dominant film traditions, an in-between location celebrated in the clumsy but enthusiastic imitation of a Bollywood musical number on the balcony of a high-rise building overlooking the city of Toronto.[7]

Another response to this precarious situation has been a renewed interest in the values and traditions of the people now known as Canada's First Nations. This interest in Native spirituality is, of course, not confined to Canada, and it has inspired large-budget co-productions, such as *Black Robe* (Bruce Beresford, 1991), *Shadow of the Wolf* (Jacques Dorfmann, 1992), *Kabloonak* (Claude Massot, 1992), and *Map of the Human Heart* (Vincent Ward, 1992). Ironically, these films are themselves hybrids: *Shadow of the Wolf*, for example, is an English-language production, directed by a Frenchman, based on *Agaguk*, a classic Quebec novel by Yves Thériault, starring American and Japanese actors as Inuit characters. Just as ironically, it proved to be a big hit in Quebec, dubbed into French, and a commercial failure everywhere else.

Rather more thoughtful treatments of Aboriginal characters appear in the films of Jean Pierre Lefebvre (see Chapter 7) and Gilles Carle (see Chapter 5), although Carle in particular tends to focus on the hybrid experience of the Métis people. These films, and many others, deconstruct the myth of the 'noble savage' to expose the hypocrisy of white society. The idea of Native people as victims of an internal diaspora has been developed in a few films that focus on life on the reservations, to which they have been assigned by the government but which also provide an environment that can protect the old traditions. Films such as Bruce McDonald's *Dance Me Outside* (1994) and Jack Darcus's *Silence* (1997) work against stereotypes but raise their own issues of authen-ticity and appropriation.[8] In the documentary field, the anthropological films of Arthur Lamothe, most notably the *Carcajou et le péril blanc* series (1971–7), offer a detailed account of the way of life of the Montagnais people in northern Quebec and an exploration of the impact of white culture and technology.

In Quebec, the issue of the treatment of Aboriginal peoples involves the need to relate their oppression to the idea of the Québécois themselves as victims of cultural oppression, a problem made thornier because most First Nations people use English as their second language and feel threatened by the prospect of an independent Quebec. The documentaries of Alanis Obomsawin, an Abenaki filmmaker at the NFB, have sought to give voice to the concerns of her people. In *Kanehsatake: 270 Years of*

Resistance (1993), she filmed behind the barricades throughout the Oka crisis, an armed confrontation in which Mohawks protested the expansion of a local golf course on their sacred land, and used the events to draw attention to a long history of exploitation.

Obomsawin came under attack for not being sufficiently objective (see Chapter 1). The CBC initially refused to show *Kanehsatake* without cuts, and many Quebec critics questioned the accuracy of her claims. Yet the use of her own voice dissociates her films from the kind of 'authority' implied by the conventional (white, male) voice-of-God commentator. As Jerry White suggests, the subjective voice contests the 'false objectivity' of the Griersonian tradition and, instead, has the effect of 'identifying whose eyes this is all seen through' (1999: 31). The result of this reflexivity is not to call into question all forms of authority; rather, it asserts the filmmaker's solidarity with her people, through what Zuzana Pick identifies as 'the storytelling tradition that is the cornerstone of First Nations' knowledge, culture, and history' (2003: 181).

The revival of an ancient storytelling tradition is central also to *Atanarjuat: The Fast Runner* (Zacharias Kunuk, 2000), the first feature film in the Inuktitut language. After falling foul of the Telefilm bureaucracy, which could only deal with major projects in English or French, the finished film won a major prize at Cannes and was acclaimed by critics in Canada and internationally. Kunuk, who began his career as a sculptor and sold his soapstone carvings to buy his first camera, was a founding member of the Igloolik Isuma co-operative that produced *Atanarjuat*. He had previously made numerous videos on Inuit life for broadcast by the Inuit Broadcasting Corporation.

The film opens with a long shot of a lone Inuit in the midst of a vast snow-covered landscape as sled dogs howl around him. This is an archetypal image of the Far North for non-Inuit audiences, who, as Kunuk himself points out, are usually unaware of the changes in the old way of life. This image is held on screen for almost a minute, and then, after we hear a voice saying, 'I can only sing this song to those who understand it', there is a cut to a dark, cramped interior, setting up the crucial contrast between inside and outside that shapes life in the North and the legend that will now be retold. There is no indication of a specific time period, and it only gradually becomes clear that the action is set in a timeless past appropriate to a legend that has apparently 'been passed down from generation to generation for four millennia' (Said, 2002: 22).

The filmmakers draw on the memories of elders who, as in all oral traditions, offered slightly different versions of the story, but the film was made possible only by digital video technology, which we see being used to shoot the film during the closing credits. By combining the traditional and the new in the production process, the filmmakers were seeking to reconcile the different forces that have shaped their lives. Kunuk thus regrets the loss of the nomadic ways of his people but also insists that the changes—the replacement of sleds by snowmobiles, for example—have not altered their fundamental values.

The legend chosen for the film involved the community in addressing the extent to which their lives had changed. As Kunuk explains, the story is 'about people who break taboos', but the filmmakers themselves had to confront the taboo introduced by Christianity against representing shamanic religious practices (Chun, 2002: 22–3). The film depicts a community divided as a result of the unjust actions of an evil shaman and the leader he supports. In this disordered world, Atanarjuat (Natar Unglaaq) himself breaks a taboo when he marries Atuat (Sylvia Ivalu) even though she has previously been betrothed to the chief's son Oki (Peter Henry Arnatsiaq). When Oki and his brothers ambush him on a hunting trip, Atanarjuat runs naked across the ice to escape and eventually returns to re-establish order.

The mythic struggle of good and evil is vividly embodied in the elemental images of the naked man racing across the vast barren landscape. This 'fight to the finish between the forces of continuity and those of destruction' attracted critics who saw its 'authentic emotion' as an antidote to the artifices of Hollywood cinema (Alioff, 2001a: 21). As one critic put it, the legend may take place in a world that is remote from the experience of most spectators, but 'the epic battle of vice and virtue makes perfect sense' (Melnyk, 2004: 261).

The difficulty of location shooting in the Arctic created a strong sense of 'authenticity' (a word that occurred in many reviews) and gave the film its power, as opposed to the Hollywood special effects that are another product of digital technology. The effect is clearly different for Inuit and non-Inuit audiences: for the former, the film reaffirms the reality of a past that is both distant and within living memory; other audiences respond to its elemental imagery, but the film also provoked discussion about its implications for Canadian cinema. In his *Globe and Mail* review, Rick Groen called it 'intriguingly exotic and uniquely Canadian' (Melnyk, 2004: 260). George Melnyk has even suggested that it offers 'the potential for recreating Canadian identity away from its Eurocentric heritage'—if the nation can embrace the 'internal foreignness' that it embodies (2004: 262-3). If this happens, it remains to be seen whether it will counter or reinforce the hybrid forms generated by Canada's diasporic cinema, which can hardly be called Eurocentric and often challenges the very notion of authenticity.

Stupid Films and Smart Films: Canadian Cinema Today

Let us encourage mediocrity and
recognize ourselves in this gallery of
coarse and stereotyped characters.

—Louis-Paul Rioux (1998: 45–6)

How does one act in a world where all is
gesture? How does one tell stories in a world
where all aesthetic and political strategies
are ultimately tired and predictable?

—Jeffrey Sconce (2002: 368–9)

In Canada as elsewhere, the national culture is often defined in opposition to popular culture. This opposition may be used to validate cultural standards seen as more worthwhile than the shoddy products of mass culture or it may be used to denigrate the national culture for failing to produce works that appeal to large audiences (see Chapter 5). Even in Quebec, where locally produced films sometimes outperform Hollywood blockbusters at the box office, the domestic share of the market reaches only about 10 per cent in a good year, and the films that succeed are usually ones about which many critics have strong reservations. Outside Quebec the box office for Canadian films falls to about 1 per cent, and the few films that do receive widespread release usually meet with strong critical resistance.

This situation has become more complicated in recent years because of the emergence of television and video as alternative forms of distribution. Yet, while Canadians now have more access than before to the products of the Canadian film industry, the viewing figures still show a clear preference for films produced elsewhere. In this chapter, I will focus on two different responses to the changing economics of film production in the global media marketplace. On the one hand, there is a growing emphasis on what André Loiselle calls 'stupid films', which are often extremely popular but excluded from the approved critical canons (1999: 75). On the other hand, the fragmentation of the traditional mass market and the blurring of the distinction between popular and art cinemas have led to what Jeffrey Sconce calls a 'shift in the strategies of contemporary "art cinema"' towards 'smart films' aimed mainly at youth audiences (2002: 350).

Boys and Girls: The Quebec Stupid Film

In a polemical article on Quebec cinema, Loiselle argues that critics have tended to focus on a canon of 'intelligent, socially-responsible, "artsy"' films rather than on the comedies and melodramas whose 'sheer popularity' provides evidence of 'how Francophone Canadians like to see themselves portrayed on screen' (1999: 75–6). He traces this tradition from the post-war melodramas (see Chapter 3) through the sex films of Denis Héroux and Claude Fournier (see Chapter 8) to the enormously popular broad comedies of the 1990s. These critically denigrated films largely account for the relatively strong box-office performance of Quebec cinema, but critics have generally ignored them or treated them as symptoms of the cultural oppression of the people who enjoy them.

Stupid films are certainly not a phenomenon unique to Quebec. Tear-jerking melodramas and vulgar comedies have long been a staple of Hollywood cinema, with the 'gross-out' teen comedies of the 1990s providing just one recent example. Stupid films are also far from absent in English-Canadian cinema, although they have rarely achieved the huge popularity of their Quebec counterparts. Yet there have been some significant commercial successes, most notably *Meatballs* and *Porky's* during the CCA period (see Chapter 3). More recently, *Duct Tape Forever* (Eric Till, 2001) and *Men with Brooms* (Paul Gross, 2002) used the appeal of popular television personalities (Red

Green and Gross, respectively) in an attempt to replicate the popular success of the Quebec films.[1] Most critics deplored these films, but in Quebec, where the nationalist cause has been built around the validation of a collective identity, the success of such films causes the most serious concerns.

As Loiselle points out, the major exception to the rule of critical disdain for this kind of cinema is a critical tradition drawing on the idea of 'carnival' in the work of the Russian theorist Mikhail Bakhtin. From this perspective, stupid films are a 'carnivalesque expression of popular culture's resistance against the ruling class' (1999: 80). Just as carnival inverted social hierarchies during a few days of licence and revelry, these works reverse and overturn such cultural values as good taste, physical beauty, social decorum, and respect for authority. In Quebec, according to Loiselle, the idea of 'subversion through laughter' has its origins in 'the old French-Canadian tradition of the burlesque' (78).

Much of the humour in the popular Quebec comedies is deliberately crude, with 'a visual emphasis on the body' and frequent allusions to bodily functions not usually mentioned in polite society or in mainstream films (Loiselle, 1999: 76). The analysis of these films becomes extremely difficult because, while their vulgarity is a challenge to established cultural norms, they also resolutely refuse to be 'politically correct', cheerfully embracing sexual, racial, and other stereotypes that have been exposed and condemned by cultural activists. Thus, although Loiselle uses these films to question the prevailing canons of film criticism, he can conclude only that they are somehow 'at once non-political and subversive, carnivalesque and conservative, progressive and sexist, liberating and alienating' (83).

The Quebec stupid film is epitomized by *Les Boys* (Louis Saïa, 1997), which proved so successful that it spawned—Hollywood fashion—two sequels (so far). It depicts a group of male misfits, played by comedians familiar to the Quebec public from film and television, whose amateur hockey team must defeat a stronger and more physical team if Stan (Rémy Girard), their manager, is not to lose his bar to Méo (Pierre Lebeau), a local gangster. The boys' victory in the climactic game thwarts the gangster's schemes, thanks to a penalty shot by Jean-Charles (Yvan Ponton), a lawyer whom the team has just learned is gay, and to a last-minute winning goal scored by Léopold (Michel Charette), Stan's overweight son.

The response of one Quebec critic illustrates the appeal of, as well as the critical contempt for, this kind of film. Louis-Paul Rioux asked, 'how could we not identify with these characters from our everyday world, a thousand miles from the inaccessible superstars of professional sport?' The question was intended sarcastically, and Rioux concluded that it all adds up to 'a stupid and insignificant entertainment' (1998: 45–6). As Loiselle points out, the utopian happy endings of this and other stupid films attract audiences because they are in marked contrast to the canonized Quebec films that 'systematically refuse to produce winners' (1999: 79).

Since English-Canadian films are equally associated with losers (or 'hosers'), the improbable triumph of the curling team at the end of *Men with Brooms* functions in much the same way. In both cases, the filmmakers came under attack for adopting Hollywood conventions, but it should be noted that the films fully exploit the loser stereotype before it is miraculously—and probably only temporarily—reversed in the final sequences. If this suggests a certain national distinctiveness, however, it should also be noted that many American teen comedies work in much the same way (albeit the final victory usually seems more conclusive).

At the opposite pole to the masculine universe of the *Les Boys* films are two films directed by Denise Filiatrault, *C't'à ton tour Laura Cadieux* (1998) and *Laura Cadieux . . . la suite* (1999). The first of these was 'freely adapted' from a novel by Michel Tremblay, and the same characters continue their adventures in the sequel. Both Tremblay and Filiatrault are 'immutable icons of Quebec culture', the former as a playwright and novelist depicting the lives of women and gays in the east end of Montreal, the latter as a stage, film, and television actress who appeared in many of Tremblay's plays, including his first big success, *Les Belles Soeurs*, in 1968 (Tousignant, 1999: 33). Laura is played by another icon, Ginette Reno, the pop singer who surprised her fans when she appeared as the fleshy mother in *Léolo* (see Chapter 6).

Tremblay's novel centres on a weight-loss clinic where a group of women (at one point in the film they are addressed as 'les girls') gather as they wait for their weekly injections. The film uses the same setting but opens it out to show Vovonne (Danielle Lorain) gambling at a casino and Madame Therrien (Pierrette Robitaille) searching the Montreal Metro system for Laura's young son, who is, in fact, not missing and whose name she does not know. Instead of the victory that provides the climax to *Les Boys*, Vovonne blows her winnings from the casino by taking the women to a Hawaiian restaurant where they forget their diets.

The film's appeal has much in common with that of the *Les Boys* films. In his review, Élie Castiel suggested it is 'like a large number of Quebec films, a film of transgressions: sex, swearing, references to a variety of bodily functions' in which the audience experiences 'a malign pleasure in seeing and, above all, hearing actors transgress the taboos that they themselves would never break' (1999: 48). Other critics felt that it failed to acknowledge the changes that had occurred since the 1970s, when the novel was written. In Montreal, 'multiculturalism is the face of the future', noted Isa Tousignant, before asking, 'where does "Laura Cadieux" fit in?' (1999: 33).

There were also complaints that the film simplified Tremblay's vision, summed up by Bill Marshall's comment that 'the ambiguities of Laura's narrative voice in the novel (for example, her popular appeal but also her racism) were lost in the film, particularly as she was played by the charismatic Ginette Reno' (2001: 206). However, the admittedly genial surface of the film is punctured by several moments that reveal the intolerance that is the other side of the community of women. As she travels to the clinic, Laura is shocked by the appearance of two punks on a Metro platform and wonders what their mothers must think of them (they, in turn, poke fun at her obesity). When she arrives, she turns and looks at a passing orthodox Jew and his son and then makes disparaging remarks about two Muslim women in the waiting room. When a nun enters, one of the women comments that the world is turned upside down when women wear veils (in the Muslim tradition) and nuns go out without them.

These moments may be somewhat anachronistic, but they do suggest a tension within the carnivalesque spirit in these films. Two critical responses nicely capture the double-edged quality of the film's humour. Louise Carrière argues that 'the theme of friendship runs beneath that of obesity', despite the many arguments and misunderstandings (1999: 31). For Isa Tousignant, what is hidden beneath the surface is much less benign: 'barely concealed under the film's main theme of obesity lie undercurrents of adultery, gambling, wife-beating and abounding prejudice against Jews, Arabs, gays, intellectual snobs and policemen' (1999: 33). The comic tone depends on the film's refusal, unlike its characters, to make judgements, and the utopian celebration of the final meal is not unmixed with a sense that the women must still cope with their obesity and a changing world they do not understand.

The celebratory meal at the end of the first film is picked up, at the beginning of the sequel, in another meal to celebrate Laura's birthday, where her friends give her a ticket for a cruise up the Saguenay River. As it turns out, the whole gang makes the trip, which culminates in a strenuous performance of the cancan at the farewell concert. The cruise functions here simultaneously as a carnivalesque release from everyday life that allows the women to satisfy their culinary and carnal appetites and as publicity for tourism in Quebec—the equivalent to the commercial sponsors that the *Les Boys* series proudly acknowledged. The mixture of carnival and commerce in these films is a major factor in their commercial appeal, but calculated to annoy defenders of auteur cinema like Roger Daudelin, who angrily dismisses 'the comedies of Madame Denise Filiatrault' as 'films without a filmmaker and without cinema' (2004: 16).

The *Les Boys* and *Laura Cadieux* films were not the first popular stupid films in Quebec. They built on the success of films such as *Ding et Dong le Film* (Michel Chartrand, 1990), based on characters established on stage by Claude Meunier and Serge Thériault, and *Louis 19, le roi des ondes* (Michel Poulette, 1994), a satire on reality television shows later remade in Hollywood as *EdTV* (Ron Howard, 1999). However, the questions generated by this phenomenon were posed in their most extreme form in a series of films involving a character called Elvis Gratton. He first appeared in a short film directed by Pierre Falardeau in 1981, which proved so popular that two more shorts followed, and the three were then edited together to create the feature-length *Elvis Gratton: Le King des Kings* (1985). Although Elvis died at the end of this film, Falardeau and actor Julien Poulin revived him in 1999 for a belated sequel, *Miracle à Memphis*, and then again in *Elvis Gratton XXX* (2004).

Falardeau is a director whose other work, in such films as *Le Party* (1990) and *Octobre* (1994), is serious and highly political, revealing a passionate commitment to the separatist cause. In principle, the figure of Elvis imitator Bob Gratton suits this political project admirably as a satiric embodiment of all the worst aspects of Quebec culture that result from its lack of autonomy. Thus when Bob wins a contest in the first film, his prize is a trip to Santa Banana, a Caribbean state that represents what Quebec will become if it accepts US cultural imperialism. Bob/Elvis illustrates the abject state of *métissage* that this imperialism entails. After he suffocates to death in an excessively tight Elvis suit, Bob's funeral procession is led by the flag of Santa Banana followed by the Stars and Stripes.

While Bob's racism and reactionary political views are the objects of satire, they are also the source of his carnivalesque energy and apparently why many in the audience identified with him. For Falardeau, the character was a response to the 'No' victory in the 1980 referendum and expressed his creators' 'immense disgust, a desire to vomit on all the Elvis Grattons' (de Blois and Racine, 1999: 10). From this perspective, these are not stupid films but quite the opposite: because 'people generally don't want to think anymore', Falardeau claims he set out 'to shake people, wake them up' (Wilson, 1986: 18). According to Marie-Claude Loiselle, he succeeded in creating films that are popular 'in the best sense of the term', because they address 'the "people" without fawning on or stupefying them', and she argues that Falardeau is simply responding to 'stupidity with derision' (de Blois and Racine, 1999: 4).

However, other critics raised questions about why the films were so popular with audiences who were the apparent targets of its satire. Thus Richard Martineau felt that, while 'the first episode undeniably constitutes a small masterpiece in itself, able to "politicize" our laughter and channel some of our frustrations and anger', the rest of the first film 'succeeds in identifying itself fully with its character and becomes the crucible of the crass idiocy it set out to denounce' (1986: 43–4). For Charles-Stéphane Roy, *Miracle à Memphis* was far from encouraging its viewers to wake up and rather asked them to 'leave their brains in the vestibule' (1999: 50). Jean Beaulieu even suggested that, 'if the majority of the people of Quebec identify with this colonized individual, it would be better to forget the very idea of independence' (1999: 31).

All of these critics agreed on the importance of the character and the phenomenon that he inspired. As Yves Rousseau suggests, Gratton is 'an authentically mythic character' (1999: 86), like Alexis Tremblay a few decades earlier, whose resonance was so powerful that he escaped from his creators' control. The problem is to account for the significance of an 'authentic myth' around a character who is the paradigm of inauthenticity. Perhaps the most balanced assessment comes from Pierre Barrette, who argues that 'Elvis Gratton was conceived as a . . . counter-model, like the fantasmatic concatenation of all the elements that work against the national emancipation of the people of Quebec' and that he is 'so seductive, even though he is detestable' because he represents contradictions that are 'the ordinary conditions of our state' (2004b: 38, 40).

After the first film, Falardeau insisted that 'it's not just Quebec, there's a kind of *global* apathy . . . no future, as the punks say' (Wilson, 1986: 18). Just over 10 years later, *Miracle à Memphis* affirms the global dimensions of stupidity and turns Gratton into an anti-artist in the spirit of punk. It begins with a montage of political leaders— Jean Chrétien, Bill Clinton, Boris Yeltsin, Jean Charest—doing things that make them appear stupid. After his resurrection at his funeral, Bob gains a reputation as a miracle worker and makes offensive remarks to the international journalists who interview him. He is signed up by a US promoter and is surrounded by well-endowed women, who also participate in his one grotesque production number. At an autograph signing to mark the publication of his memoirs, he makes jokes about his fans, including members of Quebec's multicultural communities and even a handicapped man.

The film is driven by an intense disgust with federalism and its supporters (like Bob), but as one reviewer remarked, it seems determined to make 'the characters who surround Gratton appear more stupid than he does' (Gravel, 1999: 32–3). Like punk, it becomes an essentially nihilist gesture whose refusal to be 'politically correct' seeks to expose the hypocrisy of the established order. The contradictions involved in this stand are acknowledged when, as the camera pulls back to reveal the cheering crowd at the book signing, the film suddenly grinds to a halt, and we see Falardeau and Poulin at an editing table discussing how they should end the film. They choose to do so with a farcical sequence in which Bob and his even stupider friend, Méo (Yves Trudel), try to erect a sign for the new Elvis Gratton theme park.

While the earlier Gratton films established the idea of exaggerating stereotypes for comic effect, paving the way for the later stupid films, the sequel refuses the indulgent mode of these films and subsequent successes, such as *Un Homme et son péché* (Charles Binamé, 2002) and *La Grande Séduction* (Jacques Pouliot, 2003). Its attempt to satirize stupidity involves adopting most of the elements of a stupid film, including product placements, which are satirized during Bob's performance but nevertheless exploited in the film itself. The Elvis Gratton phenomenon is, like much of contemporary popular culture, highly ambiguous, raising key questions about the possibility of satire in the postmodern media environment.

Death and Irony: Canadian Smart Films

Jeffrey Sconce defines 'smart cinema' as 'an American school of filmmaking that survives (and at times thrives) at the symbolic and material intersection of "Hollywood", the "indie" scene and the vestiges of what cinephiles used to call "art" films.' He opposes these films not to stupid films but to 'the "dumb" films of Jerry Bruckheimer, Michael Bay and James Cameron', in other words, Hollywood blockbusters. His extensive use of quotation marks testifies to the difficulty of taking these once clearly defined categories at face value, a feature that links his analysis to the phenomenon he is discussing, which 'sees everything . . . in giant quotation marks [but] still looks for art to equal sincerity, positivity, commitment, action and responsibility' (2002: 351, 358).

Sconce's long list of smart films includes one Canadian film, Atom Egoyan's *The Sweet Hereafter*, but the characteristics he attributes to this new school have much in common with those recent Canadian films that, according to Geoff Pevere, exhibit 'weirdness . . . of a strangely ordered, almost official, variety' (2002a: 101). The 'new smart cinema', Sconce argues, involves: a return to 'classical narrative strategies, instead experimenting with *tone* as a means of critiquing "bourgeois" taste and culture'; stories, 'no matter how sensationalistic, disturbing or bizarre', presented with 'a sense of *dampened affect*'; 'an overarching belief in the fundamentally random and yet strangely meaningful structure of reality (even if that "meaning" is total absurdity)'; and irony used not as 'a passive retreat from politics but a semiotic intervention within politics' (2002: 352, 359, 363, 369).

Whereas stupid films use the familiar commercial strategy of appealing to a mass audience, even if they define this audience primarily in terms of the Quebec or Canadian market, smart films exploit the emergence of 'niche' markets, but within a potentially global context. It should also be noted that smart cinema, with its often absurd and bizarre imagery, may circle round and join up with the stupid film. The gross images, stereotyped characters, grotesque bodies, implausible plots, and happy endings of the stupid film easily modulate into the unexpected images, eccentric characters, ordinary bodies, weird situations, and ironic endings of smart cinema. Films like *Scream* (Wes Craven, 1996) and *Shallow Hal* (Bobby and Peter Farrelly, 2001), for example, contain elements of both, and the divided response to the Elvis Gratton movies in Quebec may be attributed to the attempt to make smart films using the conventions and imagery of the stupid film.

Many of the films discussed elsewhere in this book might be categorized as smart cinema, Egoyan's for example (see Chapter 9). Although Sconce uses the term to describe a development within American independent cinema, his sense that these films deal with characters who are 'more acted upon than acting' (2002: 364) suggests that they move close to the territory with which Canadian cinema has been traditionally associated.

However, there are two important differences between Sconce's account of the American situation and Canadian smart films. One has to do with the audience. For Sconce, the smart films he discusses address the youth audience and, specifically, the admittedly unstable 'demographic category' known as 'Generation X' (2002: 355). The Canadian films are much less firmly directed towards youth, although some, including the films of Gary Burns (see Chapter 3), certainly are. They are, rather, products of the perennial Canadian dilemma of the lack of a national audience and become niche market films that must find or create their own niche. Perhaps related to this, the Canadian films tend to be a little less smart, in the sense that they want to hang on to a sense of the 'real', however difficult this may be in itself and especially in a culture saturated in 'hyper-real' media images (see Chapter 12).

This desire is basic to two films, *Kissed* (Lynne Stopkevich, 1996) and *Post Mortem* (Louis Bélanger, 1999), that fulfill Sconce's criterion of presenting sensationalistic material with 'dampened affect'. Both depict acts of necrophilia performed by characters whose everyday lives lack meaning and who are desperately anxious to feel something. Sandra (Molly Parker), in *Kissed*, becomes obsessed with dead animals as a child and, as an adult, takes a job in a funeral home where she has sex with male corpses. Ghislain (Gabriel Arcand), in *Post Mortem*, works as an attendant at a morgue, where he listens to mindless chatter on the radio and talks to the corpses, until he has sex with an apparently dead woman who suddenly revives during the act.

Although she begins an affair with Matt (Peter Outerbridge), Sandra finds the sex unsatisfying, and his initial fascination with her behaviour turns to frustration. He hangs himself, naked in front of her, because he thinks this will make her love him more, and the film ends with her making love to his body, accompanied by Sarah MacLachlan singing 'Fumbling Towards Ecstasy'. As Maurie Alioff suggests, 'Sandra's obsession is an extreme metaphor for any kind of human activity, from chanting to bondage, that aims at transcendence, but is deemed weird or dangerous by mainstream society' (1997: 15). The film's refusal to judge Sandra or to encourage intense emotional responses implicates the spectator in a world without moral norms or the capacity for strong feelings.

It begins with extreme close-ups of naked bodies, but we are too close to be sure what they represent; on the soundtrack, we hear Sandra describe the 'explosive' energy generated 'when life turns into death', but her voice is quiet and unemphatic. By the end, when we see Sandra making love to Matt after his suicide, we know what she means by 'crossing over', but her search for bliss (or transcendence), represented by white light, like the sublime experiences in *I've Heard the Mermaids Singing* (see Chapter 8), involves a disturbing and provocative entanglement of the physical and the spiritual.

The idea of a female necrophiliac also disturbs gender stereotypes and, in this respect, *Post Mortem* is more conventional. However, it is equally concerned to prevent easy moral judgements. Bélanger wanted to depict a situation in which it is 'very tough to draw the line between good and evil' and that raises questions about 'ourselves as a moral, ethical collectivity' (Glassman, 2000: 76–7). Whereas *Kissed* initially places us too close to the situation, *Post Mortem* holds back the necrophilia until the second of its three sections. The first sets up the difficulty of moral judgements through its depiction of Linda (Sylvie Moreau), a jobless single mother, who attacks and robs men to get money so that she and her daughter can move to the country. Her goal evokes traditional values from Quebec's past, but she gets angry with her mother for discussing religion when she babysits.

After she is beaten and left for dead by an American tourist whom she has attempted to rob, her body is taken to the morgue where Ghislain works. We see him impassively going through the admittance procedure, but we only learn about his violation of her body after his arrest. During his interrogation, flashbacks show what happened, and he is released when Linda drops the charges against him. When she resists his attempts to start a relationship, he explains that he wanted to 'join her in death', but instead it was she who 'made the journey'. The film ends a year later when she receives a letter from him, at her home in the country, in which he describes his new life caring for old people and expresses his hope that she is happy. They are both left silent and apparently thinking of each other.

The sexual encounters with dead bodies in *Kissed* and *Post Mortem* testify to an intense desire to make contact with the real in 'a world where all is gesture'. Although most Canadian smart films do not challenge taboos so directly, they often involve a crisis or trauma whose effects spread out to encompass otherwise disconnected people (with the example of Egoyan being an important factor here). They function very much like Sconce's 'random but strangely meaningful' events in a world that initially seems meaningless. In *The Five Senses* (Jeremy Podeswa, 1999), the catalyzing event is the disappearance of a young girl, while in *Maelström* (Denis Villeneuve, 1999) it is the accidental death of an old man in a car accident.

Podeswa's film is concerned less with the search for the missing girl than with interweaving the stories of characters who suffer from some form of sensory deprivation: a masseuse (Gabrielle Rose) who is out of touch with her daughter; an optometrist (Philippe Volter) who is going deaf; a woman (Mary Louise Parker) who makes decorative cakes that taste awful; a bisexual man (Daniel MacIvor) who revisits his former partners in search of the 'smell of love'. All of the characters are essentially in need of love, which they tentatively achieve by the end, as symbolized by the safe recovery of the child. According to Podeswa, the film is about the characters finding their way back to 'a more natural . . . place' (Goslawski, 1999: 21).

One reviewer complained that the characters are 'chilly ciphers' (Spencer, 2000: 50), but another enthused that the film is 'chilling in its emotional resonance' (Goslawski, 1999: 18). The key to this different effect—and affect—can be found in Barbara Goslawski's observation that the film is both 'deeply moving and intensely clever' (1999: 18). Its smartness is held in tension with its concern with natural desires and sensuous experience. In accord with Sconce's definition, tone becomes all-important: Podeswa has described his concern to balance 'a lot of different things tonally', and Daniel MacIvor, who was also credited as 'story editor', felt that the film captures 'a feeling or tone that exists inside human relationships' (Goslawski, 1999: 21, 20).

Maelström is also a film of rapidly shifting tones and a story of a character who finds a way back to nature. It is set in contemporary Montreal, but its narrator is a fish (or several fish) lying on a chopping block in a dark and archaic cellar. The opening caption is in Norwegian, and the score includes a cantata with lyrics in that language. After the fish promises to tell 'a very pretty story' there is a sudden cut to a graphic depiction of an abortion. As Bibiane (Marie-Josée Cruze) returns home from the clinic, the cheerful sounds of 'Good Morning Starshine' accompany her journey and shots of the disposal of the fetus. The fish calls her 'a young woman on a long voyage towards reality', a voyage that involves many encounters with fish, as well as the traumatic accident in which she kills an old fishmonger. He comes from Norway, and Bibiane eventually finds love with his son Evian (Jean-Nicolas Verrault). At the end, after they scatter his father's ashes on the sea off the Norwegian coast, the fish promises to reveal the secret of existence but can only say 'You are all . . . ' before the cleaver falls for the last time.

As Brenda Longfellow suggests, 'situating Norway as the site of the romantic sublime and archaic pre-modern can only be ironic given the absolute irrelevance of both to everyday life in a post-modern Québec', with the result that 'the fairy tale ending remains just that, an empty allegory' (2004: 77–8). Its emptiness—like the various 'smart' devices that lead up to it—both exposes and challenges the conditions that prevent the creation of more directly meaningful experiences. For Villeneuve, the fish functions as 'a kind of metaphor for all the storytellers from the beginning of mankind' (Amsden, 2001: 23–4), and the film thus seeks to make contact with the universal wisdom of ancient myths even as it depicts a culture losing its particular identity. The director memorably captured this tension, which underlies the whole phenomenon of smart cinema, when he said that he loves 'film that is simple and close to life, but when I write, I have a natural tendency to go in the fish direction' (24).

The appearance of fish in *Maelström*, and in three other films from the year 2000, inspired Geoff Pevere (2002a) to write a smart article called 'Fishy', about the trend towards weirdness in contemporary Canadian cinema. In more general terms, the film taps into a recurring motif in which water functions as a metaphor for the unconscious and the primal sources of life. Both Patricia Rozema's *When Night is Falling* (1995) and Léa Pool's *Emporte-moi* (1998) begin with shots of women underwater, and André Turpin's *Un Crabe dans la tête* (2001) opens with a deep-sea diver descending to dangerous depths and then depicts his problems coping with life on the surface.[2] There are many other examples, but I will deal here with two films by women directors in which the phenomenon of tides represents the realm of natural experience that lurks beneath the surface of smart cinema.

The intercutting during the credit sequence in *Black Swan* (Wendy Ord, 2001) makes it seem as if Helen (Melanie Doane) is dreaming of the black swan that, we will later learn, is the subject of a local legend. Apparently, it first appeared when Helen's mother was carried off by the powerful tides of the Bay of Fundy. Shot very quickly on digital video, the film is rather ragged, but much of its effect comes from its unusual use of intercutting and off-screen space. As Helen lies in bed, the editing moves rapidly between three actions, the robbery of a store, a speeding car, and two men clowning with a gun, but without making clear who is involved or how they are related to each other and to Helen. When Carl (Michael Riley) enters her room with a gun, he seems to be an intruder, but he turns out to be her boyfriend, and she warns him not to wake their (off-screen) daughter.

The complicated (and rather absurd) plot develops during the preparations for the Swan Festival in a fictional village (Hopeville) in New Brunswick, and the hectic events are intercut with sequences in which a young girl and boy set off along the shore to find her mother in Florida (which is where Helen was told her mother had gone after she was swept away). The girl's name is Ellie (Hannah Clayton), and she seems to be Helen's daughter, who is indeed reported missing later in the film, but her mission implies that she may be Helen as a child. After an encounter with a mysterious woman called Mara (Janet Monid), who is apparently associated with the swan and who rescues them from the tide, the children return home, and Ellie is identified as Helen's missing daughter, but her mother has just left for the city.

The memory of a woman swept away by the tides is also a key element in Manon Briand's rather more polished *La Turbulence des fluides* (2002).[3] In this film, Alice (Pascale Bussières), who works as a seismologist in Japan, is sent to investigate the sudden stopping of the tides in Baie Comeau, where she was born. She finds that many people in the town have been behaving strangely and meets Marc (Jean-Nicolas Verrault), a firefighting pilot, who is still grieving for his wife, whose body was never recovered from the river after a plane crash. The body is finally recovered, thanks to Alice's access to satellite surveillance systems, and Marc is relieved of his burden. When he and Alice make love on the exposed beach, the 'earth moves' not just as a metaphor for their passion but literally when an earthquake releases the tides. Alice, who cannot swim, is swept away but, unlike Marc's wife, she is rescued, and the gathered townsfolk watch the reunion of the couple.

Briand suggests that this ending 'opens up horizons' because, 'for the mystics, there is a solution that is very metaphoric and esoteric', but there is also enough to satisfy 'skeptics like myself, who need scientific explanations' (Castiel, 2002: 45). The film thus operates very much in the realm of the 'fantastic', in which it is impossible to decide between natural and supernatural explanations, and the affinities with Paul Almond's films (see Chapter 6) are underlined by the casting of Geneviève Bujold as a former nun who is now a waitress. A nun at the convent, which houses the seismic measuring equipment, tells Alice that people once believed the tides were God breathing. As a scientist, however, Alice's job is to discover if the stopping of the tides is a 'precursor phenomenon' that might help in the prediction of earthquakes, a hypothesis that apparently proves correct.

Another possible interpretation is provided by Catherine (Julie Gayet), a lesbian former schoolmate of Alice who is now a journalist covering the tidal anomaly. She explains the strange events by Jung's idea of 'synchronicity' whereby apparent coincidences have an underlying meaning, an idea also used by Sconce to describe the smart film's 'new realism of synchronicity' that finds meaning in apparently random events (2002: 363). Alice also encounters an old man who refers to the perception that the moon is larger when it is closer to the horizon and comments that we do not realize how much we are governed by our minds.

The idea that meaning is grounded in natural phenomena, but shaped by our perceptions, mediates between the scientific and religious outlooks and suggests that the ethics of the smart film involve a skepticism towards both forms of authority. If stupid films are simultaneously subversive and conservative, as Loiselle suggests, these smart films also contain elements of both but adopt an ironic stance that questions and complicates the terms of this opposition.

The Real and the Imaginary: Canadian Film in the Postmodern Condition

Identity is far too complex an issue
to be reduced to nationality.

—Andrew Higson (2000: 40)

What is the point, it may well be asked,
of making 'good' culture more widely available
or protecting it from the cold winds of the market
when it cannot be distinguished satisfactorily
from 'bad' culture?

—Jim McGuigan (1996: 30)

In this final chapter, I will discuss some contemporary Canadian films to bring out possible directions for the national cinema in a cultural environment shaped by global forces that have placed pressure on the ideas both of 'nation' and 'cinema'. I will use this discussion to lead into a return to the questions of value that I raised in the Introduction.

According to David L. Pike, in an article on 'Canadian Cinema in the Age of Globalization', the notorious problem of defining the national identity actually becomes an advantage in equipping Canadian filmmakers to negotiate 'a different relationship to the multi-national film production world'. They must do so, he continues, in 'a film market that no longer contains any easily delineated borders between commercial and non-commercial, Hollywood and non-Hollywood, affirmative and critical' (2001: 3, 6). The strategies they have adopted are highly varied, ranging from commercial genre films to experimentation with digital video, and some of these point to the dismantling of the borders between national cinemas.

Atom Egoyan's *Felicia's Journey* (1999), Patricia Rozema's *Mansfield Park* (1999), and David Cronenberg's *Spider* (2002) all were made in Britain, drawing on British film traditions while developing the visions of the directors' Canadian films. *The Red Violin* (1998) was a multinational production, set and shot in Italy, Austria, Britain, and China, as well as in Canada, with a Quebec director (François Girard) and an English-Canadian screenwriter (Don McKellar). Deepa Mehta has made several films in India, where she was born (see Chapter 10), while Sturla Gunnarsson, born in Iceland, also shot *Such a Long Journey* (1998) in India, based on a novel by Rohinton Mistry, a Canadian novelist born in India. While the extent to which these films, and other transnational or multinational films, can be considered as Canadian is debatable and probably different in each case, I will focus here on two directors whose films remain firmly within the national context but offer distinctive ways of articulating the local and the global.

Staging the Global and the Local: Robert Lepage and Bruce Sweeney

The debates about the relations between the local and the global in contemporary cultural theory recall, in many ways, the tension between cultural specificity and international appeal in the discourses about Canadian cinema (see Chapter 3). While Bruce Sweeney's films are resolutely local, in firm opposition to the Hollywood North productions that dominate the film industry in Vancouver where he works, Robert Lepage creates films that bring together Quebec's cultural traditions with perspectives that derive from other cultures. Their approaches are thus quite different, but both draw on a theatrical sense of performance to depict characters who must cope with what Jeffrey Sconce calls 'an inability to understand how one's tastes, gestures and actions "read" in the larger cultural field' (2002: 368).

Sweeney's three feature films—*Live Bait* (1995), *Dirty* (1997), and *Last Wedding* (2001)—show gradual increases in budget, scale, and production values, but all focus on groups of characters caught up in tangled relationships that eventually fall apart. In some ways, these films take us back to the 'realist' tradition of direct cinema films, with their emphasis on insecure and flawed young men, whose choices are shaped by the 'milieu' in which they live (see Chapter 2). Although most of the women in Sweeney's films are equally disturbed, the male perspective dominates, and there is no sign of the diasporic communities that have complicated questions of cultural identity since the direct cinema films.

Like the direct cinema filmmakers, Sweeney believes that a telling treatment of basic human problems and experiences will communicate with audiences elsewhere and that a sense of a specific local environment will enhance, rather then distract from, this appeal. In a review of *Dirty*, Jack Vermee notes that the filmmakers believe that 'mature cinema takes its "Canadianess" for granted', but he also insists that the film is 'profoundly West Coast in its attitude, the behaviour of the cast, even in its visual style' (1998: 33). The claim here is that the films are simultaneously universal, national, and regional and that the cinematic influences on Sweeney also combine the local and the international.

Live Bait, in which these influences are least fully assimilated, clearly owes much to Vancouver film pioneer Larry Kent (see Chapter 2) in its depiction of the constricting family life that drives Trevor (Tom Scholte) to leave home, a debt made even more apparent by the decision to shoot in black and white. Trevor's struggle to overcome his impotence with women his own age leads to a comedy of neurosis that derives from Woody Allen, especially in the smart remarks he uses to cover his anxiety. For example, when one potential girlfriend tells him that she has trouble ending relationships, Trevor dryly replies that he has trouble starting them. However, the deepest influence, and the one that enabled Sweeney to develop his own voice in his next films, comes from the British director Mike Leigh.

Sweeney attended a directing workshop with Leigh, who elaborates his films through a long period of rehearsals with his cast, out of which the final screenplay emerges. Working with a group of actors from the lively Vancouver theatre scene, Sweeney adapted this method to his own needs, using their personal experiences to develop situations that tend to be painful and absurd at the same time. As with Leigh's films, the rapid shifts in tone keep the spectator off balance, uncertain whether to identify with the often self-destructive characters or to find them ridiculous. In a comment that could apply to Leigh as well as to Sweeney, Tom Scholte points out that the films may appear 'misanthropic' but that, at their core, there is 'a tremendous compassion, because he sees everyone as basically a fool, and everyone is floundering in a way, and if they don't look like they're floundering, it's usually because they are putting up a good front' (Spaner, 2003: 160).

Live Bait resolves Trevor's dilemma when he makes love with Charlotte (Micki Maunsell), a much older conceptual artist, but in *Dirty*, David (Scholte again) has an intensely sexual and ultimately disastrous affair with Angela, another older woman (Babz Chula, who played his mother in the earlier film). Her lodger, Nancy (Nancy Sivak), declares bankruptcy because of her compulsive shopping habits, while his flatmate Tony (Benjamin Ratner) cannot understand why women do not respond to his clumsy advances. In this claustrophobic environment, the paths of all the characters come together in an explosive gathering at Angela's house that fully confirms Sweeney's claim that *Dirty* 'became very much about elemental, human, obsessive tendencies' (Spaner, 2003: 162).

Last Wedding similarly entwines the breakdown of three relationships. The men are close friends and, in an early sequence, they take a fishing trip, during which Noah (Ratner) announces that he is going to marry Zipporah (Frida Beltrani), with whom he has been living for the last six months. Although the others try to dissuade him as they sit in a hot tub beside a lake, the wedding takes place, and the couple quickly find that they cannot live together. Meanwhile, the relationship between Peter (Scholte), a college professor, and Leslie (Sivak) breaks down when he has sex with a student, and Shane (Vincent Gale), an architect, cannot cope when Sarah (Molly Parker) also qualifies as an architect and gets a much better job than his. It is not surprising that Vermee calls the film a 'treatise on contemporary male dysfunction' (2001: 9), but its tone is far from didactic. There is much black comedy as the complex narrative winds its way to the inevitable final shot of the three men sitting in stunned silence in the hot tub, oblivious to the natural beauty that surrounds them.

At the same time as Sweeney was making his inward-looking fables on the west coast, Robert Lepage was also translating theatrical methods into cinematic terms in Quebec. Although critics have often referred to his theatre work as 'cinematic' in its fluid juxtaposition of different times and places, it also retains 'a very theatrical spirit' (Perron, 1994: 48).[1] He has acknowledged Michel Tremblay's ritualistic plays about working-class Montreal as a major influence (see Chapter 11), but, while 'theatricality' is an important factor in his films, he echoes Sweeney when he cites 'the authenticity of his work as its main appeal to international audiences' (Dundjerovic, 2003: 10).

Lepage chooses to live in Quebec City rather than in the more cosmopolitan environment of Montreal, an apparently surprising decision for a filmmaker who firmly rejects the deep-rooted mistrust of the 'outsider' in Quebec culture (see Chapter 10). His first three films—*Le Confessionnal* (1995), *Le Polygraphe* (1996), and *Nô* (1998)— all use different cultures as a touchstone against which to measure the situation in Quebec. The characters are constantly on the move, and, as Erin Manning puts it, his films construct a vision of the nation as 'a place through which people travel and leave traces' (1998: 63). This vision does not involve a complete rejection of Quebec's cultural traditions, with their stress on remembering the past, but it does break with the idea of a pure national identity. While he notes that 'there's a generalised Alzheimer epidemic socially', this is not an invitation to nostalgia but a recognition that 'we have to be something else, we have to speak another language, accommodate new languages and new universal standards' (Dundjerovic, 2003: 154–5).

Time is of the essence in Lepage's films, although its operations often remain highly ambiguous. Whereas Sweeney's characters only make incidental references to their past and his films show no interest in placing them in a historical (or political) context, Lepage is very much concerned with the impact of the past on the present. However, because the past exists only in the memory or imagination, his films tend to combine the historical sensibility of Arcand with Egoyan's sense of subjective memories (see

Chapter 9). The idea of a past that is both oppressively present and disconcertingly absent is conveyed in a style in which long takes and tracking shots stress temporal duration, while sudden jumps in space and time suggest the fragmented experience of time associated with dreams but also with the postmodern media environment.

The importance of time (and place) to a sense of identity in Lepage's other films is underlined by the imprecision of *Possible Worlds* (2000), his one film to date made in English and not drawn from his own theatre work. Adapted from a play by John Mighton, it takes place in an unnamed imaginary setting and consists of a hybrid science-fiction/detective plot in which George (Tom McCamus) and Joyce (Tilda Swinton) meet in different, simultaneously existing worlds, with no awareness of their other lives. Their meetings may initially seem to be flashbacks, since George is found dead in the opening sequence, but the police discover that his brain is missing and has been kept alive by a scientist. The whole film is apparently imagined by this disembodied brain.

As the film constantly pulls the ground from under our feet, the characters slip between worlds defined primarily by the interests of big business and scientific research, in stylized contemporary settings that carry no markers of nationality. The different worlds show no evidence of cultural diversity, but the film creates an unsettling metaphor for a contemporary cultural situation in which, as Stuart Hall puts it, 'we are confronted by a bewildering, fleeting multiplicity of possible identities, any one of which we could identify with—at least temporarily' (1992: 277). It thus presents a postmodern version of Northrop Frye's 'obliterated environments' (see Chapter 3) in which increasingly homogenized spaces are inhabited by increasingly heterogeneous people, with the effect that the co-ordinates of location become detached from traditional national myths. Lepage's cinema responds both to the disorientation and to the possibilities inherent in this situation.

In his earlier films, the relations of space, time, and cultural identity are explored in terms of the pressures on Quebec culture. In *Le Confessionnal*, Pierre (Lothaire Bluteau) returns to Quebec City from China in 1989 to attend his father's funeral and tries to unravel the mystery of the identity of the real father of his adoptive brother Marc (Patrick Goyette). The investigation is intercut with the events leading up to Marc's birth in 1952, during the period that Alfred Hitchcock was shooting *I Confess*. In Hitchcock's film, a priest suspected of murder knows the identity of the real killer but cannot reveal what he heard in the confessional; similarly, a priest is a likely suspect when Rachel (Suzanne Clément) becomes pregnant. She is unmarried and lives with her sister Françoise (Marie Gignac) and brother-in-law Paul-Emile (François Papineau), who will soon become Pierre's parents. Rachel commits suicide after giving birth, but Pierre eventually discovers that Paul-Emile was also Marc's father.

Pierre is torn between investigating the past and trying to erase its influence on the present. He tries to paint the walls in the family home, but the marks left by the pictures that hung there keep showing through. As Christopher Gittings suggests, 'the wall, like Québec itself, is a palimpsestic text where the past intermingles with the present, structuring our understandings of both' (2002: 129). The film reinforces this idea by moving fluidly between the two periods, sometimes including both in a single shot. It also produces montage effects that yoke past and present together. Thus when the suicidal Rachel finds a razor in a bathroom cabinet in 1952, there is a cut to a red liquid running down a sink, which turns out to be paint used by Pierre in 1989. Johanne Larue nicely describes the effect when she notes that 'the flashbacks and the spatio-temporal slippages' suggest 'the indelibility of the past and its irremediable impact on the future' (1995: 29).

The implications of this strategy are rather ambivalent. Stylistically, Lepage sought to emphasize the difference between past and present by using different film stocks and filters (de Blois, 1995–6: 17). He stressed the changes in Quebec society depicted in the film: '1952, it is absolute respect for the church, but 1989, it is the absence of morality' (Caron, 1995: 29). Aleksandar Dundjerovic also describes the way in which 'the stability of the church is replaced with the 1989 instability of locations and transitional spaces, temporary places such as hotels, sleazy motels, and sauna clubs' (2003: 70).[2] For Larue, however, the film shows, despite appearances, 'how little Quebec has changed' (1995: 30). A key figure in this respect is Massicotte (Jean–Louis Millette), a diplomat and Marc's former lover who drives him to commit suicide (like his mother), and who turns out to be the defrocked priest once suspected of being his father. Is this character a sign of the decline of Quebec through its abandonment of its past values or a product of the repression on which those values depended?

A similar question also involves the relations between Lepage's film and *I Confess*, which we see in production and in extracts that further fragment the narrative. Some critics saw the relationship as one of critical opposition between a commercial thriller and an art film, but Lepage admires Hitchcock's evocative use of the Quebec City setting (Caron, 1995: 28). The two approaches are compared at the end of the film when Paul-Emile picks Hitchcock (Ron Burrage) up in his cab after the premiere of *I Confess* and tells him a 'suspense story' in which he reveals his own guilt with regard to Rachel. The story ends when the guilty man plucks out his eyes, and Hitchcock replies that it is not a suspense story but a 'Greek tragedy'. Yet the Oedipal self-punishment also refers back to Pierre's opening remarks in which he mentioned that his father went blind from diabetes (which Marc has inherited).

Lepage's film is more like a Greek tragedy than a suspense story, and this difference provides a way of understanding Quebec's contemporary situation. He explains that it deals with 'a small family unit in a small city in a small province with a small population', thus evoking 'incest, Oedipus' (Coulombe, 1995a: 22). The underlying vision rests on the paradox that, while Quebec owes its 'cultural survival' to its submission to 'the yoke of religion', it could become a modern society only by living out 'a real Greek tragedy' by killing the 'father' (Caron, 1995: 28).

This paradox may be tragic, but it is played for farce in *Nô*, in which Sophie (Anne-Marie Cadeaux) is an actress performing in an old-fashioned French farce that—absurdly—represents Canada at the 1970 World Expo in Osaka. At the same time, her boyfriend Michel (Alexis Martin) is involved in an FLQ plot that goes wrong when he uses a clock set to Japanese time as the bomb's timer. The film ends with an epilogue in which the couple watch the results of the 1980 referendum on television. Sophie suggests that the people who voted 'no' might have done so because they believe in Canada, but Michel replies that this is a 'sterile' idea that cannot be compared to the dynamic vision of Quebec that inspired the FLQ 10 years earlier.

According to George Melnyk, *Nô* shows that 'obviously Lepage preferred the "No" side', and the film appealed to 'the anti-sovereignty crowd and to anglophones because it made fun of separatism' (2004: 207). Rather, the ending offers a highly ambivalent image, in which the comfortable life into which the couple has settled is both attractive and a retreat, from the political activism of the past as well as from the broader cultural traditions to which Sophie was exposed in Japan.

In conjunction with *Le Confessionnal*, *Nô* also suggests that the difference between tragedy and farce is a matter of perspective. The shifting tones in Sweeney's films make a similar point in a much less self-conscious manner. Ironically, the English-Canadian filmmaker now seems closer to the approach of the NFB's French-language filmmakers, whose work Peter Harcourt (see Chapter 2) once described as lacking 'any reference to the larger world beyond Quebec', while Lepage seems closer to the out-ward-looking perspective he found in the Unit B films (1977a: 76). Forty years later, Canadian filmmakers are more assured and working in a wider range of genres and styles, but their films still have their roots in the uncertainties and contradictions that have shaped film in Canada throughout its history, a history that also demonstrates the close relations of tragedy and farce. These filmmakers, of course, represent only two options in the ongoing responses of Canadian cinema to the challenges of the global media marketplace, but both emphasize the need to balance an awareness of cultural traditions with an openess to change.

Body/Images: *Lulu* and *Emporte-moi*

In many Canadian films, including those of Atom Egoyan (see Chapter 9), there is a strong sense of disembodiment or bodies that cannot be contained in traditional frames of reference. This helps to explain the reputation for 'weird sex' that has grown up around Canadian cinema (see Chapter 8), often seen as out of keeping with the national 'psyche', but arguably the product of a culture whose uncertainties long prefigured the contemporary diasporic experience. These films do not simply celebrate or deplore the new media culture; rather, they ask us to think about spectatorship and the fusion of technology and subjectivity that characterizes the postmodern condition.

I will focus here on two films by directors discussed earlier in this book, *Lulu* (Srinivas Krishna, 1995) and *Emporte-moi* (Léa Pool, 1998). These films relate in uneasy, but often rewarding, ways to the cultural frameworks I have been discussing, and consequently raise important questions about defining and evaluating the national cinema. Krishna and Pool are both, to some degree, outsiders to the cultural contexts within which they work, and these films disrupt conventional patterns of response by drawing on the complex and varied intertextual associations that characterize post-modern culture. In Krishna's case, most critics proved reluctant to play the game and dismissed the film as 'bad'; Pool's film was better received, but it was not always clear how the generally positive evaluations related to its national origins.

Krishna claims that his work has nothing to do with Canadian film traditions, which he associates with documentary realism, but he also insists that 'that kind of nation-state way of dividing culture is irrelevant to my personal experience' (Bailey, 1992: 47). As we have seen, the satire in *Masala* blends Canadian iconography with Bollywood musical numbers, and the film attracted a good deal of attention because of its controversial depiction of the Indo-Canadian community and official multi-culturalism (see Chapter 10). *Lulu* received lukewarm reviews, obtained only a very limited theatrical release, and its commercial failure led to the demise of Krishna's production company.

In this respect, of course, it shared the fate of many Canadian films, and one of the reasons for its failure is its undeniably bleak depiction of multicultural and sexual relations. However, it works less as a realistic depiction of life in Toronto in the 1990s than as an allegory that builds on Stuart Hall's claim that the diasporic experience of decentring, dispersal, and fragmentation has become '*the* representative modern experience' (1993: 134). Whereas *Masala* focused on the cultural group to which Krishna himself belonged, the characters in *Lulu* come from a wide range of national and cultural backgrounds, suggesting that its failure might also derive from the sense that diasporic filmmakers should confine themselves to characters from their own communities.

The film is less concerned with the origins of the characters than with the impact on their lives of the media-saturated consumer society. It is rarely specific about where they come from: Lulu (Kim Lieu), whose real name is Khuyen, spent time in a refugee camp in Hong Kong, but she refers to the country from which she escaped only as 'back home'; another character is called Miguel (Manuel Aranguiz) in the final credits, and is apparently a refugee from Chile, but he refers only to his experiences in 'the country I come from'. The only one of the main characters who is white is Lulu's husband, Steven (Michael Rhoades), known to his friends as Lucky, ironically, because he is the stereotypical Canadian 'loser'. His best friend Clive (Clark Johnson) is a black Canadian who appears to be of Jamaican descent but whose mother is white, although again the film does not explain his background. The most explicit biographical information is provided by an Asian businessman, played by Saeed Jaffrey, who poses as a philanthropist but actually trades in illegal shipments of meat, and who describes his expulsion from Uganda by Idi Amin at some length.

The film's setting is obviously Toronto, but neither the city nor the country is ever named.[3] At one point, Lucky says, with some understatement, that he lives in a 'mixed neighbourhood'. Names are less important than images in this film, and Lulu's name is a way of making her conform to Lucky's image of her. But this is also an image that comes from the cultural memory bank. Although Clive says that it makes her sound like someone's pet, Lulu is the name of the alluring *femme fatale* figure in two plays by Franz Wedekind, an opera by Alban Berg, and the 1928 German silent film *Pandora's Box*, directed by G.W. Pabst. Krishna's Lulu wears her hair in an approximation of the style made famous by Louise Brooks, the American actress, who starred in Pabst's film as the showgirl who destroys all the men who are attracted to her.

In both films, the expressionless faces of the women make it difficult to understand their motives. The blurb on the Web site for *Lulu* emphasized the resemblance to the earlier film: 'To the men in her life, Lulu's beauty hides a complex and mysterious woman . . . . The film gradually unravels Lulu's mystery and exposes the desires and emotional hunger that, ultimately, bind the three men in Lulu's life.' It is described as 'a poignant film about the secrets and masks behind which lives are hidden'.[4] This may be an adequate description of *Pandora's Box*, but the disturbing point in *Lulu* is that there is no truth behind the mask. As in Atom Egoyan's films, it is the surface that is important; Lulu's body and her image have meaning only in the way people (including herself) look at her.

The film begins with an image of snow falling that presumably establishes the setting as Canada. As the credits begin to appear, the camera moves from the cold outside to the warm inside of a department store, where it looks down on Lulu working at the perfume counter. At first, this seems to be a conventional establishing shot, but then the image goes out of focus, and people walk in front of the woman who seems to be the object of the camera's gaze. These effects suggest a documentary look and, when the image freezes with a line across the screen, we realize that it is video image, and we may now assume that it is taken from a surveillance camera in the store.

Video images figure prominently in the film (again suggesting its affinities with Egoyan). The opening shot turns out be taken from a camera belonging to Miguel, who is making a television documentary about refugees; Lulu watches a music video with images from the Vietnam War on a bank of televisions in the store; Lucky has discovered Lulu through a video made in the refugee camp by a 'matrimonial service'. Miguel's documentary aims to capture the truth about the experience of refugees, but his claims to objectivity are undercut by his evident attraction to Lulu, and his images thus cannot be completely distinguished from the commercial exploitation of suffering in the music video or the use of video to sell Lulu to a Western husband.

The first post-credit sequence takes place in an old people's home, where Lulu visits her parents. Her father complains that they are treated like animals prepared for slaughter, and his opening words (subtitled in this English-Canadian film), introduce a concern with the breakdown of boundaries between the human, the animal, and the technological.[5] We later find that the warehouse used for the stolen meat is next door to a business that pays people to donate their bodies for medical research after they die. Clive gets a job with this company, and sells his own mother's body after he finds her dead in her apartment. When Lulu's father dies, she finds that her parents have signed a contract with this company. The film thus depicts a culture that turns bodies, on the one hand, into images and, on the other, into meat.

Emporte-moi offers a rather more optimistic take on image-making as a means of coming to terms with the diasporic experience. It is certainly a more accessible film than *Lulu* or Pool's earlier films (see Chapter 8). A Canadian–Swiss–French co-production, it can be appreciated as a nostalgic autobiographical film about a young woman's coming of age and transfers Pool's memories of her childhood in the 1960s from Switzerland, where she grew up, to Quebec where she now lives. She wrote the screenplay with Nancy Huston, a writer from Alberta who lives in Paris and writes in French, and who appears in the film as a teacher.

The theme of 'exile' figures prominently in Pool's films, but they have been more readily accepted as products of Québécois culture than Krishna's work in the English-

Canadian context. This may seem surprising, given the rather limited role of diasporic filmmakers in Quebec cinema (see Chapter 10) and may be largely explained by her francophone Swiss background. Yet it is also likely that her uprooted characters resonate with how the diasporic experience mirrors the feelings of many in Quebec of not being 'at home' in one's own culture. Her earlier films expressed this sense of homelessness through a highly poetic style in which the characters drift through environments that seem strange and unreal, but *Emporte-moi* seems to be more grounded through its apparent adoption of the narrative and stylistic qualities of European 'art cinema'.

The film begins in the countryside where Hanna (Karine Vanasse) is on vacation with her grandparents. In this traditional French-Canadian setting, she has her first period and discovers both the practical approach to the body and the inhibition about discussing it that characterize rural Catholic culture. When she returns to her family in the city, she confronts a more confusing world in which she feels out of place. Her father (Miki Manojlovic) is Jewish and her mother (Pascale Bussières) Catholic, while her friends listen to the pop music of the new youth culture, much of it emanating from the US. The city is explicitly identified as Montreal, but there is no reference to the political debates about language and culture that accompanied the 'Quiet Revolution' in Quebec during the 1960s.

Hanna resists the demands of her overbearing father, a struggling poet, and tries to make contact with her mother, who suffers from some kind of wasting disease, either caused or worsened by the long hours she puts in at a garment factory and typing her husband's poems. Her father tries to interest her in the Jewish heritage by giving her a copy of *The Diary of Anne Frank*, but Hanna finds her own role model when she sees Anna Karina in Jean-Luc Godard's *Vivre sa vie* (1962). The image of Karina, the Danish-born actress who was Godard's wife at the time, fascinates Hanna, and inserted shots from the earlier film are interspersed throughout *Emporte-moi* (compare the insertion of shots from *I Confess* in *Le Confessionnal*).

The 'art cinema' characteristics of Pool's film can thus be seen as homage to Godard, but the allusions to *Vivre sa vie* set up an intertextual dynamic that functions much like the one in *Lulu*. Karina's character is called Nana, a name, like Lulu, that has cultural associations with prostitution. In this case, the allusion is to the title character in *Nana* (1880), a novel by Emile Zola, which also is about a showgirl who destroys the men she attracts.[6] In the narrative of Godard's film, Nana becomes a prostitute but, instead of destroying men, she loses control over her own life. Hanna is, in any case, attracted less by the story or the character than by the actress as an image of energy and potential freedom, an image that functions in much the same way in *Le Chat dans le sac* when Barbara poses next to a still of Anna/Nana on a magazine cover (see Chapter 2). Whereas Gilles Groulx places this image in the context of the cultural exploitation of women, Hanna's pleasure in looking at the screen image leads to her tentative exploration of her own uncertain sexual desires.

The sequence in which Hanna sees *Vivre sa vie* echoes Nana's visit to a cinema where she is moved to tears by *La Passion de Jeanne d'Arc* (1928), the silent film directed in France by the Danish filmmaker Carl Dreyer. Although this sequence from *Vivre sa vie* is not included in *Emporte-moi*, there is an allusion to Dreyer's film when Hanna's father insists on having her hair cut short, re-enacting the famous sequence in which Jeanne's hair is cut before her execution. Ironically, although the father is apparently trying to control his daughter's sexuality, the haircut makes her look more like Nana/Anna. As an added irony, it is Hanna's teacher (or Nancy Huston) who looks more like Anna Karina, and Hanna's attraction to the actress may be a sublimation of her feelings for the teacher.

The French film and the pop songs on the soundtrack provide a framework within which Hanna tries out different possible identities. When Hanna runs away from home, the song 'Runaround Sue', by Dion and the Belmonts, begins softly on the radio in the truck of a man who drives away and abandons his dog. It then wells up on the soundtrack and becomes a non-diegetic commentary on Hanna's journey through the city at night, although it may also suggest that she replays the song in her mind as she acts out its lyrics. Similarly, inserted images from *Vivre sa vie* can be interpreted both as the film's commentary on her situation and as flashes of her memory of viewing the film.

The use of music and the montage effects in this sequence suggest the 'postmodern' aesthetic of music videos, but, where *Lulu* uses the video image as a way of exploring the compromised role of visual culture in the postmodern environment, *Emporte-moi* stresses the possibilities of the film camera as a tool for self-discovery. Hanna's teacher loans her a movie camera, and she returns to the countryside she left at the beginning. She uses the camera to film her mother, who seems to have recovered and comes to meet her at the bus stop. As we see the mother through the lens of Hanna's camera, the hand-held 8mm footage records the mother's image and relegates her to the past. The power to make images puts Hanna (and by extension Pool) in the position of Godard rather than Karina, but it remains uncertain whether the camera brings Hanna closer to her mother or allows her to see her from a distance and thus move on with her own life.[7]

Pool's film, like Krishna's, evokes a sense of an authentic but unseen elsewhere that links them to the similar feeling in earlier Canadian films. In *Lulu* it is the camp from which Khuyen 'escaped' and the lover she left behind there, as well as the country in which she was born; in *Emporte-moi* it is the Holocaust and the state of Israel, about which Hanna's father speaks, but which are not part of her own experience. The 'real' lurks outside the frame, and in both films the actual environment is less important than the interplay of the real and the imaginary.

National Values

As I noted in the Introduction, the erosion of national boundaries in contemporary cultural experience threatens the whole project of examining national cinemas. However, even though the politics of nationalism have become extremely complicated in the age of the 'war against terrorism', national identity still functions, for many people, as a major factor, politically and culturally, in trying to make sense of the postmodern condition. This is definitely the case with regard to Canadian films, which receive passionate support from a small—but perhaps growing—following as a vital expression of national distinctiveness but are still subject to an extraordinary resistance from others who also place them firmly within a national context.

The no-win situation that Canadian filmmakers often face was crystallized for me when I was researching Chapter 7 of this book. I came across a user comment on the Internet Movie Data Base entry for William MacGillivray's *Life Classes* (posted from Edmonton on 11 August 2001), headed: 'This is why nobody watches Canadian movies.' It was posted by a male contributor, who described the film as 'a jumbled, pretentious mess filled with strange performances and arty-farty messages.' His anger made him 'want to emigrate', and he warned Canadian students not to take film studies courses 'because this is the sort of fecal matter you're going to be exposed to.'[8]

As I absorbed this tirade, I remembered the very different assessment of the same film by Robin Wood, a critic not known for his sympathy for Canadian films. Wood offered an equally passionate—but far more reasoned—argument to support his claim that it is a great film by any standards. However, he firmly rejected 'any inclination to incorporate *Life Classes* into a "national Canadian cinema" as if that accounted for it: it is much too good for such a fate' (1989: 31). In other words, for the viewer who hated it, the film came to stand for all Canadian films, but, for the viewer who loved it, it had to be distinguished from other Canadian films.

In many ways, I agree with Wood that the concept of national cinema should not be used to account for, or circumscribe, a film's effects and meanings, although I think that *Life Classes* can be illuminated by reference to Canadian film traditions. The different responses to the film might be dismissed as a matter of opinion or taste, but it is also an extreme, but not untypical, example of how value judgements get entangled with questions of national identity.

According to playwright Bernie Slade, as reported by Martin Knelman, 'in England . . . you're known by your best work. In the United States, you're known by your last work. And in Canada, you're known by your worst work' (1987: 16). 'Best' and 'worst' are, of course, largely subjective categories, as the different opinions on *Life Classes* attest, and—as we have seen in many sections of this book—critics often denounce Canadian films for failings that others see as their virtues. Yet assuming the worst seems to be a characteristic not just of many Canadian films but also of the culture in which they are made.

The situation is rather different in Quebec, where there is a much stronger commitment to the need for a national cinema to articulate the values of distinctive cultural traditions. Yet Quebec critics still worry that the 'best' films do not attract large audiences. Popular films (like the *Les Boys* franchise) are often dismissed as trivial and pandering to the worst qualities of a colonized people (see Chapter 11), while films that achieve international success (such as those of Denys Arcand) are viewed with suspicion by some critics for not engaging sufficiently with the urgent cultural and political issues in contemporary Quebec (see Chapter 9).

Many of the oppositions that have traditionally organized discussions of Canadian cinema—English/French, Canada/Hollywood, realism/fantasy, auteur/genre—have become increasingly blurred, but the good/bad binary remains largely untroubled.

I have tried to circumvent it throughout this book by keeping my own value judgements implicit, but it should be obvious that I enjoy and value most of the films I have discussed. I certainly have my own preferences and feel more strongly about some films than others, but my goal has been to demonstrate that it is worth taking Canadian films seriously, both for their own sake and for what they can tell us about Canada and about films.

Many of these films are highly unstable texts, in which different discourses struggle against each other, and they belong to a national cinema riddled with contradictions and uncertainties. However, in a world in which the forms of classical Hollywood cinema or modernist art cinema are no longer what they used to be, the in-between status of Canadian cinema may no longer be quite the obstacle that it once was. The future of the Canadian film industry—as of the nation itself—remains highly uncertain, but then much the same could be said of most cultural institutions throughout the world and even of the 'real' itself. My claim is that what Canadian filmmakers have already achieved offers a perspective on the contemporary situation that needs to be taken into account and may prove more revealing than other apparently more secure vantage points. And there are some very 'good' films into the bargain!

Introduction

1. For an account of these efforts and a thorough treatment of the early history of film in Canada, see Morris (1978).
2. It is also a sign of the difficulties facing Canadian filmmakers that O'Brian began work on this film in the mid-1980s (see Knelman 1987: 39) when it would still have been fairly topical, but he had to wait 15 years to finally make it (and then the film received only a very limited release with virtually no publicity).
3. For a more detailed account of film policy in Canada, see Dorland (1998), and for closer attention to the industrial context, see Pendakur (1990) and Posner (1993).
4. Along the same lines, Tzvetan Todorov argues, allegory eliminates the 'hesitation' necessary for the functioning of the fantastic text (see Chapter 6).
5. Thomas Waugh similarly refers to 'the lingering cultural chasm between our two founding cinemas that has been so often erased at its peril by Ontario film studies' (1999: 11). I would argue that my strategy is not one of erasure but rather of bridge-building, although I am well aware of the engineering challenges involved.

Chapter One

1. The quoted comment was made in 1976 by Paul Morton, then President of Odeon-Morton Theatres Ltd, Winnipeg, to justify the lack of Canadian films in his cinemas (Tadros, 1976: 37). There have been many similar responses to Canadian cinema over the years.
2. For a thorough account of Grierson's work at the NFB, see Evans (1984).
3. For a detailed account of the film and Perrault's 'poetic documentary' style, see Clandfield (2004).
4. Alexis appeared again in two sequels directed by Perrault, *Le Règne du jour* (1966) and *Les Voitures d'eau* (1968).
5. Ancestors also figured in the title of the French version of *Alexis Tremblay Habitant: Terre de nos aïeux*.
6. Tom Daly's career provides a focus for a fascinating overview of the post-war NFB in Jones (1996).
7. A summary of the controversy can be found in Hays (2002).
8. Janine Marchessault (1995) discusses the origins of the Program and assesses the implications of its use of video to allow the people to produce their own images.
9. After some small changes, the film was eventually released by the NFB in 1976 but then almost immediately withdrawn from circulation. It was not released in a subtitled version until 1992, when the NFB released it on video under the title *Cotton Mill, Treadmill*. The original version was finally shown at an anti-censorship festival in 1994 and included in a DVD set of Arcand's documentaries released by the NFB in 2004 (in French only). See my fuller discussion of the film (Leach, 2003).

10. For a discussion of Rubbo's 'diary films', see Handling (1984). Jeannette Sloniowski (2003) provides a close reading of his methods in *Waiting for Fidel*.
11. For a close reading of *Voyage en Amérique*, see Froger (2003).
12. For an overview of King's long and varied career, see Feldman (2002b).
13. Godard's *Tout va bien* (1972) begins with the signing of cheques to cover the various costs of making the film.
14. As André Loiselle suggests, the film effectively 'exposes the very process of falsifying, altering or reconstructing history' (2002a: 82).
15. One of the most influential Canadian examples was *Hard Core Logo* (1996), Bruce McDonald's documentary-style account of the travels of a fictional rock band.
16. See Moore's *Roger and Me* (1989), *Bowling for Columbine* (2002), and *Fahrenheit 9/11* (2004). Moore is usually more aggressive than Rubbo in his questioning and in his shaping of the material.

Chapter Two

1. Four of the five 1964 feature films discussed in this chapter were nominated for the 1965 Canadian Film Awards (the exception was *Trouble-fête*). *The Luck of Ginger Coffey* won the award for best feature film, but the jury decided not to name a Film of the Year. *Sweet Substitute* won a Special Award for 'the very great promise and already substantial accomplishment clearly shown by director and actors alike, and for the sensitive and imaginative handling of the story' (Topalovich, 2000: 71).
2. For Crawley's achievements as a pioneering television producer, see Forrester (1998).
3. Brecht argued for a form of theatre in which the different elements (acting, sets, music, and so on) would not unite to create an illusion of reality but rather comment on each other, encouraging the spectator to think about how and why they relate to the play's concerns (Willett, 1964: 37–8).
4. Translated as *White Niggers of America* (Vallières, 1971).
5. Trudeau spoke of his concern for 'the protection of individual freedoms against collective tyranny' in a speech at the 1968 Liberal leadership convention. An excerpt from this speech is used as an epilogue in Jerry Ciccoritti's television mini-series *Trudeau* (2002).

Chapter Three

1. Duplessis held power in Quebec, with a brief interruption during World War II, from 1936 to 1959.
2. There were about 12 feature films in all. One of the last was *Tit-Coq* (1952), directed by Gratien Gélinas and René Delacroix and based on Gélinas's popular stage play, which presented a more overtly critical perspective on traditional values.
3. For the idea of *métissage* as a term for mixed or hybrid identities in Quebec, see Chapter 10.
4. The narrator refers to Curé Antoine Labelle, one of the most active figures in advocating the colonization of the northlands.
5. André Loiselle suggests that the setting for the final sequence is part of a strategy to distinguish between 'the stepmother's violence, which is offered as spectacle' and 'the state's violence, which remains abstract' (2003: 39).
6. The boss at the bottling plant where they work is nicknamed Frenchie, and the well-endowed secretary whom Pete takes out on a date has a French accent and is presumably from Quebec, but it is not clear how these characters relate to the regional/national tension.

7. For discussions of *Suzanne* and *The Grey Fox*, see Urquhart (2003: 71–3) and Allan (2002), respectively.
8. At the 1982 Genie Awards, Kidder won the Best Actress Award while Potts won for Best Foreign Actress.

Chapter Four

1. *Gunsmoke*, starring James Arness as Matt Dillon, ran on CBS from 1955 to 1975.
2. The tension between 'opening' and looking back in this ending recalls the ambiguity of Claude's retreat to the country at the end of *Le Chat dans le sac* (see Chapter 2).
3. David Russell describes this group as a 'New French New Wave' whose films constitute 'a form of postmodernist cinema deliberately without depth and endlessly allusive' (1989–90: 43).
4. Christine Ramsay argues that the film's 'highly stylized, ironic, and parodically condensed images' suggest the inadequacy of psychological or socio-cultural explanations of Henry's behaviour (1995b: 7).
5. For a fuller discussion of McDonald's films, see Gravestock (2002).
6. Linda Ruth Williams calls the suburb 'bland' (2001: 36); it is described as 'generic' in the entry for the film on the All-Movie Guide: <http://www.allmovie.com/cg/avg.dll? p=avg&sql=1:227026>, accessed 7 July 2005.
7. Yves Lever (1988) claims that *Le Diable est parmi nous* followed 'in the wake of the American mode launched by *The Exorcist*' even though it preceded its alleged Hollywood model (286).
8. The film thus also harks back to *La Forteresse*, a much earlier crime film set in Quebec City (see Chapter 3).

Chapter Five

1. In this respect, the alleged incoherence of Carle's films is a less overtly political version of the Brechtian 'separation of elements' discussed in Chapter 2.
2. As a student, he had already made two medium-length films, *Stereo* (1969) and *Crimes of the Future* (1970), that were experimental in form but anticipated many of the themes of the later body horror films. *Shivers* is also known as *The Parasite Murders* and *They Came From Within*.
3. Thus Reynold Humphries includes, without comment, a chapter on Cronenberg in his book on *The American Horror Film* (2002). It is not clear whether this illustrates the triumph of genre over national cinema or the familiar silent inclusion of Canada with 'America'.
4. In his book on the director, William Beard argues that 'Cronenberg is not a postmodernist but a modernist informed by the conditions of a postmodern age.' But this distinction rests on the questionable assumption that postmodernists believe that the loss of 'certainties and universalities' results in greater freedom for humanity (2001: viii). In a later article, Beard suggests that *eXistenZ* is Cronenberg's 'first genuinely postmodern film' (2002: 156). In his discussion of the early films, Christopher Sharrett calls Cronenberg 'the most "traditional" of post-modern artists' (1986: 123).
5. Linda Ruth Williams suggests that, in body horror films, 'the body has mutated into the thing to run *from*, which has serious consequences for the way we have preferred to perceive the "inner self"' (1993: 32–3).
6. *Crash* is the first, and so far the only, Canadian film to have been accorded a monograph in the British Film Institute's 'Modern Classics' series; see Sinclair (1999).

7. Lia M. Hotchkiss points out that, 'although initially siding with the Realist Underground seems to be a way to win eXistenZ, the film in the end portrays the realists as overly literal terrorists' who are 'unable to conceive of the constructedness of their own reality' (2003: 28).

8. Christine Cornea argues that the 'cyborgization process' is already apparent in *Crash*, in which 'the bodies of the performers become literally entangled with the technological bodies of the cars' (2003: 12).

Chapter Six

1. The presence of the bilingual Bujold in the films creates an impression of living between two worlds that must have resonated with Almond's situation as an English-Canadian film-maker—whose main previous experience was with CBC television—working in Quebec. Quebec critics were generally more sympathetic to the trilogy, especially *Journey*, than their English-Canadian counterparts.

2. Many Canadian films can profitably be read in the context of the Gothic tradition, but I have chosen to focus on films that, like the novels of Charlotte and Emily Brontë, explore themes of entrapment and desire through a feminine sensibility.

3. A director's cut was eventually released 10 years later, but only on video and too late to undo the damage to Jutra's career that had seemed so promising after the reception of *Mon oncle Antoine* a few years earlier. A restored 35mm print was released in 1995 by the Cinémathèque québécoise, but the film's misfortunes were not yet over. When a version of this print with English subtitles was broadcast on the Bravo network, it was cut to eliminate its more disturbing images (even though these are quite restrained by contemporary standards).

4. The film reflects George Grant's negative views on technology, which Bruce Elder used to support his arguments against realism in the 'Cinema We Need' debate (see Chapter 7). However, Elder does not mention *The Far Shore* in *Image and Identity*, his lengthy book on Canadian cinema, even though he does briefly discuss several of Wieland's avant-garde films. Presumably, the importance of narrative and the debt to Hollywood melodrama did not distance it enough from the realist tradition.

5. Leroux's indignation is rather undermined by his consistent misspelling of Tom Thomson's name.

6. In the press kit and in English-dubbed narration, this character is referred to as the 'word tamer', but the one time he is named in the French narration he is called the 'dompteur des vers'. The name is an untranslatable pun since 'vers' can also mean 'poetry'.

7. Maddin thinks that *Léolo* is 'better than anything else ever made in Canada' (Vatnsdal, 2000: 141). See also Toles (2002) for an appreciative essay on *Léolo*.

8. In his discussion of *Careful*, Darrell Varga notes that 'Maddin's films are literally shot through with veils, are about the fact of veiling, are decidedly not a narrative trajectory towards the unveiling of meaning' (1999: 62).

Chapter Seven

1. For an extensive discussion of *Neighbours* in the context of the NFB during the early years of the Cold War, see Kristmanson (2003: 49–85).

2. Elder apparently was cool towards the work of the ideological theorists (see Testa, 1985: 29, n.4), but they similarly argued that realism 'cannot deal with the real as contradictory' (MacCabe, 1974: 12).

3. Elder specifically mentions David Cronenberg's *Shivers* (see Chapter 5) and Richard Benner's *Outrageous!* (see Chapter 8).

4. For a discussion of *Wavelength* in the context of Snow's early artworks and films, see Michelson (1979).

5. For a recent overview of Elder's career, see Kashmere (2004).
6. Elder claims that the Canadian avant-garde was postmodernist from the beginning; but I would argue that filmmakers like Snow and Chambers are modernist in that their work focuses on the formal properties of the medium and stresses the need for the spectator to 'work', as opposed to the more eclectic and playful strategies of postmodern artists.
7. Lianne McLarty argues that Wieland is 'true to the "tradition" of experimental film in her use of self-reflexive forms of construction and her concern with the nature of the medium. Yet, she moves beyond most experimental films in her refusal to rely on mere abstraction and aesthetic concerns' (1982: 62).
8. This trend might be seen as a development from Elder's unspecified 'New Narrative' films.
9. For discussions of recent activities in avant-garde cinema, see Hoolboom (2001) and Zryd (2002).
10. Darcus mentioned Lefebvre, along with Larry Kent, as showing the way towards 'an indigenous cinema' that would be 'rough and fresh' (Ibrányi-Kiss, 1974: 42). MacGillivray praised *Les Fleurs sauvages* as 'one of the most perfect films I've ever seen' and admired the 'extreme simplicity and the subtlety' of Lefebvre's work (Henderson, 1987: 17).
11. Lefebvre took this position even further by arguing that, 'in essence, all cinema should be amateur because amateurism is bound up with the ideas of freedom and search' (Pageau, 1971: 97).
12. 'Right to the heart' is an allusion to the title of Lefebvre's film *Jusqu'au coeur* (1968).
13. The film is 152 minutes long, but a shorter version broadcast on CBC-Television actually seemed longer because the cuts destroyed the subtle rhythms of the original.

Chapter Eight

1. Similar arguments could be made with regard to the 'alterity' or 'otherness' represented by the immigrant communities in Quebec (see Chapter 10).
2. One of the other co-directors was Denys Arcand, and the students received help from established NFB filmmakers, including Michel Brault and Gilles Groulx.
3. For two different accounts of the goals and pitfalls of Klein's project, see Elder (1984) and Nicks (2003).
4. For a thorough analysis of the origins and implications of Poirier's hybrid and passionate film, see Loiselle (2000).
5. All of these women had more than usual opportunities to develop their talents because they were married to filmmakers. For a discussion of Marsh's *Alexis Tremblay Habitant*, see Chapter 1. The work of women filmmakers at the NFB during World War II is examined in Martineau (1977).
6. For a recent reappraisal of this film, see Loiselle (2002a).
7. For a discussion of the film as an example of 'the lesbian postmodern', see Bruce (1999).
8. On Lanctôt, see Harcourt (1999); on *My American Cousin*, see Yamaguchi (1989); and on *Loyalties*, see Wood (1989) and Longfellow (1999), as well as Susan Lord's critical survey of Wheeler's career (2002).
9. The idea of three women merging into one composite character also appeared a few years earlier in Robert Altman's *3 Women* (1977).
10. Pool also uses a (professional male) photographer in *À corps perdu* (1988) to explore questions of voyeurism and the problem of expressing 'the relations between inner experience and outer reality' (Leach 1999b: 10).
11. Waugh (2001) discusses *Outrageous!* and three other films from the 'queer Canadian canon'. See also Graham (1980).

12. *Zero Patience* has received considerable critical attention; see, for example, Gittings (2001) and Hallas (2003). Greyson's other films made less impact, although *Lilies* (1996), an English-language adaptation of a Québécois play in which male actors play the female characters, won a Genie for Best Picture. See Ramsay (2002b) for an assessment of all his films.
13. For a discussion of this film, see Bruce (2003).
14. This film, *Wolf Girl*, was shown on the network for Halloween in 2001.
15. Fitzgerald quoted from *Eye Weekly* (5 June 2003): http://www.eye.net/eye/issue/issue_06.05.03/film/wilddogs.html (accessed 17 November 2004).

Chapter Nine

1. A few years earlier, however, Peter Harcourt had complained of the 'supercilious cynicism' with which Arcand had responded to the conditions that had silenced Quebec auteurs with more integrity (2001: 41).
2. He did, however, write a six-part television mini-series, *Duplessis* (1978), on the long career of the Premier whose conservatism dominated Quebec culture in the mid-twentieth century (see Chapter 3). He also directed episodes of another mini-series, *Empire Inc* (1983), about a fictional business tycoon who operated in Quebec during roughly the same period, and he stepped in to replace Gilles Carle as director on *Le Crime d'Ovide Plouffe* (1984), set in the 1950s.
3. Egoyan's admiration for Beckett culminated in his film of *Krapp's Last Tape* (2000), made for Irish television. He has also written appreciatively of Peter Hall's 1973 film version of Pinter's *The Homecoming* (see Egoyan, 1994).
4. See Zizek's 'Lévi-Straussian' interpretation of these relationships (2004: 301). George Melnyk rather fancifully suggests that Egoyan's 'auteur vision' was shaped by the 'youthful trauma' of knowing a young woman who was abused by her father (2004: 161).
5. The only exceptions to this rule are the sequences involving the Turkish commander, who conducts his interviews, not just with the American doctor but with the Armenians, in English.

Chapter Ten

1. The opening explosion clearly alludes to the actual bombing of Air India flight 182 over the Atlantic on 22 June 1985, which also inspired the opening of Salman Rushdie's controversial novel, *The Satanic Verses* (1988).
2. Hamid Naficy comments on the 'simultaneously local and global' resonance of 'accented cinema' (2004: 134). The South Asian diaspora is an especially cogent example, with actors like Jaffrey and Segal likely to turn up in British, US, and Indian, as well as Canadian, films, thus exposing them as products of the global media marketplace but also fitting seamlessly into the local communities depicted in the films.
3. In a sense, Canadian filmmakers also suffer from a 'burden of representation'. Since most Canadians see so few Canadian films, the ones they do see come to represent the whole national cinema.
4. Many of these films are discussed in Harcourt (1998).
5. The critical failure of Srinivas Krishna's second film, *Lulu*, can also be attributed partly to its concern with characters from outside the Indo-Canadian community (see Chapter 12), and *Drive, She Said* (1997), Mina Shum's follow-up to *Double Happiness*, received little attention, perhaps because its main characters are not Chinese-Canadian.

6. Mehta was finally able to finish *Water* (2005) by shooting in Sri Lanka.

7. Guy Maddin wrote a rapturous review of Mehta's film (2003: 76–9).

8. Several films incorporate the clash between First Nations cultures and the dominant social order into generic plots, ranging from political thrillers such as *Clearcut* (Richard Bugajski, 1991) and *Windigo* (Robert Morin, 1994) to the horror film, as in *Ginger Snaps Back* (Grant Harvey, 2003).

Chapter Eleven

1. *Strange Brew* (Rick Moranis and Dave Thomas, 1983) was also based on characters from television.

2. Water imagery is prominent in the work of Robert Lepage also (see Chapter 12). In an interview, he asked, 'is it my films that tend to be watery, or is the selection of themes and subjects watery?' (Tousignant, 2001: 16).

3. Smart cinema in Quebec, especially the films of Briand, Turpin, and Villeneuve, has links to the French 'cinema of the look' of a decade or so earlier (see Chapter 4). Luc Besson, one of the filmmakers associated with this movement, was one of the producers of *La Turbulence des fluides*, a Canada–France co-production.

Chapter Twelve

1. Lepage is also an actor who regularly performs in his stage productions and has appeared in several films (including Denys Arcand's *Jésus de Montréal*). He did not, however, appear in his own films until *La Face cachée de la lune* (2003), adapted from his autobiographical one-man stage play.

2. In this respect, the film anticipates the depiction of present-day Quebec City in *Le Collectionneur* (see Chapter 4).

3. The location of the 'matrimonial service' is identified as Toronto on the video through which Lucky met Lulu.

4. www.telefilm.gc.ca/en/prod/film/film96/16.htm, accessed 24 May 2002.

5. In this respect, the film explores similar issues to Donna Haraway in her discussion of 'cyborg bodies' (1991) and can be compared with David Cronenberg's body horror films (see Chapter 5).

6. The novel had been filmed at least three times before 1962: by Jean Renoir (1926), Dorothy Arzner (1934), and Christian-Jaque (1955). Godard does not seem to allude specifically to any of these films.

7. At the time of the release of *Emporte-moi*, it was reported that Pool's next project would be a story about three immigrants from Turkey, Cuba, and Yemen. The film would be set in Quebec but, because English is the only language in which the immigrants could speak to each other, it would be made in English. Instead, Pool's first English-language film proved to be *Lost and Delirious* (2001), another story of sexual awakening and identity crises, this time set in a private school for girls; and she then went on to make *The Blue Butterfly* (2003), also in English, about a terminally ill boy who wants to find a rare butterfly in South America.

8. He also commented that he would not usually walk out of 'a movie about nude models', and I assume that it was this aspect of the film, rather than James Cameron's Canadian origins, that inspired the Web site's entry under 'recommendations': 'If you like this title, we also recommend . . . *Titanic*.'

BIBLIOGRAPHY

Alemany-Galway, Mary. 2002. *A Postmodern Cinema: The Voice of the Other in Canadian Film.* Lanham, Md: Scarecrow Press.

Alioff, Maurie. 1997. 'Sweet Necrophilia', *Take One* 5, 15 (Spring): 12–16.

———. 2001a. 'From the Edge of the Earth: Zacharias Kunuk's *Atanarjuat*', *Take One* 10, 34 (Sept.): 17–21.

———. 2001b. 'Mr. D. Takes a Pratfall: Arto Paragamian's *Two Thousand and None*', *Take One* 9, 30 (Winter): 19–21.

———. 2002. 'Gilles Carle and *La Vraie Nature de Bernadette*: Saintly Sinner, Sinful Saint', *Take One* 11, 38 (July–Aug.): 30–1.

Allan, Blaine. 2002. 'The Grey Fox Afoot in the Modern World', in Walz (2002: 117–43).

Allison, Kathryn. 1986. 'Beyond Sex and Violence: The Compassionate Filmmaking of Jack Darcus', *Cinema Canada* 132 (July–Aug.): 10–13.

Altman, Rick. 1999. *Film/Genre.* London: British Film Institute.

Amsden, Cynthia. 2001. 'Much Ado about a Fish', *Take One* 30 (Winter): 22–4.

Anderson, Benedict. 1991. *Imagined Communities: Reflections on the Origins and Spread of Nationalism*, revised edn. London: Verso.

Arcand, Denys. 1972. '*La Maudite Galette*', *Cinéma Québec* 2, 1 (Sept.): 11.

Armatage, Kay. 1971. '*Madeleine Is . . .*', *Take One* 2, 11: 27–8.

———. 2003. *The Girl from God's Country: Nell Shipman and the Silent Cinema.* Toronto: University of Toronto Press.

———, Kass Banning, Brenda Longfellow, and Janine Marchessault, eds. 1999a. *Gendering the Nation: Canadian Women's Cinema.* Toronto: University of Toronto Press.

———, ———, ———, and ———. 1999b. 'Gendering the Nation', in Armatage et al. (1999a: 3–14).

Arroyo, José. 1986. 'Jack Darcus' *Overnight*', *Cinema Canada* 136 (Dec.): 24.

———. 1987. 'The Alienated Affections of Atom Egoyan', *Cinema Canada* 145 (Oct.): 14–19.

———. 1998. '*The Hanging Garden*', *Sight and Sound* 8, 5 (May): 46.

Arsenault, André Guy. 1986. 'Yves Simoneau's *Pouvoir intime*', *Cinema Canada* 129 (Apr.): 22–3.

Austin-Smith, Brenda. 2002. '"Gender is Irrelevant": *I've Heard the Mermaids Singing* as Women's Cinema', in Walz (2002: 208–33).

Bailey, Cameron. 1992. 'What the Story Is: An Interview with Srinivas Krishna', *CineAction* 28 (Spring): 38–47.

———. 2000. 'Standing in the Kitchen All Night: A Secret History of the Toronto New Wave', *Take One* 9, 28 (Summer): 6–11.

Bakhtin, M.M. 1981. *The Dialogic Imagination*, trans. Caryl Emerson and Michael Holquist. Austin: University of Texas Press.

Banning, Kass. 1999. 'Playing in the Light: Canadianizing Race and Nation', in Armatage et al. (1999a: 291–310).

Barker, Adam. 1990. 'Actors, Magicians and the Little Apocalypse', *Monthly Film Bulletin* 57, 672 (Jan.): 4.

Barrette, Pierre. 2003. 'La Fin des bacchanales', *24 Images* 115 (Summer): 4–5.

———. 2004a. 'Le Genre sans la différence: Le Cinéma québécois à l'heure de la séduction', *24 Images* 116–17 (Summer): 8–11.

———. 2004b. 'Pierre Falardeau: 30 ans de cinéma engagé', *24 Images* 118 (Sept.): 38–41.

Barrowclough, Susan. 1982. 'Of National Cinema', *Cinema Canada* 84 (May): 25–7.

Baudrillard, Jean. 1983. *Simulations*, trans. Paul Foss, Paul Patton, and Philip Beitchman. New York: Semiotext(e).

———. 1994. *The Illusion of the End*, trans. Chris Turner. Stanford, Calif.: Stanford University Press.

Beard, William. 2001. *The Artist as Monster: The Cinema of David Cronenberg*. Toronto: University of Toronto Press.

———. 2002. 'Thirty-two Paragraphs about David Cronenberg', in Beard and White (2002: 144–59).

——— and Jerry White, eds. 2002. *North of Everything: English-Canadian Cinema Since 1980*. Edmonton: University of Alberta Press.

Beaulieu, Janick. 1992. 'Pour *Léolo*', *Séquences* 159–60 (Sept.): 52.

Beaulieu, Jean. 1997. 'Une Histoire reinventée', *Ciné-Bulles* 16, 2 (Summer): 18–19.

———. 1999. 'Si tu savais, Elvis . . .', *Ciné-Bulles* 18, 1 (Summer): 30–1.

Beaulieu, Julie. 2003. 'À la frontière des genres', *Ciné-Bulles* 21, 3 (Summer): 52–5.

Belzile, Ginette. 1995. 'Deux ou trois choses que l'on sait d'elle', *Ciné-Bulles* 14, 2 (Summer): 7–10.

Bérubé, Renald, and Yvan Patry, eds. 1971. *Jean-Pierre Lefebvre*. Montreal: Les Presses de l'Université du Québec.

Betancourt, Jeanne. 1974. *Women in Focus*. Dayton, Ohio: Pflaum.

Blumer, Ron. 1971. 'King's *A Married Couple*', in Lewis Jacobs, ed., *The Documentary Tradition: From Nanook to Woodstock*. New York: Hopkinson and Blake, 471–3.

———. 1975. '*Les Ordres*', *Cinema Canada* 17 (Dec.–Jan.): 77.

Bonneville, Léo, ed. 1979. *Le Cinéma québécois par ceux qui le font*. Montreal: Editions Paulines.

———. 1981a. 'Entretien avec Gilles Carle', *Séquences* 103 (Jan.): 4–16.

———. 1981b. 'Entretien avec Gilles Carle', *Séquences* 104 (Apr.): 4–15.

———. 1985. 'Entretien avec Léa Pool', *Séquences* 119 (Jan.): 9–14.

———. 1986. 'Entretien avec Yves Simoneau', *Séquences* 124 (Apr.): 5–10.

———. 1987. 'Jean-Claude Lauzon', *Séquences* 130 (Aug.): 10–19.

———. 1994. 'Entrevue avec André Forcier', *Séquences* 174 (Sept.–Oct.): 10–13.

Bor, Aaron. 1989–90. 'An Interview with Léa Pool', *Québec Studies* 9: 63–8.

Botting, Fred, and Scott Wilson. 1998. 'Automatic Lover', *Screen* 39, 2: 186–92.

Brault, Michel. 1975. *Les Ordres*, ed. Gilles Marsolais. Montreal: L'Aurore.

Brottman, Mikita, and Christopher Sharrett. 2002. 'The End of the Road: David Cronenberg's *Crash* and the Fading of the West', *Literature/Film Quarterly* 30, 2: 126–32.

Bruce, Jean. 1999. 'Querying/Queering the Nation', in Armatage et al. (1999a: 274–90).

———. 2003. 'Queer Cinema at the NFB: The "Strange Case" of *Forbidden Love*', in Leach and Sloniowski (2003: 164–80).

Brûlé, Michel. 1971. 'Introduction à l'oeuvre cinématographique de Jean-Pierre Lefebvre, cinéaste et Québécois', in Bérubé and Patry (1971: 17–62).

———. 1974. 'Un Constat d'impuissance à l'égard des groupes d'opposition', *Cinéma Québec* 4, 1 (Dec.): 14–17.

Brunette, Peter. 1990–1. 'Shut Up and Just Do It!', *Sight and Sound* 60, 1 (Winter): 55–7.

Brunsdon, Charlotte. 1999. 'Space in the British Crime Film', in Steve Chibnall and Robert Murphy, eds, *British Crime Cinema*. London: Routledge, 148–59.

Bujold, Geneviève, Michel Brault, and Claude Jutra. 1973. 'Interviews', *Cinema Canada* 7 (Apr.–May): 42–50.

Burgess, Jackson. 1964. '*The Luck of Ginger Coffey*', *Film Quarterly* 18, 2 (Winter): 57.

Burnett, Ron. 1993. 'Speaking of Parts', in Atom Egoyan, *Speaking Parts*. Toronto: Coach House Press, 9–22.

Byford, Chris. 1998. 'Highway 61 Revisited', *CineAction* 45 (Feb.): 10–17.

Cagle, Robert L. 1999. 'A Minority on Someone Else's Continent: Identity, Difference, and the Media in the Films of Patricia Rozema', in Armatage et al. (1999a: 183–96).

Cardinal, Roger, and Robert Stuart Short. 1970. *Surrealism: Permanent Revolution*. London: Studio Vista.

Carle, Gilles. 1972. 'Un Western religieux?', *Cinéma Québec* 1, 9 (May–June): 17.

———. 1973a. '. . . En Quête d'un film', *Cinéma Québec* 2, 5 (Jan.–Feb.): 19.

———. 1973b. 'Créer une certaine imagerie', *Cinéma Québec* 3, 1 (Sept.): 28–32.

Caron, André. 1995. 'La Première Confession de Robert Lepage', *Séquences* 180 (Sept.–Oct.): 24–9.

Carrière, Louise. 1983. *Femmes et cinéma québécois*. Montreal: Boréal Express.

———. 1999. 'Les Trois Petits Tours de Denise Filiatrault', *Ciné-Bulles* 17, 4 (Winter–Spring): 30–3.

Castiel, Élie. 1999. 'Rêves chimériques', *Séquences* 200 (Jan.–Feb.): 47–8.

———. 2002. 'Manon Briand: Les Attitances involontaires', *Séquences* 221 (Sept.–Oct.): 44–5.

———. 2003. '*Sur le seuil: Le Pouvoir du mal*', *Séquences* 227 (Sept.–Oct.): 42.

Charent, Brian, Peter Harcourt, and Margo Blackell. 1976. '*The Far Shore*', *Motion* 5, 2 (Jan.): 32–3.

Chesley, Stephen. 1975. 'It'll Bug You', *Cinema Canada* 22 (Oct.): 23–5.

Chun, Kimberly. 2002. 'Storytelling in the Arctic Circle: An Interview with Zacharias Kunuk', *Cineaste* 28, 1 (Winter): 21–3.

Clandfield, David. 1984. 'From the Picturesque to the Familiar: Films of the French Unit at the NFB (1958–1964)', in Feldman (1984a: 112–24).

———. 2004. *Pierre Perrault and the Poetic Documentary*. Toronto: Toronto International Film Festival.

Coates, Paul. 1997. 'Projecting the Exotic: Atom Egoyan and Fantasy', *Canadian Journal of Film Studies* 6, 2 (Fall): 21–33.

Conseil québécois pour la diffusion du cinéma. 1976. *Cinéastes du Québec 2: Gilles Carle*. Montreal: CQDC.

Corder, Sharon, and Jack Blum. 2001. '*waydowntown*: The Subversive Charm of Gary Burns', *Take One* 9, 30 (Winter): 8–13.

Cornea, Christine. 2003. 'David Cronenberg's *Crash* and Performing Cyborgs', *Velvet Light Trap* 52 (Fall): 4–14.

Corupe, Paul. 2003–4. 'Taking Off the Mask: Rediscovering Nat Taylor and the B-Movies of Canada's Past', *Take One* 12, 44 (Dec.–Jan.): 17–21.

Costello, John. 2000. *David Cronenberg*. Harpenden: Pocket Essentials.

Coulombe, Michel. 1995a. 'Entretien avec Robert Lepage', *Ciné-Bulles* 14, 4 (Winter): 20–4.

———. 1995b. *Entretiens avec Gilles Carle: Le Chemin secret du cinéma*. Montreal: Liber.

Crane, Jonathan. 2000. 'A Body Apart: Cronenberg and Genre', in Michael Grant, ed., *The Modern Fantastic: The Films of David Cronenberg*. Westport, Conn.: Praeger, 50–68.

Crofts, Stephen. 1993. 'Reconceptualizing National Cinema/s', *Quarterly Review of Film and Video* 14, 3: 49–67.

Daudelin, Robert. 1980. 'The Encounter between Fiction and the Direct Cinema', in Véronneau and Handling (1980: 94–106).

———. 2004. 'Cinéma en crise, cinéastes en crise', *24 Images* 116–17 (Summer): 15–17.

de Blois, Marco. 1995–6. 'L'Iconoclaste de Québec', *24 Images* 80 (Dec.–Jan.): 14–17.

———. 2001. 'Métissé(e)', *24 Images* 105 (Winter): 27.

——— and Claude Racine. 1999. 'Entretien avec Pierre Falardeau and Julien Poulin', *24 Images* 97 (Summer): 4–11.

Delahaye, Michel, and Patrick Straram. 1967. 'Le Coup de dés: Entretien avec Jean-Pierre Lefebvre', *Cahiers du cinéma* 186 (Jan.): 56–61.

de Lauretis, Teresa. 1990. 'Guerrilla in the Midst: Women's Cinema in the 80s', *Screen* 31, 1 (Spring): 6–25.

Delisle, Martin. 1987. 'Entretien avec Patricia Rozema', *24 Images* 36: 22–3.

Demers, Pierre. 1973. '*Les Corps célestes*', *Cinéma Québec* 3, 3 (Nov.–Dec.): 10–13.

Dorland, Michael. 1985. 'The Shadow of Canadian Cinema: Bruce Elder's Immodest Proposal', *Cinema Canada* 120–1 (July–Aug.): 35–6.

———. 1986. 'Renaissance Man', *Cinema Canada* 134 (Oct.): 15–21.

———. 1987. 'Jean-Claude Lauzon's *Un Zoo la nuit*', *Cinema Canada* 144 (Sept.): 37.

———. 1998. *So Close to the State/s: The Emergence of Film Policy in Canada*. Toronto: University of Toronto Press.

Douglas, Dave. 1996. 'Exile on Hastings & Main Street: The Vancouver Films of Larry Kent', *Canadian Journal of Film Studies* 5, 2 (Fall): 85–99.

Dowler, Andrew. 1981. 'George Mihalka's *My Bloody Valentine*', *Cinema Canada* 74 (May): 67.

Dundjerovic, Aleksandar. 2003. *The Cinema of Robert Lepage: The Poetics of Memory*. London: Wallflower.

Edsforth, Janet. 1972. *Paul Almond: The Flame Within*. Ottawa: Canadian Film Institute.

Edwards, Natalie. 1977. 'Who's Don Owen? What's He Done, and What's He Doing Now?', in Feldman and Nelson (1977: 160–78).

Egoyan, Atom. 1993, 'Surface Tension', in Egoyan, *Speaking Parts*. Toronto: Coach House Press, 25–38.

———. 1994. 'Holding On', *Sight and Sound* 4, 4 (Apr.): 31.

———. 1997. 'Recovery', *Sight and Sound* 7, 10 (Oct.): 21–3.

Elder, Bruce R. 1984. 'Two Journeys: A Review of *Not a Love Story*', in Feldman (1984a: 236–43).

———. 1985a. 'The Cinema We Need', *Canadian Forum* 64, 746 (Feb.): 32–5.

———. 1985b. 'A Vindication', *Cinema Canada* 120–1 (July–Aug.): 32–4.

———. 1989. *Image and Identity: Reflections of Canadian Film and Culture*. Waterloo, Ont.: Wilfrid Laurier University Press.

Ethier, Jean-René. 1973. '*Journey*', *Séquences* 71 (Jan.): 26–7.

Euvrard, Michel. 1972. '*Journey*: Eurydice deux fois perdue', *Cinéma Québec* 2, 4 (Dec.): 10–13.

Evanchuk, P.M. 1975. 'An Innerview of Michel Brault', *Motion* (Jan.–Mar.): 12–22, 31.

Evans, Gary. 1984. *John Grierson and the National Film Board: The Politics of Wartime Propaganda 1939–1945*. Toronto: University of Toronto Press.

———. 1991. *In the National Interest: A Chronicle of the National Film Board of Canada from 1949–1989*. Toronto: University of Toronto Press.

Even, Martin. 1973. 'Un Antoine Doinel québécois', *Le Devoir* (10 Feb.).

Favreau, Michèle. 1971. 'La Question du "fond" et de la "forme"', in Bérubé and Patry (1971: 85–94).

Feldman, Seth. 1977. 'Review of *The Hart of London*', in Feldman and Nelson (1977: 333–7).

———. 1982. 'Business as (Un)usual', *Cinema Canada* 81 (Feb.): 22–3.

———, ed. 1984a. *Take Two*. Toronto: Irwin Publishing.

———. 1984b. 'The Silent Subject in English Canadian Film', in Feldman (1984a: 48–57).

———. 2002a. 'Foreword', in Beard and White (2002: xi–xiv).

———, ed. 2002b. *Allan King Filmmaker*. Toronto: Toronto International Film Festival.

———. 2003. '*The Days before Christmas* and the Days before That', in Leach and Sloniowski (2003: 31–47).

——— and Joyce Nelson, eds. 1977. *Canadian Film Reader*. Toronto: Peter Martin Associates.

Fieschi, Jean-André, and Claude Ollier. 1965. 'Gilles Groulx: *Le Chat dans le sac*', *Cahiers du cinéma* 168 (July): 56–9.

Forrester, James. 1998. '"Budge" Crawley: Canada's First TV Maverick', *Take One* 7, 20 (Summer): 36–8.

Fothergill, Robert. 1972, '*Journey*', *Take One* 3, 7 (Dec.): 35.

———. 1977a. 'Coward, Bully, or Clown: The Dream-Life of a Younger Brother', in Feldman and Nelson (1977: 234–50).

———. 1977b. 'A Place Like Home', in Feldman and Nelson (1977: 349–63).

Fox, Joan. 1977. 'The Facts of Life, Toronto Style', in Feldman and Nelson (1977: 156–60).

Froger, Marion. 2003. '*Voyage en Amérique avec un cheval emprunté*: A Journey of the Mind', in Leach and Sloniowski (2003: 148–63).

Fruet, William. 1973. 'Wedding in White', in Rolf Kalman, ed., *A Collection of Canadian Plays*, vol. 2. Toronto: Simon and Pierre.

Fuchs, Cindy. 1988. '*I've Heard the Mermaids Singing*', *Cineaste* 16, 3: 54–5.

Fulford, Robert. 1974. *Marshall Delaney at the Movies*. Toronto: Peter Martin Associates.

———. 1982. 'Nothing but Heartaches', *Saturday Night* 97, 3 (Mar.): 61–2.

———. 1984. 'Canada's Trauma and Michel Brault', in Feldman (1984a: 3–5).

Frye, Northrop. 1971. *The Bush Garden: Essays on the Canadian Imagination*. Toronto: Anansi.

Gajan, Philippe. 1996. 'Cinéma de la diversité, cinéma de la collision: L'Oeuvre fictionnelle de Gilles Carle', *24 Images* 83–4 (Fall): 12–13.

——— and Marie-Claude Loiselle. 1996. 'Gilles Carle: *Pudding chômeur*', *24 Images* 83–4 (Fall): 4–11.

——— and ———. 1997. 'Entretien avec André Forcier', *24 Images* 87 (Summer): 8–13.

Garrity, Henry. 1989–90. 'Subversive Discourse in Yves Simoneau's *Pouvoir intime*', *Québec Studies* 9: 29–37.

Gaulin, Suzanne. 1984. 'Pool's Splash', *Cinema Canada* 111 (Oct.): 7–9.

Gilroy, Paul. 1997. 'Diaspora and the Detours of Identity', in Kathryn Woodward, ed., *Identity and Difference*. Milton Keynes: Open University Press, 299–346.

Gingras, Nicole. 1991. 'Figures de la mélancholie', *24 Images* 56–7 (Fall): 66–8.

Gittings, Christopher E. 2001. '*Zero Patience*, Genre, Difference, and Ideology: Singing and Dancing Queer Nation', *Cinema Journal* 41, 1 (Fall): 28–39.

———. 2002. *Canadian National Cinema*. London: Routledge.

Glassman, Marc. 2000. 'It Happened One Night', *Cinema Scope* 3 (Spring): 76–7.

Goodwin, George. 1988. 'Reclaiming the Subject: A Feminist Reading of *I've Heard the Mermaids Singing*', *Cinema Canada* 152 (May): 23–5.

Goslawski, Barbara. 1999. 'Jeremy Podeswa's *The Five Senses*', *Take One* 8, 25 (Fall): 17–21.

Graham, Alison. 1980. '"Outrageous!" and "The Boys in the Band": The Possibilities and Limitations of "Coming Out"', *Film Criticism* 5, 1 (Fall): 36–42.

Grant, Barry Keith. 2002. 'Beautiful Losers: Don Shebib's *Between Friends*', *Take One* 11, 38 (July–Aug.): 8–11.

Gravel, Jean-Philippe. 1996. 'Affreux, sales et méchants', *Ciné-Bulles* 15, 3 (Fall): 6–7.

———. 1999. 'Dr Falardeau and Mr Gratton', *Ciné-Bulles* 18, 1 (Summer): 32–3.

Gravestock, Steve. 2002. 'Outlaw Insider: The Films of Bruce McDonald', in Beard and White (2002: 242–55).

Green, Mary Jean. 1989–90. 'Léa Pool's *La Femme de l'hôtel* and Women's Film in Québec', *Québec Studies* 9: 49–62.

Grugeau, Gérard. 1989. 'Les Élans du coeur', *24 Images* 46 (Nov.–Dec.): 6–9.

———. 1990. 'De Jean Vigo à André Forcier: L'Effusion poétique', *24 Images* 50–1 (Fall): 27–31.

Gural, Anna, and Benoît Patar. 1982. 'Denys Arcand: Silence, on tourne', *24 Images* 13–14 (July–Aug.): 47–56.

Hall, Stuart. 1992. 'The Question of Cultural Identity', in Hall, David Held, and Tony McGrew, eds, *Modernity and Its Futures*. Cambridge: Polity Press, 274–316.

———. 1993. 'Minimal Selves', in Ann Gray and Jim McGuigan, eds, *Studying Culture: An Introductory Reader*. London: Edward Arnold, 134–9.

Hallas, Roger. 2003. 'The Genealogical Pedagogy of John Greyson's *Zero Patience*', *Canadian Journal of Film Studies* 12, 1 (Spring): 16–37.

Handling, Piers. 1982. 'Don Shebib's *Heartaches*', *Cinema Canada* 83 (Apr.): 48.

———, ed. 1983a. *The Shape of Rage: The Films of David Cronenberg*. Toronto: General Publishing.

———. 1983b. 'A Canadian Cronenberg', in Handling (1983a: 98–114).

———. 1984. 'The Diary Films of Michael Rubbo', in Feldman (1984a: 205–16).

———. 1986. 'Larry Kent Lost and Found: A Critical Rehabilitation', *Cinema Canada* 127 (Feb.): 10–16.

Haraway, Donna. 1991. *Simians, Cyborgs, and Women: The Reinvention of Nature*. New York: Routledge.

Harcourt, Peter. 1977a. 'The Innocent Eye: An Aspect of the Work of the National Film Board of Canada', in Feldman and Nelson (1977: 67–77).

———. 1977b. 'Men of Vision: Some Comments on the Work of Don Shebib', in Feldman and Nelson (1977: 208–17).

———. 1980. '1964: The Beginning of a Beginning', in Véronneau and Handling (1980: 64–76).

———. 1981. *Jean Pierre Lefebvre*. Ottawa: Canadian Film Institute.

———. 1984. 'Pierre Perrault and *Le cinéma vécu*', in Feldman (1984a: 125–35).

———. 1987. 'Planting Pictures: An Appreciation of the Films of William D. MacGillivray', *Cinema Canada* 146 (Nov.): 14–21.

———. 1998. 'Faces Changing Colour Changing Canon', *CineAction* 45 (Feb.): 2–9.

———. 1999. 'Two plus Two: Contesting the Boundaries of Identity in Two Films by Micheline Lanctôt', in Armatage et al. (1999a: 244–52).

———, ed. 2001. *Jean Pierre Lefebvre Vidéaste*. Toronto: Toronto International Film Festival.

Hardy, Forsyth. 1966. *Grierson on Documentary*. London: Faber and Faber.

Harkness, John. 1982. 'Notes on a Tax-Sheltered Cinema', *Cinema Canada* 87 (Aug.): 22–6.

———. 1983. 'The Word, the Flesh and the Films of David Cronenberg', in Handling (1983a: 87–97).

———. 1989. 'The Improbable Rise of Denys Arcand', *Sight and Sound* 58, 4 (Autumn): 234–8.

Harris, Lesley Ellen. 1991. 'Atom Egoyan: Laughter in the Dark', *Canadian Forum* 70, 805 (Dec.): 15–17.

Harrison, Marion. 1989. 'Mermaids: Singing Off Key', *CineAction* 16 (Spring): 25–30.

Haskell, Molly. 1974. *From Reverence to Rape: The Treatment of Women in the Movies.* New York: Holt, Rinehart and Winston.

Hays, Matthew. 2002. 'On Ethics and Aesthetics: *The Things I Cannot Change* and *Courage to Change*', *Take One* 11, 38 (July–Aug.): 32–3.

Henderson, Colin. 1987. 'Inter-View', *Cinema Canada* 146 (Nov.): 15, 17, 19, 21.

Higson, Andrew. 1989. 'The Concept of National Cinema', *Screen* 30, 4 (Autumn): 36–46.

———. 2000. 'The Instability of the National', in Justine Ashby and Higson, eds, *British Cinema, Past and Present.* London: Routledge, 35–47.

Hodgins, B.W., R.P. Bowles, J.L. Hanley, and G.A. Rawlyk, eds. 1974. *Canadiens, Canadians and Québécois.* Toronto: Prentice-Hall.

Hookey, Robert. 1977. 'Backtalk . . . with David Cronenberg', *Motion* 6, 4–5 (Nov.): 16.

Hoolboom, Mike. 2001. *Inside the Pleasure Dome: Fringe Film in Canada.* Toronto: Coach House Press.

Hotchkiss, Lia M. 2003. '"Still in the Game": Cybertransformations of the "New Flesh" in David Cronenberg's *eXistenZ*', *Velvet Light Trap* 52 (Fall): 15–32.

Howell, Peter. 2003. 'A Director in His Prime: Denys Arcand's *Les Invasions barbares*', *Take One* 12, 43 (Sept.–Dec.): 28–31.

Hudecki, John. 1972. '*Wedding in White*/One', *Take One* 3, 7: 29–30.

Humphries, Reynold. 2002. *The American Horror Film: An Introduction.* Edinburgh: Edinburgh University Press.

Hynam, Penelope. 1981. 'Beryl Fox', *Cinema Canada* 73 (Apr.): 26–30.

Ibrányi-Kiss, A. 1974. 'Filmmaking West Coast Style', *Cinema Canada* 13 (Apr.–May): 42–5.

———. 1977. 'Mireille Dansereau: *La Vie rêvée*', in Feldman and Nelson (1977: 250–8).

Irving, Joan. 1980. 'To Berlin with Love', *Cinema Canada* 63 (Mar.): 11–15.

Jaehne, Karen. 1988. '*I've Heard the Mermaids Singing*: An Interview with Patricia Rozema', *Cineaste* 16, 3: 22–3.

———. 1992. 'David Cronenberg on William Burroughs: Dead Ringers Do *Naked Lunch*', *Film Quarterly* 45, 3 (Spring): 2–6.

Johnson, Ian. 1965. '*The Luck of Ginger Coffey*', *Films and Filming* 11, 11 (Aug.): 31.

Jones, D.B. 1996. *The Best Butler in the Business: Tom Daly and the National Film Board of Canada.* Toronto: University of Toronto Press.

Jutra, Claude. 1966. 'Les 101 questions: *À tout prendre*', *Objectif* 37 (Nov.–Dec.): 24–30.

Jutras, Pierre, Réal La Rochelle, and Pierre Véronneau. 1987–8. 'Conversation autour d'un plaisir solitaire', *Copie Zéro* 34–5 (Dec.–Mar.): 4–12.

Kael, Pauline. 1974. *Deeper Into Movies.* New York: Bantam.

Kashmere, Brett. 2004. 'R. Bruce Elder: In the Realm of Mystery and Wonder', *Take One* 12, 45 (Mar.–June): 36–8.

Kelly, Virginia. 1981. 'Pressed to Wrap', *Cinema Canada* 74 (May): 61–2.

Kemp, Philip. 2004. 'The Last Laugh', *Sight and Sound* 14, 3 (Mar.): 36–7.

Knee, Adam. 1992. 'The Metamorphosis of *The Fly*', *Wide Angle* 14, 1 (Jan.): 20–34.

Knelman, Martin. 1984. 'Mum's the Word', in Feldman (1984a: 21–3).

———. 1987. *Home Movies: Tales from the Canadian Film World.* Toronto: Key Porter.

Kracauer, Siegfried. 1947. *From Caligari to Hitler: A Psychological History of the German Film.* Princeton, NJ: Princeton University Press.

Kristmanson, Mark. 2003. *Plateaus of Freedom: Nationality, Culture, and State Security in Canada, 1940–1960.* Toronto: Oxford University Press.

Kroker, Arthur. 1984. *Technology and the Canadian Mind: Innis/McLuhan/Grant.* Montreal: New World Perspectives.

Lan, Stephen. 2002. 'In Search of Wonder: Peter Mettler's *Gambling, Gods and LSD*', *Take One* 11, 39 (Sept.–Nov.): 14–17.

Landy, Marcia. 1994. *Film, Politics, and Gramsci*. Minneapolis: University of Minnesota Press.

Larue, Johanne. 1991. '*Archangel* et *La Liberté d'une statue*: Fictions expérimentales de jeunes cinéaste', *Séquences* 150 (Jan.): 45–6.

———. 1992. 'Contre *Léolo*', *Séquences* 159–60 (Sept.): 53.

———. 1995. 'Lepage/Hitchcock: Leçons d'histoire(s)', *Séquences* 180 (Sept.–Oct.): 28–31.

Lavoie, André. 2002. 'Chaire fraîche et Vieille capitale', *Ciné-Bulles* 20, 2 (Spring): 6–9.

Leach, Jim. 1980. 'Don Owen's Obliterated Environments', *Dalhousie Review* 60, 2 (Summer): 277–89.

———. 1990–1. 'Habitant and Missionary: Ideology and the Voice-of-God in Two 1943 Films on Quebec', *Journal of Canadian Studies* 25, 4 (Winter): 100–10.

———. 1999a. *Claude Jutra, Filmmaker*. Montreal and Kingston: McGill-Queen's University Press.

———. 1999b. 'Lost Bodies and Missing Persons: Canadian Cinema(s) in the Age of Multi-National Representations', *Post Script* 18, 2 (Winter–Spring): 5–18.

———. 2003. 'Dark Satanic Mills: Denys Arcand's *On est au coton*', in Leach and Sloniowski (2003: 87–102).

——— and Jeannette Sloniowski, eds. 2003. *Candid Eyes: Essays on Canadian Documentaries*. Toronto: University of Toronto Press.

Lefebvre, Jean Pierre. 1965. 'La Crise du langage et le cinéma canadien', *Objectif* 32 (Apr.–May): 27–36.

———. 1968. 'Les Quatres Saisons', *Cahiers du cinéma* 200–1 (Apr.–May): 108–9.

———. 1975. 'Notes pour la C.E.C.O.', *Cinéma Québec* 4, 7: 28–30.

———. 1976. 'La Cohérence dans le cinéma québécoise', *Cinéma Québec* 4, 9–10: 42–5.

Leroux, André. 1971. 'Une Expérience de démystification: *Les Maudits Sauvages*', *Cinéma Québec* 1, 3 (Aug.–Sept.): 20–3.

———. 1975. 'Cri de coeur', in Brault (1975: 119–20).

———. 1976. '*The Far Shore*', *Séquences* 86 (Oct.): 41–3.

Lever, Yves. 1988. *Histoire générale du cinéma au Québec*. Montreal: Boréal.

Lévesque, René. 1968. *An Option for Québec*. Toronto: McClelland & Stewart.

———. 1975. 'Pourquoi Les Ordres?', in Brault (1975: 124).

Lockerbie, Ian. 1995. '*Les Bons Débarass* ou l'état d'une nation', *Ciné-Bulles* 14, 1 (Winter–Spring): 36–40.

Loiselle, André. 1995. '"I only know where I come from, not where I am going": a conversation with Denys Arcand', in Loiselle and Brian McIlroy, eds, *Auteur/Provocateur: The Films of Denys Arcand*. Westport, Conn.: Praeger, 136–61

———. 1999. 'Subtly Subversive or Simply Stupid: Notes on Popular Quebec Cinema', *Post Script* 18, 2 (Winter–Spring): 75–84.

———. 2000. *Mourir à tue-tête/A Scream from Silence*. Trowbridge: Flicks Books.

———. 2002a. '*Madeleine Is* . . . Worth a Second Look', *Take One* 11, 38 (July–Aug.): 34–7.

———. 2002b. 'Michel Brault's *Les Ordres*: Documenting the Reality of Experience and the Fiction of History', in Walz (2002: 74–96).

———. 2002c. 'The Radically Moderate Canadian', in Beard and White (2002: 256–69).

———. 2003. *Stage-Bound: Feature Film Adaptations of Canadian and Québécois Drama*. Montreal and Kingston: McGill-Queen's University Press.

Loiselle, Marie-Claude. 1991. 'Le Mal d'une époque', *24 Images* 56–7 (Fall): 55–9.

———. 1994. 'L'Arpenteur de tous les possibles', *24 Images* 73–4 (Sept.–Oct.): 16–19.

——— and Claude Racine. 1988–9. 'Survivre par l'imagination', *24 Images* 41 (Winter): 6–9.

——— and ———. 1991. 'Entretien avec Léa Pool', *24 Images* 56–7 (Fall): 45–9.

Longfellow, Brenda. 1987. 'Mireille Dansereau: A Phase Apart', *Cinema Canada* 146 (Nov.): 10–11.

———. 1992. 'The Melodramatic Imagination in Quebec and Canadian Women's Feature Films', *Cineaction* 28 (Spring): 48–56.

———. 1996. 'Globalization and National Identity in Canadian Film', *Canadian Journal of Film Studies* 5, 2 (Fall): 3–16.

———. 1999. 'Gender, Landscape, and Colonial Allegories in *The Far Shore*, *Loyalties*, and *Mouvements du désir*', in Armatage et al. (1999a: 165–82).

———. 2004. 'Counter-Narratives, Class Politics and Metropolitan Dystopias: Representations of Globalization in *Maelström*, *waydowntown* and *La Moitié gauche de la frigo*', *Canadian Journal of Film Studies* 13, 1 (Spring): 69–83.

Lord, Susan. 2002. 'States of Emergency in the Films of Anne Wheeler', in Beard and White (2002: 312–26).

Lowenstein, Adam. 1999. 'Canadian Horror Made Flesh: Contextualizing David Cronenberg', *Post Script* 18, 2 (Winter–Spring): 37–51.

Luke, Timothy W. 1991. 'Touring Hyperreality: Critical Theory Confronts Informational Society', in Philip Wexler, ed., *Critical Theory Now*. London: Falmer Press, 1–26.

Lyotard, Jean-François. 1984. *The Postmodern Condition: A Report on Knowledge*, trans. Geoff Bennington and Brian Massumi. Minneapolis: University of Minnesota Press.

McBride, Jason. 2002. 'Betting on Transcendence: Peter Mettler on *Gambling, Gods and LSD*', *Cinema Scope* 12 (Fall): 26–9.

———. 2003. 'The Music Men: Guy Maddin and George Toles on *The Saddest Music in the World*', *Cinema Scope* 16 (Fall): 5–12.

MacCabe, Colin. 1974. 'Realism and the Cinema: Notes on Some Brechtian Theses', *Screen* 15, 2 (Summer): 7–27.

———. 1976. 'Theory and Film: The Principles of Realism and Pleasure', *Screen* 17, 3 (Autumn): 7–27.

McCullough, John. 1999. '*Rude*; or the Elision of Class in Canadian Movies', *CineAction* 49 (June): 19–25.

McGregor, Gaile. 1992. 'Grounding the Countertext: David Cronenberg and the Ethnospecificity of Horror', *Canadian Journal of Film Studies* 2, 1: 43–62.

McGuigan, Jim. 1996. *Culture and the Public Sphere*. London: Routledge.

McLarty, James. 1974. 'Larry Kent', *Motion* (May–June): 19.

McLarty, Lianne M. 1982. 'The Experimental Films of Joyce Wieland', *Ciné-Tracts* 17 (Summer–Fall): 51–63.

McSorley, Tom. 2002a. 'Faraway, So Close: Atom Egoyan Returns Home with *Ararat*', *Take One* 11, 39 (Sept.–Nov.): 8–13.

———. 2002b. 'Time and Space: Goin' Down the Rails with *Stations*', *Take One* 11, 38 (July–Aug.): 44–5.

Maddin, Guy. 2003. *From the Atelier Tovar: Selected Writings*. Toronto: Coach House Books.

Magder, Ted. 1993. *Canada's Hollywood: The Canadian State and Feature Films*. Toronto: University of Toronto Press.

Manning, Erin. 1998. 'The Haunted Home: Colour Spectrums in Robert Lepage's *Le Confessionnal*', *Canadian Journal of Film Studies* 7, 2 (Fall): 49–65.

———. 2003. *Ephemeral Territories: Representing Nation, Home and Identity in Canada*. Minneapolis: University of Minnesota Press.

Marchessault, Janine. 1995. 'Reflections on the Dispossessed: Video and the "Challenge for Change" Experiment', *Screen* 36, 2 (Summer): 131–46.

Marcorelles, Louis. 1973. *Living Cinema: New Directions in Contemporary Film-making*, trans. Isabel Quigly. New York: Praeger.

Marshall, Bill. 2001. *Quebec National Cinema*. Montreal and Kingston: McGill-Queen's University Press.

Marsolais, Gilles. 1968. *Le Cinéma canadien*. Montreal: Éditions du jour.

———. 1975. 'Démasquer les faux maîtres', in Brault (1975: 11–14).

———. 1978. 'Le Temps d'un échec: un jeu de mort', in Marsolais, ed., *Le Temps d'une chasse*. Montreal: Les Éditions le Cinématographe, 13–14.

Martin, Paul-Louis. 1966. 'Sérieux trop sérieux', *Cahiers du cinéma* 179 (June): 76–7.

Martineau, Barbara Halpern. 1977. 'Before the Guerillières: Women's Films at the NFB During World War II', in Feldman and Nelson (1977: 58–67).

Martineau, Richard. 1983. '*Maria Chapdelaine*: Carle versus Louis Hémon', *Cinema Canada* 97 (June): 17–20.

———. 1986. '*Elvis Gratton—Le Film*', *Séquences* 123 (Jan.): 43–4.

Melnyk, George. 2004. *One Hundred Years of Canadian Cinema*. Toronto: University of Toronto Press.

Mercer, Kobena. 1994. *Welcome to the Jungle: New Positions in Black Cultural Studies*. New York: Routledge.

Metz, Christian. 1974. *Film Language: A Semiotics of the Cinema*, trans. Michael Taylor. Oxford: Oxford University Press.

Michelson, Annette. 1979. 'About Snow', *October* 8 (Spring): 111–24.

Moen, Kristian. 2001. 'The Polyphonic Prairies: The Creation and Re-Creation of *Drylanders*', *Canadian Journal of Film Studies* 10, 1: 28–47.

Monk, Katherine. 2001. *Weird Sex and Snowshoes and Other Canadian Film Phenomena*. Vancouver: Raincoast Books.

Morris, Guy. 1968. 'Focus', *Cinema Canada* 36 (Sept.): 18–19.

Morris, Peter. 1978. *Embattled Shadows: A History of Canadian Cinema 1895–1939*. Montreal and Kingston: McGill-Queen's University Press.

———. 1984. *The Film Companion*. Toronto: Irwin Publishing.

———. 1989. 'The Uncertain Trumpet: Defining a [Canadian] Art Cinema in the Sixties', *CineAction* 16 (Spring): 6–13.

———. 1994. 'In Our Own Eyes: The Canonizing of Canadian Film', *Canadian Journal of Film Studies* 3, 1 (Spring): 27–44.

———. 2002. 'Canadian Gothic and *Les Bons Débarras*: The Night Side of the Soul', in Walz (2002: 99–113).

Moses, Michele. 1975. 'A Glimpse of the Far Shore', *Cinema Canada* 23 (Nov.): 41.

Nadeau, Chantal. 1992. 'Women in French-Quebec Cinema: The Space of Socio-Sexual (In)difference', *CineAction* 28 (Spring): 4–15.

Naficy, Hamid. 2004. 'Epistolarity and Textuality in Accented Films', in Atom Egoyan and Ian Balfour, eds, *Subtitles: On the Foreignness of Film*. Cambridge, Mass.: MIT Press, 131–51.

Neale, Steve. 2003. 'Questions of Genre', in Barry Keith Grant, ed., *Film Genre III*. Austin: University of Texas Press, 160–84.

Nicks, Joan. 2003. '*Not a Love Story: A Film about Pornography*—Tabloid Rhetoric in Interventionist Documentary', in Leach and Sloniowski (2003: 131–47).

Northey, Margot. 1976. *The Haunted Wilderness: The Gothic and Grotesque in Canadian Fiction*. Toronto: University of Toronto Press.

O'Neill, Edward R. 1997. 'Identity, Mimicry and Transtextuality in Mina Shum's *Double Happiness* and Quentin Lee and Justin Lin's *Shopping for Fangs*', *CineAction* 42 (Feb.): 50–62.

O'Pray, Michael. 1984. 'Primitive Phantasy in Cronenberg's Films', in Wayne Drew, ed., *David Cronenberg*. London: British Film Institute, 48–53.

O'Regan, Tom. 1996. *Australian National Cinema*. London: Routledge.

Ord, Douglas. 1977. 'An Essay on Canadian (Film)', *Cinema Canada* 38–9 (June–July): 40–4.

Owen, Don. 1971. *Nobody Waved Good-bye*, ed. Herbert Voaden. Toronto: Macmillan.

Pageau, Pierre. 1971. 'Jean-Pierre Lefebvre, critique (essai de montage)', in Bérubé and Patry (1971: 95–107).

Pendakur, Manjunath. 1990. *Canadian Dreams and American Control*. Detroit: Wayne State University Press.

Peranson, Mark. 2000. 'Calgary Everyman: Gary Burns Works *waydowntown*', *Cinema Scope* 5 (Fall): 5–9.

Perreault, Luc. 1972. 'Une grosse machine appelée *Kamouraska*', *La Presse* (Montreal) (13 May).

Perron, Bernard. 1994. 'Les Aveux de Québec', *Ciné-Bulles* 13, 4 (Fall): 46–9.

Pérusse, Denise. 1987–8. '*Le Déclin*: Une Stratégie filmique oscillant entre le cliché et l'ironie', *Copie Zéro* 34–5 (Dec.–Mar.): 49–51.

Pevere, Geoff. 1993a. 'Cliffhanger: Cronenberg and the Canadian Cultural Consciousness', *Take One* 3 (Fall): 4–9.

———. 1993b. 'Who's the Boss? Do Canadians Have a Problem with Authority?', *Canadian Forum* 72, 822 (Sept.): 28–9.

———. 1995a. 'Middle of Nowhere: Ontario Movies after 1980', *Post Script* 15, 1 (Fall): 9–22.

———. 1995b. 'No Place Like Home: The Films of Atom Egoyan', in Atom Egoyan, *Exotica*. Toronto: Coach House Press, 9–41.

———. 2002a. 'Fishy', in Beard and White (2002: 100–4).

———. 2002b. 'History and Mystery: Atom Egoyan on *Ararat*', *Cinema Scope* 12 (Fall): 15–20.

——— and Wyndham Wise. 2004a. 'Atom Egoyan: Face the Strange', *Take One* special issue (Sept.–Nov.): 63–94.

———. 2004b. 'Mermaids Don't Sing the Blues: The Films of Patricia Rozema', *Take One* special issue (Sept.–Nov.): 5–34.

Pick, Zuzana M. 2003. '"This Land is Ours"—Storytelling and History in *Kanehsatake: 270 Years of Resistance*', in Leach and Sloniowski (2003: 181–96).

Pike, David L. 2001. 'Canadian Cinema in the Age of Globalization', *CineAction* 57: 3–10.

Porton, Richard. 1997. 'Family Romances: An Interview with Atom Egoyan', *Cineaste* 23, 2 (Dec.): 8–15.

Posner, Michael. 1993. *Canadian Dreams: The Making and Marketing of Independent Films*. Vancouver: Douglas & McIntyre.

Pratley, Gerald. 1973. '*La Vraie Nature de Bernadette*', *International Film Guide*: 124.

Prédal, René. 1967. *Jeune cinéma canadien*. Lyon: Premier Plan.

Racine, Claude. 1989. 'Entretien avec Atom Egoyan', *24 Images* 43 (Summer): 10–11.

———. 1992. 'Entretien avec Jean-Claude Lauzon', *24 Images* 61 (Summer): 4–11.

Ramsay, Christine. 1995a. 'Léo Who? Questions of Identity and Culture in Jean-Claude Lauzon's *Léolo*', *Post Script* 15, 1 (Fall): 23–37.

———. 1995b. 'Social Surfaces and Psychic Depths in David Wellington's *I Love a Man in Uniform*', *Canadian Journal of Film Studies* 4, 1 (Spring): 3–25.

———. 2002a. 'Canadian Narrative Cinema From the Margins: The "Nation" and Masculinity in *Goin' Down the Road*', in Walz (2002: 3–24).

———. 2002b. 'Greyson, Grierson, Godard, God: Reflections on the Cinema of John Greyson', in Beard and White (2002: 192–205).

Rioux, Louis-Paul. 1998. 'Hommage au génie québécois!', *Séquences* 195 (Mar.–Apr.): 45–6.

Rodley, Chris, ed. 1992. *Cronenberg on Cronenberg*. Toronto: Knopf.
———. 1999. 'Game Boy', *Sight and Sound* 9, 4 (Apr.): 8–10.
Romney, Jonathan. 2003. *Atom Egoyan*. London: British Film Institute.
Roscoe, Jane, and Craig Hight. 2001. *Faking It: Mock-Documentary and the Subversion of Factuality*. Manchester: Manchester University Press.
Rosenthal, Alan. 1970. 'The Fiction Documentary: Interviews with the Makers of *A Married Couple*', *Film Quarterly* 23, 4 (Summer): 9–19.
Rousseau, Yves. 1999. 'Le Temps des bouffons', *24 Images* 98–9 (Fall): 86–7.
Roy, Charles-Stéphane. 1999. 'Séparer le subtil de l'épais', *Séquences* 204 (Sept.–Oct.): 50.
Russell, David. 1989–90. 'Two or Three Things We Know about Beineix', *Sight and Sound* 59, 1 (Winter): 42–7.
Russell, Delbert W. 1983. *Anne Hébert*. Boston: Twayne.
Said, S.F. 2002. 'Northern Exposure', *Sight and Sound* 12, 2 (Feb.): 22–5.
Saunders, Doug. 2001. 'The Myth of Hollywood North', *Report on Business Magazine* 17, 10 (Apr.): 96–101.
Sconce, Jeffrey. 2002. 'Irony, Nihilism and the New American "Smart" Film', *Screen* 43, 4 (Winter): 349–69.
Sharrett, Christopher. 1986. 'Myth and Ritual in the Post-Industrial Landscape: The Horror Films of David Cronenberg', *Persistence of Vision* 3–4 (Summer): 111–30.
Shaviro, Steven. 2002. 'Fire and Ice: The Films of Guy Maddin', in Beard and White (2002: 216–21).
Shuster, Nat. 1973. '*Kamouraska*: Wuthering Heights on the St. Lawrence', *Motion* (Nov.–Dec.): 28–9.
———. 1974. '*La Mort d'un bûcheron*', *Motion* (Jan.–Feb.): 49–50.
———. 1975. 'October 1970, Revisited', *Motion* 4, 2: 23–4.
Silverman, Michael. 1984. 'A Post-modern Cronenberg', in Wayne Drew, ed., *David Cronenberg*. London: British Film Institute, 31–4.
Sinclair, Iain. 1999. *Crash*. London: British Film Institute.
Sloniowski, Jeannette. 2003. 'Performing the Master Narratives: Michael Rubbo's *Waiting for Fidel*', in Leach and Sloniowski (2003: 103–14).
Spaner, David. 2003. *Dreaming in the Rain: How Vancouver Became Hollywood North by Northwest*. Vancouver: Arsenal Pulp Press.
Spencer, Liese. 2000. '*The Five Senses*', *Sight and Sound* 10, 1 (Jan.): 49–50.
Spencer, Michael, with Suzan Ayscough. 2003. *Hollywood North: Creating the Canadian Motion Picture Industry*. Montreal: Cantos International.
Stone, Tammy. 2003. 'The King of Cinéma-Vérité: An Interview with Allan King', *Take One* 11, 41 (Mar.–May): 31–5.
Straw, Will. 2002. 'Reinhabiting Lost Languages: Guy Maddin's *Careful*', in Walz (2002: 305–17).
Strick, Philip. 1970. '*A Married Couple*', *Sight and Sound* 39, 4 (Autumn): 219–20.
Suner, Asuman. 1998. 'Postmodern Double Cross: Reading David Cronenberg's *M. Butterfly* as a Horror Story', *Cinema Journal* 37, 2: 49–64.
Sutherland, Ronald. 1971. *Second Images: Comparative Studies in Québec/Canadian Literature*. Don Mills, Ont.: New Press.
Sussex, Elizabeth. 1965. '*The Luck of Ginger Coffey*', *Sight and Sound* 34, 3 (Summer): 149.
Szeman, Imre. 1994. 'Tracing Patterns of Flight: Ethnicity, Multiculturalism, and *Masala*', *Reverse Shot* 1, 2 (Summer): 13–17.
Tadros, Connie. 1976. 'Reflections on Our Home Movies', *Cinema Canada* 27 (Apr.): 33–7.

Tadros, Jean-Pierre. 1972a. 'Entretien avec Denys Arcand', *Cinéma Québec* 1, 9 (May–June): 27–9.

———. 1972b. 'Rejoindre le mythe par le quotidien: Une entrevue avec Gilles Carle', *Cinéma Québec* 1, 9 (May–June): 18–21.

———. 1973. 'Gilles Carle: Face à un Québec déchiré', *Cinéma Québec* 2, 5 (Jan.–Feb.): 20–6.

Tasker, Yvonne. 1996. 'Approaches to the New Hollywood', in James Curran, David Morley, and Valerie Walkerdine, eds, *Cultural Studies and Communications*. London: Arnold, 213–28.

Taubin, Amy. 1989. 'Memories of Overdevelopment: Up and Atom', *Film Comment* 25, 6 (Nov.–Dec.): 27–9.

———. 1992. 'Burning Down the House', *Sight and Sound* 2, 2 (June): 18–19.

Testa, Bart. 1985. 'So, What Did Elder Say?', *Cinema Canada* 120–1 (July–Aug.): 27–9.

———. 1995. 'Arcand's double-twist allegory: *Jesus of Montreal*', in André Loiselle and Brian McIlroy, eds, *Auteur/Provocateur: The Films of Denys Arcand*. Westport, Conn.: Praeger, 90–112.

Thérien, Gilles. 1990. 'L'Empire et les barbares', *Cinémas* 1–2 (Fall): 9–19.

Tierney, Kevin. 1981. 'Interview: Gilles Carle', *Cinema Canada* 74 (May): 40–4.

Todorov, Tzvetan. 1973. *The Fantastic: A Structural Approach to a Literary Genre*. Cleveland: Case Western Reserve University Press.

Toles, George. 2002. 'Drowning for Love: Jean-Claude Lauzon's *Léolo*', in Walz (2002: 275–301).

Topalovich, Maria. 2000. *And the Genie Goes To . . .: Celebrating 50 Years of the Canadian Film Awards*. Toronto: Stoddart.

Tousignant, Isa. 1999. 'Denis Filiatrault's *C't'à ton tour, Laura Cadieux*: A Woman of Substance?', *Take One* 23 (Spring): 32–4.

———. 2001. 'Fated Possibilities: A Conversation with Robert Lepage', *Take One* 9, 30 (Winter): 14–18.

Tremblay-Daviault, Christiane. 1981. *Un cinéma orphelin: Structures mentales et sociales du cinéma québécois*. Montreal: Québec/Amérique.

Tudor, Andrew. 2003. 'Genre', in Barry Keith Grant, ed., *Film Genre III*. Austin: University of Texas Press, 3–10.

Turim, Maureen Cheryn. 1985. *Abstraction in Avant-Garde Films*. Ann Arbor: UMI Research Press.

Turner, Graeme. 1993. 'The Genres Are American: Australian Narrative, Australian Film, and the Problem of Genre', *Literature/Film Quarterly* 21, 2: 102–11.

Ty, Eleanor. 1999. 'Spectacular Pleasures: Labyrinthine Mirrors in Atom Egoyan's *Exotica*', in Lynne Van Luven and Patricia L. Walton, eds, *Pop Can: Popular Culture in Canada*. Toronto: Prentice-Hall, 4–12.

Urquhart, Peter. 2003. 'You Should Know Something—*Anything*—About This Movie. You Paid For It', *Canadian Journal of Film Studies* 12, 2 (Fall): 64–80.

Vallières, Pierre. 1971. *White Niggers of America*, trans. Joan Peckham. Toronto: McClelland & Stewart.

———. 1974. 'Brault a manqué son coup', *Cinéma Québec* 4, 1 (Dec.): 18–20.

Varga, Darrell. 1999. 'Desire in Bondage: Guy Maddin's *Careful*', *Canadian Journal of Film Studies* 8, 2 (Fall): 57–70.

Vatnsdal, Caelum. 2000. *Kino Delirium: The Films of Guy Maddin*. Winnipeg: Arbeiter Ring.

Vermee, Jack. 1998. 'Bruce Sweeney Gets *Dirty*', *Take One* 7, 21 (Fall): 32–4.

———. 2001. 'Bruce Sweeney's *Last Wedding*: Dumpster Sex, Leaky Condos and Relationships Gone Bad', *Take One* 10, 34 (Sept.): 8–11.

Véronneau, Pierre. 1987–8. 'De l'Incertitude au paradoxe: De l'Histoire, ou la singularité originelle d'Arcand', *Copie Zéro* 34–5 (Dec.–Mar.): 24–6.

———— and Piers Handling, eds. 1980. *Self Portrait: Essays on the Canadian and Quebec Cinemas*. Ottawa: Canadian Film Institute.

Walton, Glenn. 1997. 'Thom Fitzgerald's *The Hanging Garden*', *Take One* 6, 17 (Fall): 34–7.

Walz, Gene, ed. 2002. *Canada's Best Features: Critical Essays on 15 Canadian Films*. Amsterdam: Editions Rodopi.

Waugh, Thomas. 1999. 'Cinemas, Nations, Masculinities', *Canadian Journal of Film Studies* 8, 1 (Spring): 8–44.

————. 2001. 'Fairy Tales of Two Cities, or Queer Nation(s)/Urban Cinema(s)', *Canadian Journal of Film Studies* 10, 2 (Fall): 102–25.

————. 2002. 'Home Is Not the Place One Has Left or *Masala* as "a Multi-Cultural Culinary Treat"?', in Walz (2002: 254–72).

Wedman, Les. 1976. '*The Far Shore*', *Cinema Canada* 32 (Oct.): 30.

Weinmann, Heinz. 1990. *Cinéma de l'imaginaire québécois: De La Petite Aurore à Jésus de Montreal*. Montreal: L'Hexagon.

White, Jerry. 1999. 'Alanis Obomsawin, Documentary Form and the Canadian Nation(s)', *CineAction* 49 (June): 26–36.

Williams, Linda Ruth. 1993. 'A Virus is Only Doing Its Job', *Sight and Sound* 3, 5 (May): 31–3.

————. 2001. 'Blood Sisters', *Sight and Sound* 11, 6 (June): 36–7.

Wilson, Neil. 1986. 'Up Yours!', *Cinema Canada* 129 (Apr.): 17–18.

Wise, Wyndham, ed. 2001. *Take One's Essential Guide to Canadian Film*. Toronto: University of Toronto Press.

Wood, Robin. 1975. 'New Cinema at Edinburgh', *Film Comment* 11, 6 (Nov.–Dec.): 25–9.

————. 1983. 'Cronenberg: A Dissenting View', in Handling (1983a: 115–35).

————. 1984. 'An Introduction to the American Horror Film', in Barry Keith Grant, ed., *Planks of Reason: Essays on the Horror Film*. Metuchen, NJ: Scarecrow Press, 164–200.

————. 1989. 'Towards a Canadian (Inter)national Cinema Part 2: *Loyalties* and *Life Classes*', *CineAction* 17 (Summer): 23–35.

Woods, Lysandra. 2002. 'Srinivas Krishna and the New Canadian Cinema', in Beard and White (2002: 206–15).

Yakir, Dan. 1978. '*Ciné-transe*: The Vision of Jean Rouch', *Film Quarterly* 31, 3 (Spring): 2–11.

Yamaguchi, Joanne. 1989. 'Who is the American Cousin? Canadian Cinema, Cultural Freedom and Sandy Wilson's *American Cousin*', *CineAction* 16 (Spring): 70–2.

Zeldin, Toby. 1989. 'Jack Darcus' *Kingsgate*', *Cinema Canada* 168 (Nov.): 24.

Zizek, Slavoj. 2001. *The Fright of Real Tears: Krzysztof Kieslowski Between Theory and Post-Theory*. London: British Film Institute.

————. 2004. 'The Foreign Gaze Which Sees Too Much', in Atom Egoyan and Ian Balfour, eds, *Subtitles: On the Foreignness of Film*. Cambridge, Mass.: MIT Press, 285–306.

Zryd, Michael. 2002. 'A Report on Canadian Experimental Film Institutions, 1980–2000', in Beard and White (2002: 392–401).

FILMOGRAPHY

This filmography is divided between Canadian and non-Canadian films. With the proliferation of co-productions and Canadian filmmakers working abroad, this distinction sometimes becomes rather arbitrary. Unlike government institutions, I have not used a points system to determine whether a film qualifies as Canadian, but I have taken into account such factors as the sources of funding, the geographical setting, and the creative personnel involved.

Canadian Films

Funding for film production in Canada is a very complicated business. This filmography attempts to include all the production companies involved with each film but does not list the numerous government agencies that also supported many of the films. (Numbers indicate pages where films are discussed or mentioned in this book.)

À corps perdu (*Straight for the Heart*), dir. Léa Pool (Les Films téléscène/Xanadu [Switzerland], 1988)
The Act of the Heart, dir. Paul Almond (Quest Film, 1970), 76–9
The Adjuster, dir. Atom Egoyan (Ego Film Arts, 1991), 119, 121
Aerial View, dir. William MacGillivray (Atlantic Fimmakers' Cooperative, 1979), 92, 94
Alexis Tremblay Habitant: The Story of a Farmer in Quebec, dir. Jane Marsh (NFB, 1943), 13–14, 38
L'Amour humaine (*The Awakening*), dir. Denis Héroux (Cinépix, 1970), 102
L'Ange de goudron (*Tar Angel*), dir. Denis Chouinard (Max Films, 2001), 132
Ararat, dir. Atom Egoyan (Alliance Atlantis/Serendipity Point/Ego Film Arts/ARP [France], 2002), 118, 121–3
Archangel, dir. Guy Maddin (Cinephile/Ordnance Pictures, 1990), 85
À Saint-Henri le 5 septembre (*September Five at Saint-Henri*), dir. Hubert Aquin (NFB, 1962), 15
Atanarjuat (a.k.a. *The Fast Runner*), dir. Zacharias Kunuk (Igloolik Isuma/NFB, 2001), 111, 134–5
À tout prendre (*Take It All/ The Way It Goes*), dir. Claude Jutra (Jutra, 1963), 25
Au clair de la lune (*Moonlight Bowling*), dir. André Forcier (Les Productions Albinie, 1982), 84, 86
Aujourd'hui ou jamais (*Today or Never*), dir. Jean Pierre Lefebvre (Les Productions Vent d'Est, 1998), 97
Back to God's Country, dir. David M. Hartford (Canadian Photoplays, 1919), 103–4
Bar salon, dir. André Forcier (Les Films André Forcier/Les Ateliers du cinéma québécois, 1973), 84, 86
Because Why, dir. Arto Paragamian (Aska Film/Cinoque Films, 1993), 132
Beefcake, dir. Thom Fitzgerald (Alliance Independent Films/Channel 4 Films [Britain]/ La Sept-Arte [France]/Emotion Pictures [USA], 1998), 110

Non-Canadian Films

INDEX